ALSO BY JACQUES ELLUL

The Technological Society (1964)

Propaganda (1965)

These are Borzoi Books, published in New York by Alfred A. Knopf

THE POLITICAL
ILLUSION

THE
POLITICAL
ILLUSION

BY

JACQUES ELLUL

TRANSLATED FROM THE FRENCH
BY KONRAD KELLEN

New York: Alfred A. Knopf

⌈1967⌉

L. C. Catalog Card Number: 66–19375

THIS IS A BORZOI BOOK
PUBLISHED BY ALFRED A. KNOPF, INC.

MANUFACTURED IN THE UNITED STATES OF AMERICA

FIRST AMERICAN EDITION

Originally published in French as *L'Illusion politique*
© 1965 by Robert Laffont

TO

Bernard Charbonneau,

my friend

Translator's Introduction

The Political Illusion is the third of Jacques Ellul's books to be presented to the American public. The first, *The Technological Society,* was essentially an overview of the conflict between technology and human freedom; the second, *Propaganda,* showed how modern man, surrounded and seized by propaganda, more often than not surrenders himself to it only too willingly even in democracies, even if he is educated; this third volume, *The Political Illusion,* examines modern man's passion—political affairs—and the role he plays in them and in the modern state.

As before, Ellul uses logic rather than facts, though he illustrates his thoughts with many examples and quotations (thus remaining within the web of contemporary thought on his subject). And he concludes that all facets of political activity as we know it today are a kaleidoscope of interlocking illusions, the most basic of which are the illusions of popular participation, popular control, and popular problem-solving in the realm of politics.

The first great evil from which most other evils spring is politization (the act of suffusing everything with politics and dragging it into the political arena). In our modern world, contrary to what was the rule in all previous ages, everything is politized: men seek political solutions for everything, whether the problem be freedom or justice or peace or prosperity or happiness.

Anything not political does not arouse widespread interest; it is not accorded any independent existence in our politized world.

As a result of this politization of all aspects of life and of the orientation of all thought and energy toward politics, men increasingly turn to the state for a solution of their problems, though the state could not solve them if it tried. And everywhere in the world this increasing inclination to turn to the state leads to three evils: boundless inflation of the state's size and power; increasing dependence on it by the individual; and decreasing control over it by the "people" who think they control it, whereas in reality they merely surrender all their powers to it.

This state, then, engages in politics. But even though the state ceaselessly talks through the mass media—through those who represent it, whether they are democratically elected or not—of noble things and cherished values, momentous decisions and great goals, essentially it deals with tinder. Two things limit all its political endeavors: on the one hand, politics inexorably follows certain patterns over which the politicians have absolutely no control—they do what they must; on the other, where a certain margin of freedom of action remains, they deal with ephemeral, basically unimportant things that are made to seem important for public consumption. The political leaders merely manipulate the images among which modern man dwells. Whereas in the Middle Ages man had direct knowledge of the limited range of things that concerned him, he now lives in a world of images reflecting faraway places, people, and conditions brought to him as "information" by the mass media. This universe is not, Ellul says, a tissue of lies, "but it permits any and all interpretations and translations," and the graver the situation the more "managed" and "edited" will be the version fed to the public. The whole of these images is then translated by contemporary men into a view of the world.

Are "the people" then without any influence upon the course

of political events? On the contrary, Ellul says, but their influence is all for the worse; for if public opinion is not aroused, nothing can be done in democracies, and if it is aroused, moderate, equitable, and provident solutions are no longer possible. Public opinion will either disregard something altogether or demand a drastic—i.e., unjust and undesirable—solution.

In the second half of the book, Ellul arrives at what he considers the three essential aspects of the political illusion. The first concerns control of the state. Ellul rejects the idea that in a democracy as we know it "the people" control the state with their ballots. They do, he says, control to some extent who is on top of the pyramid, but that does not mean control of the state; the elected representatives have no way of controlling—or even thoroughly knowing—the behemoth under them. To change those in office means to change nothing: these men inevitably are faced with *le politique,* which by Ellul's definition is either dealing with ephemeral matters or moving along "iron rails," for which reason they are not effective leaders. And in our technological age they are the creatures of the technical experts they employ.

The second essential aspect of the political illusion is that of popular participation; if "the people" cannot control the state, do they not at least participate substantially in its doings? No, Ellul says. Just as their ballots cannot control the course of events, their organizations, such as parties or trade unions, do not channel popular desires so as to make them effective. The principal reason is that these organizations require men at the top who are professional politicians concerned with little else than the eternal struggle to attain and retain power against rivals in their own and all other camps. These men are interested only in having the support of numbers, and the hopes and aspirations of the rank and file are filtered, not up but out. Moreover, members of the rank and file in an organization, like the citizens in a state, are dependent upon the information fed them, and the party or union hierarchs are expert in managing information and in preventing all nonconforming forces from emerging.

The third aspect of the political illusion is the eternal, illusory quest for "political solutions." This is the greatest pitfall of all. After peace or freedom, education or the living standard, or even the law has been advertised and accepted as a polititcal problem, people demand political solutions. But there are no political solutions for these problems; in fact there are none even for genuine political problems. For while, say, arithmetical problems indeed have a solution, political problems have none; indeed Ellul's definition of a genuine political problem is that it consists of truly contradictory given facts, i.e., that it is insoluble in the precise meaning of that term. Political problems merely permit equitable settlements. Yet the technicians more and more present all political problems as solvable equations. And because we believe them, or the politicans who obey them, we expect *la politique* to find solutions for everything, and we therefore make it and the state the guardian and executor of all values—which, as a result, wither away.

What is the solution? To depolitize? On the contrary, Ellul says. Too many people already have abdicated their political heritage and, by so doing, have committed the inexcusable political act of giving the state even more power. Depolitization is merely an escape brought about by indolence or cowardice. The only possible course to take is, first of all, to demythologize politics and put it into its proper, limited place. For that we must reject modern—particularly American—attempts to "adjust" the individual through psychological means to a situation against which he would do better to rebel if he wants to maintain or attain his freedom and fulfill himself as an individual. On the contrary, strong and productive *tensions* (by which Ellul means foci of strong interest and concern) must be built up or be permitted to build up, springing from adherence to genuine values and convictions, and faith must be restored in other avenues of human effectiveness than the illusory means of what nowadays goes by the name of political action and engagement. These tensions might be genuine tensions between church and state, or labor and state, or the military and civilians, rather than peaceful cooperation at the top in the face of illusory tensions below. Without saying so, Ellul seems to think that the "establishment" is evidence that genuine tensions on real issues no longer exist and that the establishment keeps them from arising and fertilizing our society.

But to arrive at genuine tension, it is also necessary to shed all such prejudices and commonplaces as: history travels along a predestined road . . . man is good . . . man is made for happiness . . . technology is neutral and can be controlled . . . moral progress follows material progress . . . work is virtue . . . no more words, action. . . . These are just clichés, Ellul says, and must be discarded, hard though that may be, if politics is to be put into its proper place, the individual again to come into his own, and democracy to flourish in our age, in which technology controls man, propaganda his mind and soul, and the political activity he so fervently pursues, like the role he believes himself to be playing in the political order of things, is a mere illusion. As Ellul phrased it (in a letter of May 27, 1966): "To me this appears to demand a more genuine, more personally involved approach to democracy—which seems to me possible only by a re-formation of the democratic citizen, not by that of institutions."

Konrad Kellen

July 1966

Author's Preface to the English Translation

The American reader must understand that this is a typically French book, that is, the situation it describes pertains to the evolution of French institutions, and the problems it treats are the effects of specific characteristics of the French state and administration. But these characteristics are to a large extent the result of history; I hardly need recall Tocqueville's accurate judgment that the French Revolution did not change the French state in any substantial way. To be sure, doctrines were modified, a ruling social category was abolished, and one form of politics substituted for another, but nothing fundamental in the course of political power changed; the general trend followed by the state—not the monarchy—set by Richelieu and Louis XIV was continued by the Jacobins and the Directory. The transition from monarchy to republic did not change the centralization, the authoritarianism, or the stringencies of the existing political system—on the contrary. The Revolution, and later the Empire, furthered Louis XIV's ideas in truly remarkable fashion. Louis XIV himself was actually prevented from putting his intentions into operation by three obstacles. There were, first, institutions outside the political realm which had great force (for example, the Catholic Church); second, a historical tradition at work, stronger than the strongest king, which he was unable to undo (for example, the historical obligation to respect local freedoms, the officers' corps); and finally there was not yet enough sheer physical capability behind the instruments of power (a small police force, absence of telecommunications).

However, precisely these obstacles were to disappear between 1789 and 1848. In order to assure national unity, the Revolution suppressed all independent bodies, broke the power of the Church, the officers' corps, and the *parlements*—all in order to give unlimited power to the revolutionary state, but also because the ideology of national sovereignty assumed that all citizens should be considered in their individuality and never incorporated into bodies that would determine their fates. At the same time, the Revolution destroyed, for reasons of its own inherent logic, all traditions that the king had had to respect. Finally, at just that epoch, new physical means of exercising power made their appearance, either in the form of deliberate creations (national army, popular police) or as consequences of technological progress (development of a press permitting propaganda, more rapid means of communication, such as Chappe's aerial telegraph). As a result, the state that followed in the wake of the Revolution became much more authoritarian than the state that had preceded it, because it was endowed with much more powerful means of action, and because the growth of the state in France was not so much the work of theoreticians (Richelieu and Louis XIV were not primarily theoreticians or Machiavellians) as the fruit of practical and efficient men seeking to make the state apparatus as efficient as possible; this general trend on the part of the monarchy was merely resumed by the regimes following it, even if constitutional theories were different by then.

But what were to become the French state's specific characteristics? First of all, *centralism*. The monarchic view was that nothing in the nation could function properly unless there was one and only one method for making decisions. This view was the fruit of actual observation. In feudal society, when there had been a great number of political decision centers, there had been disorder, incessant conflicts, and the resulting disadvantages for the population. As a result, the king had come to believe that singleness of the center of decision was the only remedy. This belief had then come to be expressed in theories and images which, however, were of secondary importance—for example the image of the human body in which the brain was the will's one and only center. A society was then envisaged in which every movement and every reform would receive its impetus from such a political center. It seemed no longer necessary that local powers should have any autonomy, but necessary that they should become instruments of the central will. This quest for centralization and reduction of all political life to a single point was accentuated during the Revolution by the conflict between the Jacobins and the Girondists.

There are many causes for that conflict—it has even been claimed that the Girondists were federalists—but the result of the Jacobin victory is inescapable: accentuation of centralization. Only the power of the Assembly was a political power of decision, and all political life led back to that in the capital. Federalism became a crime. Obviously, under Napoleon, this centralization could only become more pronounced; all strands of the political system had to be held in one hand. But it must be reiterated that this was not the feat of one man, either king or dictator, but the organic process of the state's development; the Directory, for example, was no less bent on centralization (and authoritarianism) than the empire had been. The state, responding to what its responsibility was considered to be, had to centralize. It is well known that Hegel's thinking was influenced by this example, and that German theories of state in the nineteenth century had the French state for their model. In France it was overwhelmingly clear that this concept would never be questioned again, even when the ideology of the liberal state was dominant, even when, as was the case on several occasions, there was the will and the intention to decentralize. But that aim was never to be attained. And the Second Republic in 1848 was even more bent on centralization than the Restoration had been. It is also important to remember that the horror and hatred leveled at the Commune were aimed just as much against their aim of doing away with the state as against their anticapitalist ideology.

A second important aspect of French institutions is their rationalism. Beginning with the Revolution, and in the wake of *Aufklärung,* people tried to think rationally about political, juridical, and administrative institutions. Old influences were at work, too, derived from Descartes and from Roman Law. From then on there was a reaction against all irrational elements that had been part of the *ancien regime*—in that regard the Revolution was truly something new. It was assumed that the Law and the State should be based on reason and rationally organized. For the men of 1793, everything was rational, or rather, was to become rational. The idea was that everything in society and man not subject to reason had to be eliminated. Men became convinced that truth could be discovered only through reason, and that reason, moreover, conformed to nature: therefore the more rational all institutions would become, the more they would conform to nature (whose rational character was discovered by science at that time) and the more just and efficient would they be. In the domain of the law, this led to an increasing suppression of all historical, pragmatic, customary law and to the creation of an entirely rational law. Similarly, it was considered necessary to divide French national territory into segments in no way congruous with history or geography, but with mathematical criteria (this went so far that a proposal was made to make the departments simply into equal squares). In any event, it is remarkable how important mathematics became in the political, administrative, and economic realms at the very time of the Revolution of 1789. The true political thought of the time (not activities in front of the curtain, such as those by Marat or Danton!) was that all would be solved if politics could be reduced to mathematics. From then on, administrative units were to become abstract and to turn into perfectly rational organizational systems; and corresponding theories were propounded. The aim was to construct a perfectly coordinated machine, single, hierarchized, and cohesive, in which the human element would be reduced to a minimum; to establish a mechanical administration that was anonymous and would eliminate every element of chance afforded by ideas, passions, sentiments, or personal interests.

Eventually Napoleon progressively established an administrative system that came as close as possible to such a rational model. But what the revolutionaries had overlooked was that such a machine was identical with an authoritarian state. It was the ideal instrument in the hands of a central authority that knew how to use such a device to organize an entire nation. True, a single, centralized seat of political power needed rational and vigorous means of action. Those means, at the same time, required a political power center invested with an authority none could challenge.

After Napoleon, this became the great conflict and adventure of our French Institutions in the nineteenth and twentieth centuries. On the one hand, there was, generally speaking, liberalism's triumph, which was not only economic but also political. To be sure, there were periods when power still tried to be authoritarian (the July Monarchy, the beginnings of the Second Republic, the first part of the Second Empire) but such authoritarian power collided with a general conviction that political liberalism was the truth: authoritarianism could not develop fully; it had to return to liberalism. After that there arose the remarkable conflict between a liberal state and an administration made to fit an authoritarian state. But there was no question of changing the form, the structures, of that administration, which in fact was by far the most effective, advanced and satisfactory. To destroy such a rational organization would have been regarded as retrogression. The only way out was to perfect it—and that is precisely what happened during the entire nineteenth century; but the more the system was perfected, the more its character was reinforced.

Max Weber's description of the bureaucracy applies even more aptly to French administration than to German, which, moreover, was a copy of the French. And during the entire Third Republic we had a politically very liberal regime that rested on very rigorous organization and ended up by functioning almost like a closed circuit. Such are the historic characteristics that determine the institutional problems of contemporary France. I wrote this book with them in mind, and with reference to them.

But, if the book is tied to a reality specifically French, can it have other than purely documentary interest for the foreign reader? It seems to me that it can, after all, have the value of example and serve as a warning. For I am not so sure that this French history is only French and only history. Does not the entire world experience the temptations that were experienced by the men of the French Revolution? Should this be so, France, for once, would have been ahead of other nations, though not necessarily for the best!

Let the reader ask himself only two questions: first, are we not witnessing a general trend toward statism, even in liberal, entirely democratic countries? The latter are without a doubt witnessing the growing prestige enjoyed by the centralized state. Peoples with strongly federal structures are trying to leave federalism behind; Swiss citizens care less and less for local life and local political issues, and instead, take on the belief that only the central authority is important; as a result, local powers are gradually being transferred to the federal center, which, little by little, is ceasing to be "federal" and is becoming "central." People are under the impression that in a world in which all problems are vast and extremely complex, local organs have neither the means nor the competence to do justice to such problems—a central power seems needed, for it alone has all the means to face these problems and solve them.

In a world in which interdependencies have become more and more stringent, in which every local decision has national, and sometimes even international repercussions, a central authority seems needed, one which takes these interdependencies into account, balances them, and compensates for them, since it seems that spontaneity of political play suffices less and less to bring about a correlated development of the different sections of the economy or to reconcile opposed viewpoints on such problems as that of the free economy in France or that of the colored people in the United States. In a society in which socio-political trends unceasingly accelerate, people constantly have the feeling of losing time when beginning to study problems on the local level, or when engaging in long debates on matters that require rapid decisions. This "acceleration of history" also favors the establishment of a single political power center, capable of rapid action and more efficient technical surveys that can be contained in ordinary speeches by politicians, and capable of facing sudden crises that cannot be resolved at the local level.

In a society in which the growth of technology demands ever greater efforts and in which the great technological enterprises demand the centralization of all possible documentation, of all researchers (working in a coordinated manner, rather than individualistically or dispersedly), and of all financial resources (given the enormously great costs involved), only a central power can satisfy all these exigencies. The fact is that in order to implement technological progress, literally all the nation's resources must be mobilized. It is no longer possible to leave that to amateurs, to private enterprises, or to men who do not hold the entire machine in their hands; one can no longer afford to lose time in areas in which a single technological delay quickly causes a cumulative effect. Here, too, only a centralized state can bring about the needed mobilization.

To be sure, such a state can leave a certain number of tasks to private enterprises which already have the capability to take care of them. But the fact that certain enterprises, even of considerable size, are given particular tasks does not make centralization any less important; on the contrary, the more such decentralization is promoted, the more the state needs a stringent organization capable of putting all the pieces of the puzzle together. The more the various services and local enterprises of different importance are drawn in, the more a general, rational framework is needed. This leads to the second question: must an administration be slow, uncoordinated, or incompetent? Can a politician be a truly good administrator? Does he not need an enormous array of offices and experts? Must he not try to make his administration ever stricter and to reduce the various elements of human weakness in the process?

An administration must become more and more rationalized in order to respond to the multiplicity of its tasks, and this rationalization almost inevitably leads it along the road of bureaucracy. It seems to me that all countries in the Western and Soviet worlds are traveling in that direction, at different rates and in different ways. Nowadays one can scarcely avoid the centralized state and rationalized administration. But I do not mean that the French type is inescapable (and thus prophetic) or that the institutional structures operative in France must arise everywhere.

The French type, to the extent that it is a century and a half old, is obviously obsolete, which causes specific problems in France that are unique to that country; but I have addressed myself little in this book to these specifically French problems. In France this purposeful neglect has aroused some criticism to the effect that I did not deal with the real problems. But I omitted them because to me they seemed secondary as compared with the more permanent aspects and profound implications of the problems involved. It is not particularly important to analyze, as Michel Crozier does, the style of French bureaucracy; to do so means to stick to details of structure and behavior, ultimately of no importance, because determined by special circumstances. But if the specific type of the French centralized state or its bureaucracy is obsolete, it nevertheless yields a model, a schema, both in theory and with respect to possible further development, which makes it a valuable example for other countries faced with the problem of centralization, of the application of technological means in administration, of adjusting bureaucracy to the growth of the economy, and so on.

Yet there definitely exists the possibility that different kinds of institutional structures could spring from that same centralizing and rationalizing orientation. But such diversity can affect only secondary elements, and only if it does not interfere with the system's efficiency. For rationalization in a technological society consists in reducing the element of chance (quite accurately, economic planning has been defined as "anti-chance") and in the reduction of inefficiency. But up to the present, and in spite of all efforts on the part of social and political scientists to show that free democratic play is more efficient than any other form, it nevertheless seems that the application of conscious, directive rationalization is more efficient. Take the example of war, where the efficiency test is clear: every war entails in every government a growth of its powers and a rational coordination of all activities. Thus, the more the technological character of society increases, and the more its need to be efficient grows, the more all real forces outside the central power structure tend to diminish. Only apparent divergencies remain—ones that have no true impact.

For this reason, the analysis contained in this book, though at first glance closely tied to French experience and to the political administrative history of my country, may ultimately be of wider value. I don't say that things are necessarily unfolding in other countries as they are described here. But that face to face with the same necessities, the political powers run the risk of ending up traveling along the same road, in which case there is a good possibility that things will take the same course as they did in France.

Anyone who holds the view that planning, in whatever domain, is both efficient and inevitable cannot, for example, evade the controversy about the relation between democracy and planning or the attempt to find possibilities of democratic planning, and he will then necessarily encounter the arguments and points found in this book. It is not an exhaustive analysis, but considering the actual state of affairs, for France it is. It is not impossible to find another road for democratic planning, but it must, in any case, be realized that the actual experiences related are proof of the conflict between planning and the practice of true democracy. Put differently: for those not yet committed to the road of centralization and rationalization, the book may be, on the one hand, a warning, and on the other, a basis for reflection in their effort to find other answers without first losing time exhausting oneself "on roads leading nowhere" (*Holzwege*).

JACQUES ELLUL

January 1966

Contents

THE POLITICAL
ILLUSION

The people will fancy an appearance
of freedom; illusion will be their na-
tive land.

Saint-Just

In the seventeenth century we could have written of the comic illusion. In our day the illusion has become tragic. It is political.[1] People in our time, with even greater zeal than in the nineteenth century, invest political affairs with their passions and hopes, but live in a peculiarly distressing political trance. Despite past experiences we have not attained a realistic view of our situation, and the interference of myths constantly frustrates political impulses and renders our thoughts out-of-date. To be sure, circumstances have made us question yesterday's political certainties; we are now aware of the tenuous nature of public opinion even if strongly affirmed in some

------

[1] No definition for the word "political" can be found that would be both exhaustive and universally acceptable. Differences of opinion in this field are well known. Still, I will employ this term partly in the ordinary sense, partly in a restricted sense, i.e., not only with reference to a particular system. For example, as far as I am concerned, political matter ("*le* politique") is the domain and sphere of public interests created and represented by the state. Politics ("*la* politique") is action relative to this domain, the conduct of political groups, and any influence exercised on that conduct. I therefore include in this last term the conduct of "public affairs" as a form of competition between groups that claim to provide solutions to problems raised in a society.

glorious plebiscite; we know that the sovereignty of the people is an etiological myth without possible realization; we know that "the popular vote is not an effective process for controlling or passing judgment on a regime, or an effective means of arbitration in the struggle between opposed political and social forces, nor a process suited to select the ablest leaders." [2]

Although the events of the twentieth century have made it clear that the political notions treasured as truths in the nineteenth century are but faded myths for us, the majority of our fellow citizens still live by them. Among them are sentimental democrats, idealistic Christians, and those so devoted to the past that they accept as evidence of change no political events subsequent to the French Revolution. And yet the old shibboleths have been violated by events. The juridical and constitutional structures corresponding to the old myths had to become ever more complex in order to retain an appearance of effectiveness. But even the appearances have lost their power of seduction. As a result, in the last twenty years we have seen new stars rising on the horizon, a slow creation of new myths taking the place of those now defunct, a creation of a new political illusion destined—as always—to veil a reality that haunts us and that we cannot control. It therefore seems to me that if we have any chance at all to rediscover some value in collective life, we must reject past and present myths and attain full consciousness of the political reality as it actually exists.

But I do not believe that this reality can be grasped by the tool that is most widely accepted today: mathematical, experimental, and microscopic sociology. Such efforts, so impressive in some respects, produce solid results only at the price of abandoning the object of the study. To disregard many factors in order to study only one, to schematize behavior in order to classify it, to indulge in prejudices carefully camouflaged by extremely objective methods—such are the shortcomings, among many others, of this type of sociology.[3] Its methods do not en-

---

[2] *L'État et le citoyen,* publ. under the direction of Club Jean Moulin (Paris: Editions du Seuil; 1961).
[3] Pitrim Sorokin: *Tendances et déboires de la sociologie américaine* (Paris: Editions Montaigne; 1959), orig. publ. in U.S. as *Fads and Foibles in Modern*

title us to pass from microscopic analysis to macroscopic conclusions. A recent study [4] has shown us the complexity of the
problem and revealed how the extrapolation of the results of
microscopic analysis leads to a strange world in no way coinciding with political reality. Attempts such as these superimposed certain images on political reality and try to establish
certain patterns, but without ever coming to grips with genuine
political matter: some essential element is always lacking, some
basic aspect is always neglected! The discursive method, though
seemingly less precise, is, in the end, more exact.

Like some Christians who constantly speak of God, Christianity, and their faith because they would find themselves confronted with an immense void if they stopped talking, we talk
endlessly of politics in an unconscious effort to hide the void in
our actual situation. The word is compensation for an absence,
evocation of a fleeting presence, a magic incantation, an illusory
presence of what man thinks he can capture with the help of
his language. There is auto-suggestion in it: I say it and repeat
it; it therefore exists. It is true that man's words exist and, in a
way, we can be satisfied with just that. Perhaps our words are
the unconscious reaction of a slow and critical awakening of
our consciousness. Because it would be too awful if the void
were an inescapable fact, we must destroy the silence by our
talk and fill the void with sound to keep it from being too
frightening. The use of sound and speech as substitutes for
substance are rites that go back to the beginnings of the human
race. Sade wrote his diary to elevate mediocre experiences and
compensate for the absence of his *amours ancillaires*. In the
middle of the nineteenth century, people began to talk of culture, only to deplore at the same time that culture was in a state
of crisis. And the endless talk contributed to culture's rapid
deterioration, just as the country that arms on a grand scale is
the one that continually talks of peace and keeps showing the

---

Sociology (Chicago: Henry Regnery; 1956). Jacques Ellul: *Propagandes* (Paris:
A. Colin; 1962), Annex I, publ. in U.S. as *Propaganda* (New York: Alfred A.
Knopf; 1965).
[4] François Bourricaud: *Esquisse d'une théorie de l'autorité* (Paris: Plon; 1961).

dove and the olive branch; and it is the dictator with his police and party organization who will stimulate his most fervent zealots to make speeches to the effect that freedom has finally been assured and democracy finally been realized.

If one has attained an object, why talk about it? If one really lives in peace and freedom, why make them the subject of speeches? Their very existence and the pleasure of enjoying them should be enough. When there is plenitude, what can be added to it? The lover united with his beloved never writes poems; poetry is produced only as a result of absence and loss. Poetry is only a verbal affirmation of love when love is no longer anything but a cloud, regret, anxiety attacking the individual's uncertainty.

Sometimes we see a Machiavellian will at work, a deliberate cheating of people by those fully aware of the real situation—the rule of a dictator, magic incantations—and the people effectively experiencing, through the mediation of the inspired word, a reality simulating what has been taken from them. Freedom can be even more real when proclaimed by a chief in the shadow of his Gestapo than in the paralysis resulting from the various possibilities offered to our enfeebled decision-making abilities. But, more frequently, the verbalization by a political leader comes from a man's heart as a spontaneous, profound response meant to veil the intolerable situation in which what we cherish more is in danger of ultimately being revealed as defeat, shadow, absence, illusion. But we cling to this illusion; we have chosen it as our value; we must believe in it; it must remain an independent and constant object on which we can lean, for which we can live. We will then talk about it and repeat it in the form of an incantation to assure ourselves that we have it, know it, live it. It becomes a profound rule, constantly verified, and should also become a theorem of political interpretation: A regime that talks most of some value is a regime that consciously or inconsciously denies that value and prevents it from existing. And this concerns us at the humble political level. Every day, scientific, polemical, didactic, philosophic studies on politics and democracy are appearing. Every one of these studies—my own above all—testifies to our attachment to these works of man —politics and democracy—and the fear that haunts us because we know well at the bottom of our souls that nothing is left of them but words.

INTRODUCTION

POLITIZATION

It is a stereotype in our day to say that everything is political. We were reminded only recently that politization is "denounced by both official moralists and the good people."[1] But what is politization? We have been given two of its dimensions: Politization is represented by the importance and growing frequency of ideological debates; and it is manifested by the tendency to treat all social problems in the world according to patterns and procedures found in the political world.

Though these two characteristics are indeed part of the phenomenon of politization, they are much too limited and specific to provide a full description. It is quite true that one of the aspects of politization in our society is the volume of ideological debate, doctrinal conflict, systematic argumentation along certain lines. But politization also exists in countries where ideological debates do not occupy an important place; what is more, we must ask *why* these ideological debates have increased and what attitude people assume with regard to political matters, and not just to one or another doctrine. On the other hand, it is also true that there is a tendency to treat all social problems

---

[1] François Bourricaud: *Esquisse d'une théorie de l'autorité* (Paris: Plon; 1961), p. 326.

within the procedural framework of politics, that is, with debates, conferences, and so on. But this is an extremely narrow
and limited view of politization, for it must be stated first that
all problems *have,* in our time, become political. It is not
just a question of accepted political procedures being applied
to questions that at first glance do not seem political. The point
is that these questions *are* by now in the political realm, and
political procedures are applied to them because they have
become part and parcel of political affairs.[2]

The essential element that must be taken into consideration
if we want to understand the *total* phenomenon of politization
is a fact that is, if not the cause at least the moving force of this
phenomenon. The fact is the growth of the state itself. Governmental action is applied to a constantly growing number of
realms. The means through which the state can act are constantly growing. Its personnel and its functions are constantly
growing. Its responsibilities are growing. All this goes hand in
hand with inevitable centralization and with the total organization of society in the hands of the state.

The nation-state is the most important reality in our day. It is
much more fundamental in our world than economic reality.
Nowadays the state directs the economy. To be sure, the state
must take economic factors into account. The economy is not
an inert object in the hands of an arbitrary and capricious
ruler. But the ruler versed in economic techniques determines the economy much more than the economy determines
the state. The state is not just a superstructure. Marxist analysis
was valid only in the nineteenth century, when the emergence
of uncontrolled, explosive economic power relegated a weak,
liberal, and unclearly delineated state to the shadows and sub-
jugated it. But today the major social phenomenon is the state,
becoming ever more extended, ever more assured, and everywhere standing in the limelight. Of course, Lenin knew well
that every revolution must be political, but in his last letter (his

---

[2] We have not spoken here of the country's high standard of living that has
permitted the development of a true democracy, the establishment of a stable
government, and the development of socio-political techniques.

"Testament") he admitted that the emergence, evolution, and persistence of the Soviet state was for him a surprising and disturbing phenomenon. It was not as a result of a crisis, accident, or a disagreeable necessity in the pursuit of the highest objectives that the Soviet state has never ceased becoming stronger, despite its illusory reduction in power since the days of Khrushchev. Only the believers can still accept the dogma of the state's "withering away"; it seems clear today that the Soviet state's concern with the administration of all things by no means signifies its decline but rather its having become absolute. This development could take place only as a result of man's need to conform, which is the aim of all propaganda. In this confirmation of its power, the Soviet state is not fulfilling a special destiny. Soviet society is not evolving according to special laws, and the transition to socialism has not modified general socio-political trends. What we see in Soviet society is the general development of the state in our world, its growth and structure. To be sure, we are aware of all the differences that may exist between the Soviet state and the American state, the British state, or the French state. There are juridical and constitutional differences, differences of practice and intention. They exist, but are of little consequence compared with the similarities, and particularly with the general trend. There are more differences between the American state of 1910 and that of 1960 (despite the constitutional sameness) than between the latter and the Soviet state (despite the constitutional differences).

The idea that the state has become a phenomenon in itself— the most important in our society—is still expressed by certain Marxists in the well-known analysis of the emergence of a third class (the bureaucracy, the great cadres, the major technicians) —the class of those constituting the real political power. The fact that this political power eventually produced its own class is probably the most telling sign of society's takeover by the state.[3] And in our days the individual's seizure by the political powers is much graver and more decisive than economic aliena-

---

[3] Milovan Djilas: *The New Class* (New York: Frederick A. Praeger; 1957).

tion. The substitution of political slavery for economic slavery is the current fraudulent exchange.

At present the greatest problem is the citizen in the clutches of political power. In one sense we can feel reassured, for here we return to well-known problems always debated by political men and philosophers: the relation of man to state power? Let us call upon Plato and Montesquieu for assistance. The danger of the individual being absorbed by the state? Let us appeal to Hobbes and Rousseau. But I want to stress that aside from the customary reflections on the nature of power (to which insufficient attention is being paid in our day), the uniqueness of our situation must be taken into account. The given facts of the problem have changed and past political philosophy can be of little help. It seems to me that there is an entire, so far little explored, *intermediary* zone between the zone studied by political scientists, who often remain at the surface of the events, and the zone of pure political thought—I could almost say political metaphysics—that has a certain permanence. I shall try to keep myself in the zone between the two.

The other element (the growth of the state is the first) that conditions and determines the politization of society is the growth of the individual's participation in political life. It is a doctrinal offshoot of democracy—of various arrangements in different republican states, of demographic growth that brings the masses closer to the seat of power, of speedier communications, development in education, and, finally, of the fact that the state's decisions increasingly concern everybody, and that the state does not feel assured of its legitimacy except by the expressed support of the people. These are the reasons for and symptoms of this growing participation.[4]

All this forms a solid body of evidence. But one neglected fact must be stressed. It is accepted that since the eighteenth century the individual's participation in political affairs has increased. But while this is generally admitted (before the eighteenth century there was little such participation in the West), the corollary is generally omitted: except on rare occasions, political

[4] Jacques Ellul: *Propaganda* (New York: Alfred A. Knopf; 1964), Chap. iv.

affairs in and by themselves, and in the eyes of man, formerly had little importance. In view of the fact that *we* judge everything in relation to political affairs, this seems unbelievable. How can we admit that in those past centuries political affairs were not a subject of interest, of passion—that lack of public participation was much less the result of the autocratic character of the prevailing regimes than of great indifference on the part of the public itself? Nevertheless, it seems that for centuries political affairs, except for rare moments, produced little activity, were the care of specialists in a specialized domain, or a princes' game that affected a very limited number of individuals. True political revolutions were palace revolutions, and when they took place the masses were rarely more than extras or stage decorations. However that may be, even if this claim does not ring quite true, active participation in political affairs by the masses is a new phenomenon.

To think of everything as political, to conceal everything by using this word (with intellectuals taking the cue from Plato and several others), to place everything in the hands of the state, to appeal to the state in all circumstances, to subordinate the problems of the individual to those of the group, to believe that political affairs are on everybody's level and that everybody is qualified to deal with them—these factors characterize the politization of modern man and, as such, comprise a myth. The myth then reveals itself in beliefs and, as a result, easily elicits almost religious fervor. We cannot conceive of society except as directed by a central omnipresent and omnipotent state. What used to be a utopian view of society, with the state playing the role of the brain, not only has been ideologically accepted in the present time but also has been profoundly integrated into the depths of our consciousness. To act in a contrary fashion would place us in radical disagreement with the entire trend of our society, a punishment we cannot possibly accept. We can no longer even conceive of a society in which the political function (on the part of the governmental authority) would be limited by external means: we have arrived at the monistic idea of power that stops power. We can no longer conceive of a society with autonomous "in-between" groups or diverging activities. The primary role of political affairs is one of the common sociological presuppositions shared by all and growing in all countries.

We consider it obvious that everything must be unreservedly subjected to the power of the state; it would seem extraordinary to us if any activity should escape it. The expansion of the state's encroachment upon all affairs is exactly paralleled by our conviction that things *must* be that way. Any attempt on the part of any enterprise, university, or charitable enterprise to remain independent of the state seems anachronistic to us. The state directly incarnates the common weal. The state is the great ordainer, the great organizer, the center upon which all voices of all people converge and from which all reasonable, balanced, impartial—i.e., just—solutions emerge. If by chance we find this not so, we are profoundly scandalized, so filled are we with this image of the state's perfection. In our current consciousness no other center of decision in our social body can exist. To repeat: it is not just the fact of the state being at the center of our lives that is crucial, but our spontaneous and personal acceptance of it as such. We believe that for the world to be in good order, the state must have all the powers.

Conversely, we find a rather curious attitude among certain social psychologists who regard every phenomenon of authority, at whatever level, in whatever groups, or in whatever way it manifests itself, as never anything but an accident whose paradigm is the state. If a leader emerges in a group, or if a father exercises his authority in the family, or if a technician imposes himself upon a corporation, the phenomenon of authority is taken out of its proper context and traced back conceptually to approximate that of the state, so that *all* instances of authority are microcosms of central authority.

The place we accord in our hearts to the state and political activity leads us to an interpretation of history which we regard primarily as political history. For a long time only events concerning empires and nations, only wars and conquests, only political revolutions were taken into account. Undoubtedly that conception of history is obsolete: it has been replaced by the importance attributed to political and administrative structures. A society has no reality for us except in its political institutions, and those institutions take precedence over all others (despite the importance assumed by economic and social history). Above all, we cannot escape the strange view that history is ultimately a function of the state. Only where the state is, is history worth the name. The Merovingian times are so dark only because the state was inconsequential. The "Middle Ages" are merely an intermediary age, a period without name, only because they unfolded between two periods when the state was glorious: the Roman and the Monarchistic. Between the two there was this regrettable interlude in which the historian must look at society as unformed because it was not directed from a summit, animated by a single will, or centrally organized. Fortunately the kings restored the state with iron hand. France again became a property of value and the superiority of that restoration was contrasted to the disorderly dissolution of the Holy Roman Empire. To be sure, because we are democrats, we are against Louis XIV's monarchic authoritarianism. But he retains our secret affection because he was The State.

And we are profoundly irritated with de Gaulle because he promised—but failed to produce—the centralized, impartial, all-powerful state, so powerful that it would have only to show its power without exercising it: the unchallengeable and sure state that would have given us pride and peace of mind. How many times have we read and heard of efforts that would finally give the state all the needed authority! We are poor, lost children who seem no longer to remember what the means and the price of that would be! This aspiration, this unconscious assigning of the supreme role to the state leads us immediately to the consideration that everything is now its business. The question returns again and again, like some evidence that it would be absurd to protest: "But after all, what is there that is *not* political?"

To be sure, if we begin by conceiving society as a whole made up of dead pieces without autonomy, receiving an active place only in a coherent system, and obtaining life only from the supreme impetus of political power, then we must accept the

suggested answer as evident. And it *is* evident for us contempo-
raries. But one should be aware of the fact that it is based on a
prejudice, on adherence to a preconception. What we see here
is the result of the process of politization in our selves: the
penetration into our unconscious of the "truth" that an ultimately
political process rules our lives. As a result we are lead to render
all questions political. Those which are not must then be politicized because our frame of mind dictates that ultimately everything is political. This is not only fixed in the minds of the masses
but is stated to be so—and justified—by the intellectuals. Take
Talcott Parsons: "Political affairs are the center of intergration
of all analytical elements of the social system, and not one of
these particular elements." [5]

If art is not part of this, that is only because we do not notice
it. To notice it more clearly one need only encourage attributing
political sense or value to art—make the artist feel that his
efforts are vain if he is not "engaged" or does not manufacture
doves that can be plastered on all the walls. This constant confusion between political affairs and society is a new phenomenon
in history. Undoubtedly there were some earlier models: the Az-
tec Empire, Egypt, perhaps China, and, to some extent, Rome.
But there we must make two major reservations: in those days
the state did not have the means to execute its intentions. The
mass of the people did not spontaneously—or, one might say,
ontologically—offer its faith and ideology to the state. If there
was a religion sanctioned by the state, there was not, ordinarily,
a *religion* of state (worship of the state). In other eras, a man
could be regarded as being committed by being involved in the
structure and the collective life of his society—in the arts,
science, religion, etc. He is no longer considered "committed,"
however, unless the implications of his activity are directly
political.[6] To participate in non-political activities that are never-

---

[5] Talcott Parsons: *The Social System* (Glencoe, Ill.: The Free Press; 1951), p.
126.
[6] The term "political" must be taken here in its precise and restricted sense, i.e.,
with relation to the state and not to just any power, or just any social activity.
Max Weber's definition is both classic and excellent: "Politics is the leadership
by a political body called the state, or any influence exerted in that direction."
I also agree with Weber that the state can be defined sociologically only by its

theless definitely related to our society is regarded as without value. A poet restricting himself to being a poet without signing petitions or manifestos would immediately be accused of retiring to his ivory tower. Nowadays we prefer Aristophanes' political pieces to Aeschylus. As the renowned and very politized French actress Simone Signoret said: "We want to bring a message to the world."

In this general trend, values are also being politicized. As Jean Barets has said, all values have a political connotation—in fact, a political content—in our eyes. Liberty? We jump with both feet from the haziest metaphysical discussion to the concept of political regimes, and from this to a political definition of freedom, which in our eyes is negligible unless it is officially incorporated in a regime, or the fruit of a constitution, or represented by the participation of a citizen in state power. To say that freedom simply means that the individual can escape the power of the state and decide for himself on the sense of his life and his works seems in our day a simplistic, ridiculous, and adolescent reaction. Similarly, justice no longer exists as a personal virtue or as the more or less attained result of the law. When we take it seriously, justice unfortunately must be endowed with some adjective, particularly the adjective "social," i.e., it is ultimately regarded as political. It is up to the State to make justice prevail: there is only *collective* justice, and the difficult questions by legal philosophers of past centuries make no more sense to us now than does the Christian affirmation that justice is the individual's miraculous transformation by the grace of God. In our day values that cannot be given political content or serve some political activity are not longer taken seriously.

In fact, values no longer serve us as criteria of judgment to determine good or evil: political considerations are now the

---

specific means, which is force. Obviously, force is not the state's only normal means, but it is its specific and exclusive means. The definition of politics by François Goguel and Alfred Grosser is also acceptable (see *La Politique en France* [Paris: A. Colin; 1964]). "It is the whole of behavioral patterns and institutions concerning public affairs which help create power, control actions through such power, and ultimately try to replace those who exert it."

pre-eminent value, and all others must adjust to them. Politics and its offspring (nationalism, for example) have become the cornerstone of what is good or represents progress. Political concerns are thought to be inherently excellent. Man's progress in today's society consists in his participation in political affairs. How many articles and declarations have we not read on that subject! For example, women finally become human beings because they receive "political rights." To say that woman, mother of the family, exerting a profound effect on the development of her children was the true creatress in the long run, the true force from which all politics originated, is now just reactionary talk. A person without the right (in reality magical) to place a paper ballot in a box is nothing, not even a person. To progress is to receive this power, this mythical share in a theoretical sovereignty that consists in surrendering one's decisions for the benefit of someone else who will make them in one's place. Progress is to read newspapers. The political scientist Rivet meant it seriously when he said: "A man who cannot read a newspaper [Rivet was talking about Africa] to be informed is not a man." What a strange conception of manhood! This is the political trinity: "Information—Participation—Action." That is now the order of the day and the nature of progress.

People fight for economic democracy, which is expected to give them an opportunity to express their desires on affairs that touch them most closely, and this economic democracy, concerned with working conditions, distribution channels, plan requirements, prices and tariffs—all things that are infinitely concrete—is now contrasted with the political democracy of a former time, which is today regarded as merely abstract and theoretical. But let us turn the clock back two hundred years. What did those who clamored for this political democracy have in mind? To attain direct and effective control over the police; not to pay taxes except those one had agreed upon (which then seemed like a voluntary contribution); not to go to war except when the people themselves wanted it; to be able to express one's ideas freely and publicly; for each and every person to be able to affect and form public opinion. Were these abstract matters? By no means. They were terribly precise and concrete. We know how important such things are. But, except for ideologists who only see things in their dreams and imagination, we also know that economic democracy is in the process of failing now, at the very moment when it is being built, and that the power attributed to the "toilers" in Yugoslavia, the Soviet Union, or France is only theoretical and apparent. The process by which, in the nineteenth century, political decisions became a mere abstraction is being repeated in identical form, before our eyes, in connection with economic decisions now allegedly entrusted to the individual. The same farce takes place in the economic realm, always under the pretense of giving man powers in relation to the state. But it should be understood first that in the case of the modern state, powers granted to the individual are never anything but innocuous concessions, mere powers to endorse what is good for the state—the latter being the sum of all the social good.

However, the masses, who do not actually participate in political affairs, firmly believe that they do; and, in addition, make their illusory participation their principal criterion of dignity, personality, liberty. Colonial people finally become civilized people because they join the United Nations; Africans finally attain dignity because they share political power; and, solemnly, the thinkers tell us: "They are entering into History." For those thinkers no history exists where there is no politics. Who can fail to be struck by such profound politization! To claim that the complex social organization of the Bantus or the transformation of a continent by the Manchus are not part of our history would be ridiculous. Yet it is the most profound conviction of our time that such peoples enter into history only when they begin to adapt their state structures and political life to the Western model. The reference to *political* affairs is what really counts. Now, finally, these people will "make their voices heard."

This judgment, only mildly exaggerated, has its corollary: the severe condemnation of "apolitical people." In our society anyone who keeps himself in reserve, fails to participate in elections, regards political debates and consitutional changes as superficial and without real impact on the true problems of man, who feels that the war in Algeria deeply affects him and his children, but fails to believe that declarations, motions, and votes change anything will be judged very severely by every-body. He is the true heretic of our day. And society excommuni-cates him as the medieval church excommunicated the sorcerer. He is regarded as a pessimist, a stupid fellow (for he fails to see the very deep and secret mores in the political game), a defeatist who bows his head to fate, a bad citizen: surely, if things go badly, it is his fault, for if he were more civic minded, the vote would turn out differently (it is not enough to have 80 per cent of the voters cast their vote; no, we need 100 per cent!), and democracy would be more effective. Negative judgments rain down on him; his effectiveness and his morality are judged; even his psychic health is questioned (the unpolitical man is obviously a little paranoid or schizophrenic!). Finally the ulti-mate condemnation of our day and age is hurled at him: he must be a reactionary.

This shows us that man in his entirety is being judged today in relation to political affairs, which are invested with ultimate value. In our judgment everything has become political and political affairs are the ultimate guidepost. Beyond them there is nothing. And political affairs can be judged only by political considerations. One may say, of course, that politics should be in the service of man or of the economy, but that does not de-tract from the fact that the greatness of the state, its power to organize, and man's participation in the collective *via political channels* are the ultimate value symbols and criteria of our time, substituted for the religious symbols and criteria of the past.

One must reach the same conclusions if one considers not just the presuppositions, prejudices, and unconscious motiva-tions of modern man, but his conscious emotional attitude. As soon as this man involves himself in politics he is animated by a passion without measure. In our day political conflict has defi-nitely become the decisive and ultimate form of conflict. It is enough to have been in contact with the Fascists in 1934, the Communists, or the Gaullists to understand to what extent dis-agreements nowadays over forms of government, or the European Defense Community, or other limited concerns are more fundamental than disagreements over the ultimate ends of man. It is celebrated as a victory of the spirit when anti-Christian materialists and fervent Christians collaborate, when bourgeois intellectuals and factory workers sit on the same committees, when Fascists and Mohammedans, or Christians and Mohammedans work in fraternal harmony. But it should first be asked, what *is* this powerful cement that permits men to overcome race and class differences and eliminates the most violent metaphysical and religious differences? There is only one: politics. Compared to a similarity of views for or against a decision regarding some war, how significant can differences be on the meaning of life? It should also be asked whether this beautiful accord, celebrated with such enthusiasm, is not dearly paid for by concomitant divisions. In fact, such accords can be established only at the price of designating a common enemy—a political enemy—and the accord will be all the closer as the hatred against "the other" becomes more violent. As a result, Christians will drive Christians from the church and Mohammedans will kill Mohammedans. Political disputes today are what disputes between Christians were in the sixteenth century. But perhaps to know whether it really is Christ who saves us is ultimately much less important than the conclusion of a treaty or the choice between permanent revolution and other ways of doing things.

But do not the lives of millions depend on such political decisions? They do because our political passion creates such dependence. But this dependence need not exist. For political conflicts, political solutions, political problems, political forms are ultimate, not in themselves or by the nature of things, but by the glory we attribute to them, by the importance assigned to them by every one of us, by the frantic trembling exhibited each time the political sacrament—the flag, the chief, the slogan— comes near us. We may say that the basis for this is the factual situation of the expanding state. That is true. But this state has no powers except those recognized by its subjects. I do not say it exists by virtue of what we yield; much rather, it exists by virtue of our loyalties and our passions. But the remedy Marx considered a cure for political alienation no longer applies. It is no longer sufficient that man deny the state his confidence or reject its authority (as observed already by Father Suarez) for the state to appear clearly as an empty phantom. Nowadays the crystallization of political structures, the growth of means of actions on the part of the state, and the creation of a new political class are irreversible phenomena to the extent that they exist; in any case, one's feelings cannot change them.

Thus our passions can only reinforce political affairs, and never weaken them. Traveling along this road, we are, in order to survive without an internal split, forced to attribute great good sense to political conflicts and, proceeding in the reverse direction from what was always man's course in such matters, to jump from the expanded political sphere into metaphysics, from politized history into metahistory that knows no miracle, no ends. Moreover, instead of the consoling presence—that experience so much desired by religious people—man now experiences faith and religious conversion thanks to his participation in politics. What was lost by the church has been found by the parties, at least those worthy of the name. Faith in attainable ends, in the improvement of the social order, in the establishment of a just and peaceful system—by political means—is a most profound, and undoubtedly new, characteristic in our society. Among the many basic definitions of man, two are joined together at this point: *homo politicus* is by his very nature *homo religiosus*. And this faith takes shape in active virtues that can only arouse the jealousy of Christians. Look how full of devotion they are, how full of the spirit of sacrifice, these passionate men who are obsessed with politics. But people never ask whether all this is worthwhile. Because these witnesses are so devoted, they invest the object of their service with their passion. In this fashion a nation becomes a cult by virtue of the millions of dead who were sacrificed for it. It must all be true, as so many agreed (did they?) to die for it. The same goes for the state, or national independence, or the victory of a political ideology.

Those who are thus devoted do not remain without compensation or profit: here they find the communion that escaped them everywhere else. On the level of political action, or in the

Resistance, or in the well-known solidarity of parliamentarians among themselves, or in Communist cells or O.A.S. groups, or in great, solemn, vibrant meetings in defense of the republic man can experience the communion that he absolutely needs but no longer finds in his family, his neighborhood, or his work—a common objective, some great popular drive in which he can participate, a camaraderie, a special vocabulary, an explanation of the world. Politics offers him these joys and symbols, these indispensable expressions of communion.

These are, it seems to me, the various aspects of politization, constituting a whole. But we still must find out whether man, once politicized, is not victim of a hoax or trapped in a *cul de sac*.

Contrary to what we have just said, some speak nowadays of modern man's *de*politization. By merely looking at the distress displayed by the political scientists and essayists who analyze this depolitization, we can measure to what extent politics have become value. If man were depolitized, what a disaster; it is as though he should cease being an artist, intelligent, or sensitive. Depolitized? An entire dimension of man would disappear. Surely, political affairs are neither a game nor a useful, only moderately important, pragmatic activity: they represent a genuine value and appear to give man control over his destiny. But, it seems to me, if it is true that depolitization is only a temporary and local phenomenon, it must be understood in any case that it can be discerned only in relation to politization. Because modern man is politicized as he presumably never was before, any retreat from political affairs becomes very noticeable and visible, and we experience it as a retrogression. But it is not only with regard to the general movement of politization that we can discern depolitization; it is also within the compass of the former that the latter takes place. Depolitization is not a phenomenon of similar magnitude: it is more limited than politization, affects only certain areas, certain forms of behavior, and certain attitudes. Politization, on the other hand, affects the whole conception of actual life and even gives depolitization a significance different than it seems to have at first glance.

In order to judge the nature of depolitization more specifically, some observations must be made: on the one hand, there really is a certain depolitization in the form of "*de*participation," "*de*ideologization," "*de*partisanization," and a certain reluctance to vote. On the other hand, there is apolitization of new groups that take the place of weakening older political groups, and a growing interest in political problems. S. M. Calvez has said it very well: "A politicized mind is not the opposite of a depoliticized mind. A politicized mind is an invaded, crushed, passively submissive mind, even where this submission provokes agitation and violence." [7]

On the other hand, we cannot assume the presence of just any depolitization. Most authors wrestling with the problem (many of whom are convinced, a priori, that there is depolitization) admit that the term covers variable realities (with the Left complaining of the growing apathy of its militant members, parties of the loss of adherents, and so on), but ultimately depolitization is seen as a decline of political participation in its older and more traditional forms, not as the refusal of all participation (Calvez). This is true even when there is some skepticism or indifference with regard to political activity (Merle), a "relativization of political affairs" (André Philip), or an "empirical political existence that is ambiguous, prudent, and a little facetious" (Georges Lavau). All this does not imply genuine depolitization, and above all does not signify a breach in the phenomenon of politization as we have described it earlier. Depolitization as discussed by most political scientists is really concerned only with actual participation of a democratic nature. Yet, for example, to put oneself in the hands of the state not by default but because of loyalty is the height of politization (Alfred Grosser); similarly, in a democracy politization in the general concept of social life is more important than participation in election meetings. There can be, simultaneously, a disinterest in politics and an overevaluation of political affairs. There can be a "*de*ideologization" of controversies by the surrender of old doctrines, and at the same time a "mythization" of

---

[7] Taken from an article by S. M. Calvez in Georges Vedel (ed.): *La Dépolitisation: Mythe ou réalité* (Paris: A. Colin; 1962).

the state and an emotionalization of its problems. In such instances depolitization is superficial and, as soon as circumstances change, a violent and massive *"repolitization"* will appear on the very level of activity which seemed to have been abandoned.[8]

The point is to try to penetrate to a certain reality of political affairs within, but also outside of, the philosophy of politics, outside the "framework of a positive conception of history, that imaginary shelter to which we are led equally by the theory of the proletariat as the universal class, and by the religious idea of the 'becoming of the spirit,'" in Clement Lefort's remarkable formula.[9] Here the point is to reject at the same time the conviction that the ultimate questions are answered and the conviction that there is nothing except questions of fact. Besides, these two orientations lead to the same result, as was noted by Lefort: "Political reflection takes place within a limited horizon. . . . Political science and Marxist ideology have come to be two examples of contemporary conservatism."

To sum up: political analysis is generally conducted on either a philosophic level (political philosophy) or on a scientific level (political science). On the former level are, for example, such remarkable works as those of Eric Weil.[1] But I do not agree with him that today's central problem is to reconcile historical customs—with the state as their guardian—with a world organization fighting to control the forces of nature by means of contemporary technology. That is a theory of political phenomena which will not be adopted in this book.

The second type of analysis attempts to use a scientific method to describe and analyze the same phenomena. Innumerable works of that kind exist, but I will try here to use a different approach. My essay will be neither scientific nor philosophical and will therefore hardly be regarded as serious. And yet I believe it has substance.

---

[8] In this connection, see David Riesman: "Criteria for Political Apathy," who thinks that visible participation in elections and public expression of political opinions can hide deep political indifference and an absence of political engagement.
[9] Clement Lefort: "La Pensée de la politique," *Lettres nouvelles* (1963).
[1] Eric Weil: "De la politique" (1956).

[I]

THE NECESSARY
AND THE
EPHEMERAL

Let us first recall two traditional characteristics of politics, implicitly recognized but rarely expressed. 1. To have political processes it is necessary that there be an effective choice among several solutions. These solutions are not all equally just, or effective, or pleasant, but all are possible and, generally, no one solution can be selected as absolutely superior to all others. Here evaluation of the circumstances and the necessities they impose will play an important role. Among the various possible solutions, one may be preferable for moral reasons, another for reasons of utility. And each decision can be criticized from some point of view. Recent studies on decision-making attest to this variable and "chancy" character quite clearly (see, for example, the excellent work of *Société d'études et de documentation économique, industrielles et sociales* (s.e.d.e.i.s.).[1] The true political man will be the one who perceives the solution—not necessarily the middle solution incorporating most of the possible advantages; nor the most efficient solution, or the one that best expresses certain values; but he will be the man who, taking all facts and opinions into account, will find the response that wins the consent of the greatest number, while opening new possibilities for the future, i.e., possibilities for development.

But this choice must pertain to solutions that really exist: to have a choice—the eminent function of politics—it is necessary that there *really* be several solutions from which to choose. When a nation is crushed militarily, several solutions no longer are possible; it is then forced to accept the conqueror's conditions. (Take, for example, Poland in 1940.) At such a moment no political decisions can be made. To make them it is necessary to have what is called freedom. Real political decisions can be made only by men who are not too much tied down by their constituents, or by legal texts, or too conditioned by a monolithic civilization, or ruled by circumstances. They must be made by men who have some latitude in that they possess effective means of action, the ability to influence public opinion, and can dispose of a set of combinations and elements that can be used in different ways. To be sure, such men may make mistakes, but that does not make their decisions less political. True political decisions can never obey necessity. Political man cannot limit himself to being a machine simply endorsing inexorable events.

Moreover, a political man cannot limit himself to partial choices. Political decisions inevitably encompass choices of ends and choices of means; the dissociation of the two is absolutely artificial in political affairs. All great political figures were men who had extraordinary understanding of the major importance of means and knew that no true decision can be made without a choice, a definite extension of means; they knew that political decisions cannot be "general ideas," mere choices of ends, which

---

[1] Cf. Michel Massenet: "L'Avenir de la Liberté politique," in *Bulletin* s.e.d.e.i.s. (1962).

leave the selection of means to so-called executives. This, however, is a completely outmoded view, belonging to an epoch in which the means had not yet attained such importance, and did not yet directly influence ends. Moreover, if the choice of ends is to be a genuine choice, an exact knowledge of the contemplated means is necessary. And the politician's task will be precisely to subordinate the means to the ends on which he decides; but he will not decide on those ends except in conjunction with the means that he can put into motion. Thus political decisions are at the same time profound and general, actual and detailed. They emerge from a series of partial choices ultimately forming the decision. Let us remember Hegel's remarkable formula summing up this entire process: "The man of action, political man, must be certain that as a result of his action necessity will become a contingency, and contingency a necessity."

2. On the other hand, to render a political decision a certain duration of time necessary; the decision cannot concern an immediate event. It assumes a posture for the future, and sets a people's or government's image for some time to come. A political decision, in the true sense of the word, includes not only the inescapable nature of its execution, which is its most clearly apparent element, but also the establishment of a continuity, for from this decision a given situation will result which does not begin at point zero (I am thinking here of an absurd headline of June 30, 1961, declaring "Algeria at Point Zero"), but at a point on a curve, implying an elapse of time. Just like a law, a political position necessarily contains a position with regard to the future. It is not inevitable that the constant fluctuations of times and circumstances jeopardize what was decided yesterday; it is not inevitable that the hazards of public opinion modify the ends worked out or the means selected (this has been analyzed in detail in my book on propaganda); for if such is the case we are no longer actually involved in political affairs. The little demagogues gravely say that the government must be a simple expression and instrument of what public opinion desires. This formula, resting on the unproved presupposition of public opinion's wisdom and the equitable distribution of universal reason, is the very negation of true politics. For politics to

exist there must be control, not of men or forces, but of a continuing process.

Of course, it might be said that all this is artificial, and contrasts with the fluid course of life, the constant progress of technology, the organizing action of our administration or law. But as Marx very well observed, it is on the basis of this continuity of law and the political decisions encompassing a future brought under control that technological or economic progress can take place. It cannot take place except in a certain sequence, within a certain framework. Moreover, a political decision encompassing the future is not a simple anticipation of that future, anymore than it is a holding back of the future. It is a control over the future. The foresight exercised by a political man, necessarily chancy, is not the same as that of the political scientist who limits himself to predicting the most probable development. The political man aims at the realization of his anticipation: he aims at bringing the future to bay and making it conform to his wishes. Without such aim, there would be no politics. For a time, political activities do establish a regime, an institution, an agreement, a treaty, but such established practices are obviously only part of an evolutionary process. As prescribed points of reference they are part of the future, and with their help the political man can better gauge his course. Obviously, these points of reference are not eternal. But they represent a certain machinery with whose principles the political man is familiar; in the midst of fluctuating developments and uncontrollable phenomena, he knows his course. Thus the role of politics is not to "freeze" a society into a certain shape, but to introduce into it factors of continuity without which the coherence and continuity of a group would become too much a matter of chance. Finally, permanent arrangements always lead rapidly to an exhaustion of human and social substance.

But in our day the combination of these two elements of true political activity really no longer exist, or at least are in the process of disappearing. Choices take place in our society, but they no longer belong to the political realm as I have just described it. Continuities become ever firmer, but they no longer represent real political positions with regard to the future. On the contrary, they are new continuities, pre-empting true political activity. Politics nowadays is more frequently restricted to a field of limited powers and is no longer able to change given situations, a process whose efforts wove a rich fabric in another day.

The only domain in which politics can still act is the domain of current events, i.e., the sphere of the ephemeral and the fluctuating. As a result, the feeling that a political decision is truly serious has been lost. What becomes visible is no longer anything but appearance. The futility of acting within this vacuum is compensated for only by the extreme agitation of the politicians. Thus, the decisive trait of today's politics is the fusion of two contradictory elements: the necessary and the ephemeral.

1. The Necessary

To be sure, political decisions are still being made. But these are really pseudo-decisions because they are so rigorously determined as to give their initiators neither latitude nor choice. I am not speaking here of the doctrine of predetermined history. Everybody is familiar with the collective belief, springing from Marxism, that there is a particular direction to history, a rigorous mechanism of historical movement *necessarily* leading to socialism. What really seems remarkable about this belief is that the most fervent adherents to this doctrine of historical necessity are inevitably the ones acting with the greatest vigor to effect that very history! The doctrine itself did not foresee such a possibility, but frequently doctrines engender actions contrary to those which could logically have been expected. This has been true of Calvinism and Buddhism, as well as of Marxism; Lenin has probably best operated within the possible range of political choices in an otherwise contingent universe. And, establishing a method, he made it possible for his successors to follow a surprisingly effective political course. But one must not delude oneself. In the Soviet Union, too, the possibilities of choice are becoming progressively restricted. Communist politics, too, is encroached on nowadays by necessity, and by no means the kind of necessity for which its doctrine could have prepared it, but more and more by the kind imposing itself on every state. Therefore the thought of a predetermined course of history is not what I think decisive or disturbing. What is really disturbing is that the political game is played as if predetermined doctrine and necessity dictated the conditions, even though no true sense is at all apparent from the sequence of events. No doctrine has influenced the situation. Doctrine has not even expressed its direction and evolution; doctrine has merely reified ongoing situations insofar as the conditioning of people and the absence of any true political activity is concerned.

To have true choice in a political decision, the possibility must exist of combining various given factors and even facts of differing nature. And to make it really political, these given factors must not be imaginary, theoretical, or ideal, but must correspond to reality—either to facts or to real beliefs. But one of the considerable limitations of political choice is the elimination of what can be called values from the collective conscience, the current mentality, the spontaneous attitudes of the man in the street. Despite all criticism that can be leveled at Max Weber, his theory of the tension between facts and values (as a belief, not as a metaphysic) is not only useful but certainly valid. No matter how shocking or unlikely this may appear, the man of our day, indifferent to values, has reduced them to facts.[2]

Justice, freedom, truth are words still useful in propaganda. But these terms have new connotations: justice now means happiness produced by equal distribution of material goods; freedom has come to mean high living standards and long vacations; and truth, more or less, has come to mean exactness with

---

[2] A corollary development has turned political facts into values. For example, the fact of national existence turns into the value of national existence, which produces nationalism. Thus, the *fact* of the state becomes a value, and produces statism. I will not explore this phenomenon here, but instead refer the reader to my study: "Nation and Nationalism," *Revue de l'Évangélisation* (1962).

regard to facts. I could multiply these examples and expand the analysis; but basically, for many reasons, our time lacks guideposts and aims. Reference points selected are themselves closely dependent on facts, and do not furnish criteria of judgment with regard to those facts or a distant enough vantage point from which to view events. It is exactly at this point that the political leader finds himself extremely weakened: his capacities of decision are greatly limited in that he no longer can, in the eyes of public opinion or in his own, set values against facts. Strangely enough, politicians sometimes consider themselves liberated—more independent and more effective—when values have been jettisoned and they find themselves engaged in pure realism, cynicism, and skepticism. How often do we find this said about Machiavelli! Why do people not see that, quite to the contrary, despoiling politics of values means to relegate it to the domain of pure facts, which gives politics a chance to act without moral rules, to be sure, but at the same time considerably reduces its choices and decisions. Facts narrow politics down more than values; the results of acts committed by the prince are heavier if the prince adopts the conduct of a Machiavelli than if he adopts that of a Louis IX.

Naturally, if we judge in this fashion, we are thinking of believed, adopted values, accepted by all or almost all in a society or nation. Those which are specific only to the prince—an esoteric religion or a sophisticated philosophy—have no weight at all, and offer no possibility of combinations or latitudes of choice. That is why the public's dislike of values is so great. Values are thought to be part and parcel of an antique mode of thought, existing only as appearances to which credence is no longer given, having been rediscovered, as they were, under France's Third and Fourth republics as "Sunday sermons" that nobody considered worth basing his conduct on. And yet the "liberation" from the tutelage of values only leads to submission to a much more stringent necessity, which is, however, felt less because it no longer leaves any choice.

In fact, as we try to understand the progressive elimination of true political decisions, we must observe that the political man does not suffer at all as a result. He no more aspires to political freedom than anybody else does. Freedom always confronts the individual with painful contradictions and with responsibilities that he must exercise in the face of choices and risks. The individual never likes that; he much prefers a necessary, inevitable, clear course: in this way at least no time is lost in deliberation, and there is no binding responsibility. The individual is always ready to submit to necessity, as long as freedom's vocabulary is preserved, so that he can equate his servile obedience with the glorious exercise of a free, personal choice.

Along various routes, the nineteenth and twentieth centuries have become extraordinarily clever in practicing this terrible hypocrisy. And the political leader is no exception. He will not make true decisions as long as appearances will save him. He does not miss values which, if they were present, believed and accepted, would force painful choices upon him. I think Gaston Bouthoul [3] is in error when he thinks that governments have the grand choice: either power or happiness; either subjugate neighbors or raise the living standard. In the actual concrete situation the choices are already made: all governments are in favor of raising the living standard, and the kinds of power politics practiced today are only the means to that end, means that in many cases are still very necessary.

On the other end of this scale another evolution also tends to pre-empt decisions and make the course of political events inevitable. We still live within national frameworks. And, considering the wild growth of nationalism, that situation is not at the point of disappearing. Governments are national. But nowadays political decisions are made on a global level. Every nation that wants to be sovereign, whose government wants to engage in politics, is really part of a bloc that prevents it from making its own decisions. In appearance each nation can do what it wants with regard to NATO or Comecon. But in reality it has no choice at all. The decisions government must make are necessary decisions. If the French government withdraws from the Euro-

[3] Gaston Bouthoul: *L'Art de la politique* (Paris: Éditions Séghers; 1962).

pean Defense Community,[4] people are scandalized, consider it treason, and the matter must immediately be taken up under another name, in another form, to obtain the same result: France's place inside the bloc makes it unthinkable and even unrealizable for it to reject what that bloc requires. Every effort toward independence is a blow struck against an inherited situation, and will not be tolerated for long.

Those holding different views will cite at this point innumerable political decisions that did, or could have, come to pass: Yugoslavia leaving the Cominform, the patient and voluntary creation of a united Europe, Britain's hour of choice to join or not to join Europe, France's decision concerning Red China, and so on. But it would be easy to point out the higher necessities that imposed those choices. Of course political decisions still are possible. The point here is merely to demonstrate the growth of limitations weighing them down. Such limitations have always existed. The question is: are they more inevitable today than yesterday? Must we recall that as far as a united Europe is concerned, innumerable writers neither particularly wanted it to come about (which is of little importance), nor did they theorize much about it, but saw such a development as inevitable, as inscribed in the logic of facts? Thirty years ago, Ortega y Gasset wrote that "the probability of a general European state imposes itself mechanically." But when we talk of necessity, we do not mean to say that the political man limits himself to letting things take their course. He can also make absurd decisions preventing some development, as in France today, or he can excite himself greatly, talk a great deal, try to convince, set up committees or institutions, and use the mass media of communication. He fights to build Europe. But if he pursues this goal, it was imposed on him by the facts. When he commits himself, he does so out of the necessity created by the already present objective. He fights, but for an objective that is the fruit of prior circumstances and is reached mechanically, a little ear-

---

[4] The E.D.C. case, in which the technicians, after having been defeated by a political decision, finally won out in the Paris Accords, was well analyzed by Jean Meynaud: *La Technocratie: Mythe ou réalité* (Paris: Payot; 1964), p. 122.

lier or a little later. His agitation only hides from him his object's inexorable character. But one more qualification is in order here, so that the reader will not draw a hasty and general conclusion: I have no mechanical, fatalist, or organicist view at all. I only say that most of the time, in our days, things are that way. Genuine independent political decisions are more and more limited and rare. We can cite cases in which previously this rule was so common and general that one would not even have thought of giving examples! [5]

The point is that the integration of nations and peoples into power blocs very greatly reduces possibilities for independent decisions. A typical case is that of the new nations. Three months after Fidel Castro came to power I wrote (and received no praise and much criticism for my "simplistic" views) that he would be forced to enter into the Soviet bloc; that he would not be able to carry out his personal policy; and that this alignment would lead to internal communization. In the same way, the much discussed *tiers monde* (Third World—the uncommitted nations) exists only to the extent that it does not yet exist, and where, as a result, imaginary constructions still are possible and words have free reign. Once the African and Arab people have consolidated themselves, they will be obliged to enter a rigorously closed and determined system. Let no one say at this point that the entrance of nations into a vast body only shifts the locus of decisions, and that decisions can be made just the same. Some say: "We are only going through a period of adaptation. Political decisions thus far taken on the national level now become decisions at a higher level, but remain just as free. A difficulty arises only from the inconsistency between these two levels, and the difficulty of bringing them together." We know that argument; but we are referring only to one of the constants that cannot be demonstrated here for reasons of space: every

---

[5] A good example of idealism was furnished by Ludovic Tron (in *Le Monde*, February 19, 1963), who believes that the concept of "Europe" was a victory of public opinion and affected various governments. Such a claim is really surprising. It must not be forgotten that the "European" concept is the work of economic and military technicians. The amorphousness of public opinion is demonstrated by polls. What Tron calls "public opinion," "movements," or "circles" is precisely those little general staffs where the technicians dominate.

time an organism increases in dimension and complexity, the rate of necessity increases and the possibilities of choice and adaptation decline. In reality, big blocs obey much more rigorous mechanisms and their political actions become increasingly simplistic and predictable. The size and complexity of the mechanism is such that, if we want it to function, it must function in an autonomous fashion, with the fewest possible decisions and innovations.[6]

From the moment efficacy becomes the criterion of political action, new limitations restrict all decisions. That is exactly what is happening today. Even with the best of intentions, no one nowadays could select any other political criterion than efficacy. Already democracy's game rests entirely on success. The man will be elected who can bring some project to its successful conclusion, who is the most likely to succeed; a goverment that fails in some enterprise will inevitably be overthrown. Failure is never forgiven; the leaders of a defeated state are judged as war criminals, though they would have been the judges had they won. In times when people oriented themselves by other values it was possible to preserve a government that had been defeated but was legitimate. Jean II, the Good, remained king of France, as did Francis I; honor was saved, therefore everything was possible though all had been lost. This would be unthinkable today. The law of politics is efficacy. It is not the best man who wins, but the most powerful, the cleverest; and all these terms can be reduced to one: effectiveness. Despite its doctrine, the Soviet regime has gained a place of respect in the eyes of non-Communists because it won the war and increased production. In fact, in a technological world of implacable competition efficiency has become the sole criterion of a government's legitimacy. And how could one make a different choice as long as the challenge, leveled at us by someone who selects the route

---

[6] A remarkable example is the Ecumenical Council of Churches. In the beginning, when this council was very simple and animated by spiritual concerns, it provided opportunities for "informal" meetings. But the more the number of churches adhering to it increased, the more the council became structured and rigid, and the more the ability to fulfill its mission at the spiritual level declined.

toward efficiency, cannot be met except by taking the same road? If one nation decides to take that road, all others will follow suit; even if they are not being overwhelmed by the most efficient nation, the domestic populations themselves, jealous of their own prestige and success, will demand such an orientation.

Because of external competition and internal pressure, efficiency must become the primary aim. But this means that one must adopt the system of the enemy, and that those we hate will still win in the end. We have known for a long time that only a dictatorial regime can oppose a dictatorial movement on the rise (Rumania between 1935 and 1939, for example); that only propaganda can oppose propaganda; that only a rationalized—a planned—economy can withstand the competition of another planned economy. All of which means that ultimately Hitler really won the war. To be sure, one can dissemble for a while and maintain a liberal appearance, but, in the long run, competition becomes overwhelming and one must pick the shortest route. Yet the choice of efficiency, if not dictated in advance or unanimous, is, at a given moment and under the prevailing circumstances, not a free choice at all. At the same time, the penalty for not making it is all the harder and faster: simply to disappear from the surface of the earth. The time is over when men could say: "After me the flood." The flood now comes before our end. Thus we can formulate another constant with regard to contemporary political affairs: efficiency renders our choices more limited and the penalties harder and more immediate. The political man cannot choose between what would be more or less efficient. The choice is made independently of him. Because he may err in evaluating a situation, he must take recourse to men who are more competent than he, and place the choice in the hands of technicians.

Here we encounter a problem that has often been discussed in the last few years.[7] I will insist on only two points: the true

---

[7] Cf. Jacques Ellul: *The Technological Society* (New York: Alfred A. Knopf; 1964). Also reports from the Fifth Congress of the International Political Science Association, particularly Vedel's and Grégiore's papers. See also Raymond Boisdé: *Technocratie et Démocratie* (Paris: Albin Michel; 1963) and Jean Meynaud: *La Technocratie.*

choice today with regard to political problems depends on the technicians [8] who have prepared a solution and technicians charged with implementing the decisions. This leads to a " professionalization of the political function." Thus the margin of new moves open to the political man becomes even more reduced. One can say: "The great choices are in fact limited, their implementation requires modern techniques . . . not essentially different from one political party to another"—or from one government to another. Politics hardly retains any longer 'the illusion of initiative in regard to political choices.' " . . . "Even a Minister must ask somebody to advise him, in order to be able to choose between various possibilities proposed by other technicians." [9] In reality, today's actual decisions have no bearing on the spectacular and exciting questions agitating public opinion and perhaps becoming the arenas for great debates; rather, the decisions fundamentally affecting the future of a nation are in the domains of technology, fiscal techniques, or police methods; choice between electrification or prospecting for oil in the Sahara; implementation of a five-year plan, and so on. But these innumerable decisions are the fruits of the technician's labors. The political man is remarkably incompetent in these fields unless he is a specialist: but even if he is a specialist he will be a specialist in a particular field and leave all the rest to his colleagues. And the decision will no longer be taken on the basis of a philosophic or political principle or on the basis of a doctrine or ideology, but on the basis of technicians' reports outlining what is useful, possible, and efficient.[1]

Of course technicians can propose different solutions. And some cling to that fact in order to say: political man remains master of his decision after all. That is a fallacy. The politician

---

[8] The term "technician" is used in a general sense. For a more detailed definition, see J. Meynaud: *La Technocratie.* I entirely agree with his conclusions: a distinction must be made between specialized technicians, "generalists" (the latter being charged with producing syntheses), and, finally, experts. According to Meynaud, we have a technocracy when technicians of real or imagined competence participate in decisions and when technical competence enters into all organisms charged with decisions. Meynaud also shows how frequent that participation is.

[9] *L'État et le citoyen,* publ. under the direction of Club Jean Moulin (Paris: Éditions du Seuil; 1961), p. 168.

[1] J. Meynaud: *La Technocratie,* pp. 70 ff.

finds himself inside a framework designed by technicians, and his choice, if it is serious, will be made on technological grounds: he will have another technician establish what is "the best technique." Surely there can be errors. I have never said that technology was infallible.[2]

The important thing is that necessity subordinates political decisions to technical evaluations [3] with the consequence that "Political" decisions become increasingly rare. If politics is still defined as the art of the possible, nowadays it is the technician who determines with growing authority what is possible. All this is the result of innumerable forces that I cannot analyze at length: the increasingly technological nature of society at the moment when the state takes charge of that society, glorification of the technicians in public opinion, which, in turn, has been pushed to the point at which nothing is taken seriously that is not the fruit of technology, etc.[4] However that may be, the importance of the technicians in every political decision brings

---

[2] Examples of errors made by technicians, or aggravations of existing situations as a result of their recommendations are easy to produce; for example, the massive orientation toward dam construction in 1945 in France; the 1954 decision to apply intensive agriculture to the virgin territories in the Soviet Union; the decision to grow corn in the Soviet Union, and so on. But the fact remains that nothing can be opposed to a technical study on some problem; even if the conclusions are wrong, almost no one can dispute them. The fact is that the psychological and social current invariably leads us to place our confidence in the technicians, and for that reason their power is practically absolute.

[3] André Philip is right when he says that "at present property is no longer the most important thing, but rather the power of decision which is steadily becoming dissociated from it." The power of decision, accurately analyzed by Jean Barets, dominates our present economy and politics.

[4] A good example of the authoritarian nature of the technicians' activities is contained in Jean Barets: *La Fin des politiques* (Paris: Calmann-Lévy; 1962), a work that is both perfectly logical and superficial, coherent and unrealistic (under the appearance of statistical and pseudo-analytical realism). But despite all errors, it presents a good picture of the technicians' dictatorial power. The technicians' power with regard to political affairs emerges very clearly from the famous Stanford University report, *The Development of Scientific and Technological Progress and Its Effects on U. S. Foreign Policy* (1960). Still, agreeing with Meynaud, I do not think that power wielded by the technicians is a government by technicians. Rather, because of shifting competence, and not because of a change in regime, we see an increasing influence of technicians in political decisions, as was also shown in Bernard Gournay's analysis in *La Science administrative* (Paris: Presses Universitaires de France; 1962). Gournay believes that their power rests on an entire ideology of technologization, though without any conspiracy on the part of the technicians to take over. Theodore Caplow (*Arguments* [1962]) correctly stresses that technicians have a tendency to retire into "civic apathy," which also makes a technocratic regime unlikely.

opposite regimes closer together. All far-seeing political men desire a technological apparatus, and the United States, like the U.S.S.R., is traveling along the road leading to the increasing subordination of politics to technology. *Despite appearances* to the contrary, Pierre Mendès-France and President de Gaulle conceive of politics really in the same way, because they both insist on the pre-eminent role of the technician. Moreover, they are thinking of the same technicians.

Despite appearances? They are not just appearances: for example, we see a parliament receiving bouquets from Pierre Mendès-France, contempt from de Gaulle—but equally impotent in either instance; an executive apparently sovereign in the one case and responsible in the other, but, in each case, entirely dependent on the technological structure; and the great decisions really being necessities in all instances.[5]

Another important aspect of the technological apparatus that we attempt to retain is the necessary continuity of decisions once they have been taken. Precisely because the decisions are based primarily on technical considerations and are of technical content, they cover a long space of time and presuppose some continuity. No political change can alter what has been done or what must be done in the future, for technological factors condition each other. Will a change in government or the legislature, or even a change of regime, modify an established plan? Can it change decisions concerning the petroleum industry or atomic research?

Work on the controversial Pierrelatte project[6] (France's atomic energy installation—Tr.) was begun in 1955 and carried forward by all subsequent governments[7] i.e., even by those who had opposed it earlier on the grounds that it was militarist. This well illustrates the fragile nature of political opinion when faced with the continuity of technological steps already set in motion.

---

[5] Meynaud frequently stresses the politician's impotence in the face of the experts' conclusions: even where the latter are not really conclusive, the politician is not equipped to dispute them. Also see Michel Debré: *La Mort de l'état républicain* (Paris: Gallimard; 1947).

[6] Pierre Mendès-France: *La République moderne* (Paris: Gallimard; 1964), p. 124.

[7] Daniel F. Dollfus's article in *Le Monde*, July 1963.

Moreover, an enterprise of that kind is of course not "militarist" in itself; there is no clear delineation between peaceful and military uses. Whatever the political orientation of a government may be, however, it cannot modify what has already been begun, though the decisions involved are actually the most important facing the nation. But decisions that seem to be largely based on political judgment are hard to realize because of the weight of technological continuity incorporated in them. A government of the Right must endorse nationalization of enterprises, not for reasons of doctrine, but mainly for technical reasons, just as it is forced to maintain Social Security provisions. The unsuccessful British attempt to shift into reverse shows the extent to which governments have become powerless to make truly political decisions.

In all this we have limited ourselves to drawing the general and most obvious conclusions from processes that are known, described, and analyzed. Most of the time we do not dare really to look things in the face: generally, we limit ourselves to seeing in them a displacement of decision-making in the direction of the executive branch,[8] but we feel that the decision still remains *inside* the political realm. But this displacement toward the executive branch is only a stage in the progressive elimination of political action itself. Therefore efforts to bring parliament and the executive back into balance seem vain: the problem has gone beyond that.

Michel Crozier [9] is of the opinion that the role of experts is transitory and never determining. He says that in the exercise of "ultimate power" (the power to arbitrate in uncertain situations, i.e., true political power), after certain periods of uncertainty, the technicians change, and as soon as the work has been scientifically organized or the understanding of existing economic phenomena has allowed the government to make rational pro-

---

[8] See, for example, André Hauriou's article in *Le Monde*, December 1962.
[9] Michel Crozier: *Le Phénomène bureaucratique* (Paris: Éditions du Seuil; 1964), p. 220.

jections in a particular area, the power of the experts declines. In a rapidly changing society the technicians' success leads, according to Crozier, to the destruction of their real power:

> The process of rationalization gives the expert his powers, but the results of rationalization limit them. As soon as one field is seriously analyzed and known, as soon as the first intuitions and innovations have been translated into rules and programs, the expert's power tends to disappear. In fact, the experts have no real social power except at the beginning of progress, which means that this power is changeable and fragile. . . .

Their power, he says, becomes increasingly fragile, "to the extent that methods and programs based on science and technology can be utilized and directed by people who are not experts."

But Crozier fails to distinguish between experts and technicians. Undoubtedly the expert is being summoned, quite incidentally, to give his opinion in a situation of uncertainty. But the role of the technician, who, incidentally, can also be summoned as an expert, is not limited to that. And the influence of the technician does not diminish because the situation ceases to be uncertain. Besides, we are very far from an easy, simple application of techniques. Crozier speaks of the technique of economic anticipation: he forgets that the more it develops, the less is it within reach of just anybody. Second, as the techniques become well known and more ingrained, the technician is called in less as an expert to render his occasional and somewhat mysterious service; he is integrated into the whole of the state on a permanent basis (but not absorbed by the bureaucracy), and in fact his power increases, for he participates constantly in decisions: economic anticipation leads to the constant existence of a corps of planners. And the technician's techniques, being his own, are as mysterious to the political man as the skills of the expert in Crozier's narrow sense. Finally, the more the state's interference increases in domains where techniques are necessary, the more it needs technicians and also experts. Even if Crozier's analysis were correct, it would not be so for the reasons he gives, i.e., because the expert disappears from a certain sec-

tor and is replaced by another in another sector, but because
the basic situation changes, and particularly the relationship
between the political power and its technicians and experts.

But I know the argument well: we must distinguish between
ends and means.[1] The technician is only a means. The politician
retains his choice and decisions in the area of ends, of general
options, of the over-all direction of national development. Parliament must and can assign objectives to a plan, "objectives the
people choose to make theirs." The plan would then be limited
to coordinate measures so as to obtain these objectives. To effect
this choice one can even appeal to the country itself. By simpli-
fying the debate one will arrive at the conclusion that the
determination of the needs to be satisfied remains a political
act, and that recourse can be had to universal suffrage to answer
the question, as, for example, choosing from among various
objectives of consumption, or the desired ratio between consumption and reinvestment, or the length of the working day.
But all this is terribly illusory, for the choice is limited in all its
dimensions. On the policy level, the general orientation already
has been laid down. Nobody can shift into reverse; watchwords
such as "rapid economic expansion, satisfaction of collective
needs, help to underdeveloped countries"[2] are, for example,
three objectives (and we could name many others) on which
nobody has to make a decision, for the chips are on the table.
On the operational level, the decision depends very heavily on
basic feasibility, resources, or technical capabilities (in the
stricter sense of the word). Even there the technician will tell us

---

[1] Grégoire, among others, speaks of the need to "separate fundamental options,
i.e., the responsibilities of leading politicians, from minor decisions that should
be left to the experts." He gives an example: the implementation of great public
works should be left to the experts once the broad lines of an economic plan
have been laid down. But who analyzes conditions, formulates possibilities, and
sets the trends underlying such an economic plan? *Other experts,* of course.
Meynaud has produced a valid critique in this connection in *La Technocratie,* p.
266.
[2] The idea that the great decisions are inescapable because they are dependent
on the international system is well known, even though nobody draws the
conclusions therefrom. See André Hauriou's articles in *Le Monde* (December
1962), and Michel Massenet's discussion in "L'Avenir de la Liberté politique,"
Bulletin s.e.d.e.i.s., II (1962).

what is possible. It is superficial to distinguish between political ends and technological means; nowadays the means limit these ends, but they also permit us to define them. Between the policy and operational levels that we have just indicated, however, can we believe that even relatively general political decisions are free? In reality, other inescapable necessities exert their pressure here, as, for example, such an inexorable sociological current as urbanization, which can only be accepted.[3] And even if it is only a question of establishing priorities among several equally desirable objectives, the most powerful argument, in connection with problems that may appear very political, is always the sliding scale of the technical ability to realize them. As a result, it is again the technicians who show how successive implementations are mutually conditioned. For example, if it is necessary to build an atomic plant first, it is because its products will permit something else, which in turn will again lead to something else.

Where there are no judgments by technicians we see in the political realm a strange impotence with regard to decisions. The examples cited by Jean Meynaud, showing that political power, contrary to that of the technicians, remains autonomous, only confirm this judgment: problems concerning social tensions, parochial schools, decolonization, or the European Defense Community (EDC) show to what point political man is disarmed when he cannot lean on, or hide behind, a seemingly sure technical expertise. Thus Meynaud is right when he says that in many cases in which the role of the technician is not indispensable, politicians avail themselves of technicians anyway.[4] This is particularly noticeable in international organisms. Faced with "purely" political problems, such as Algeria or the Berlin crisis, politicians are unable to make decisions, as we can observe every day. But, it will be said, then you *do* recognize

---

[3] Joseph A. Schumpeter has produced the following admirable formula: "If results giving people long-term satisfactions were to serve as touchstones *for* a government for the people, a government *by* the people would not always emerge victorious from such a test." See *Kapitalismus, Sozialismus, Democratie* (Bern: A. Francke; 1946); publ. in U.S. as *Capitalism, Socialism, Democracy* (New York: Harper & Bros.; 1950).

[4] J. Meynaud: *La Technocratie*, p. 100.

the existence of purely political problems and possible initiatives on the part of the politician? Certainly, but with the following double reservation: the politician's uncertainty stems from the fact that he no longer has his tutor and habitual counselor, and above all, from the fact that he finds himself delivered to other necessities which we have mentioned earlier. In the Algerian affair, there was not a single decision that was not the result of necessity; no political man was able to alter the course of events. Could it have been otherwise? I do not think so. Thus, those who predicted from the beginning that an F.L.N. victory was inevitable and claimed to be on the side of peace asked their listeners to comply with a probable necessity and presented as a free and independent act what was only a calculation of the greatest probability. But were they as accurate with regard to the immediate present? They did not take into account that in 1956, and still in 1958, 70 per cent of all Frenchmen were firmly in favor of French Algeria and that the army was even more so— not to mention the Frenchmen in Algeria. Necessity, foreseeable from the beginning, took hold and revealed itself gradually to a growing number of people until it became a *fait accompli*. All attempts at original solutions made between 1956 and 1960 failed.[5]

To be sure, the political world has not become a "machine." I am well acquainted with the sociological school that insists on the fluent and malleable character of the world of politics and public opinion, on social mobility, and "informal" relations.

I know of course that feverish agitation prevails in all political settings; there are innumerable committees and commissions, and innumerable decisions are made; a great number of manifestos are signed, alliances concluded, budgets discussed, candidates eliminated, officials named, procedures established,

---

[5] See Pierre Viansson-Ponté's excellent description (*Le Monde*, May 8, 1962) on the evolution of the political structure in France, under the title "Lobbies et Technocrates." But he may be wrong in saying that this is only an occasional, accidental evolution: in reality, it is an adjustment by the French state to current political conditions.

actions planned, and programs begun.[6] This great activity reinforces the illusion of action; this mass of words, papers and
committees gives us the illusion of decisions. In reality, this
activity itself greatly contributes to a sociology that devotes
little attention to initiative or freedom. Such political activity
unfolds according to rigid norms and obeys the very necessities
I mentioned earlier. But it must be understood that there remains the mass of micro-decisions affecting the general trend,
micro-decisions that express the politicians' choices and innovations. Their true significance is minuscule.

Yet, it will be said, are not ideological debates in progress?
Are not political men obeying an ideology? And, if they are, is
that not to escape necessities? Without wanting to enter into a
general discussion of ideology, I want to say only that the only
ideology that counts—Marxism—is imposed by facts and situations, not at all by voluntary adherence. Moreover, Marxism
is today regarded as a "valid" and proper ideology exactly with
respect to those of its features which are outmoded. Marxism is
an ideology expressing the economic, legal, and political situation in the middle of the nineteenth century. It permitted, at
that time, explanation and control of the situation. In 1870 a man
who committed himself to Marxism committed a voluntary act
and sought to control the course of events. But this ideology no
longer explains anything. It is in no way connected with actual
reality—neither in its philosophy, its economy, its over-all view
of history, nor its conception of society, state, or law. A century
ago, Marxism allowed people to foresee what was likely to
happen, and actually did happen (except for some relatively
minor points). But just because these predictions came true,
Marxism, as a body of thought, had simultaneously exhausted
itself. There is no longer any ideological debate, and the debates in which people engage are completely academic. The
masses accept Marxist ideology because events have confirmed
it; they therefore merely give in to events, i.e., to the strongest
current. Those who become Marxists mainly do so because the

---

[6] See J. Meynaud: *La Technocratie,* p. 72.

Soviet Union has the strongest batallions, which has always been the sign of a profound philosophy and the expression of perfect liberty. But there is a complementary reason: the masses adopt this ideology precisely because it is obsolete, precisely because it no longer really relates to prevailing social reality and the present political situation. It has become a reassuring screen to hide—and hide from—reality. It has become a protective device against confronting actual problems that men cannot see, because they think that they already hold the key to everything. Here we find, in the realm of politics and economics, the accusation so often leveled at Christians: Your Christianity, having become a theology, a system, a moral, contains beforehand the solution to all spiritual and moral problems; therefore you can avoid these problems; they do not exist for you. Such ease and security are sought by those who nowadays throw themselves into the arms of Marxism. But there is no expression of human freedom there, no attack on political affairs by men trying to control and change them.

This vacuity of current ideology does not imply a disappearance of beliefs, presuppositions, and so on, but mainly the disappearance of an authentic revolutionary power, a passion for radical transformation. One cannot simply say, with Meynaud, that people are adhering to a dominant ideology that would imply statism. The point is that we have here an adherence to the ongoing socio-economic development generated by technological motives enforced by technological means, moving in the direction of a technological continuity: there is no longer room for ideological debate.

All this does not imply a rigid division between technicians and politicians, or that all technicians are on one side, all politicians on the other when a decision is to be made. There are divisions among technicians just as among politicians. It is also true that sometimes the political powers bypass the technicians' advice when making decisions. But when I am given such examples as political action in Algeria, or Mr. Khrushchev's hasty decisions—made contrary to the technicians' advice, which, in all probability, eventually caused his dismissal—I ask if they were successful.

Let us admit that one might reserve the term "political affairs" for the domain where the technician has not automatically the last word, as Jean Meynaud says, or where he is subordinated to a political design. Still, even there, his role is considerable; and a completely independent political decision is ephemeral. It just does not exist. It is quite true that about problems traditionally called "political" the technician does not know more than the politician, but the important point, the great change, is that, as a result of the general devotion to efficiency, the growth of technological sectors, and the habit of seeking aid from technicians, so-called political problems have been downgraded in the eyes of public opinion and the politicians themselves have become the object of anger, disappointment, and disapproval. This essential fact must be kept in mind: the sector in which, formerly, only political considerations could decide has not only been shrunk, but also has come to be considered secondary and frustrating.

All public opinion analysis shows the error in Jean Moulin's thesis that public opinion is hostile to the experts.[7] True, it is easy to say that sometimes public opinion takes pleasure in an expert's failure, but that is a special instance of opposition to "authority." As between the expert and the politician, public opinion almost always favors the technician. Naturally we can always hope that the politician will regain control over the technician. But we must admit that it is merely a pious wish. Even Meynaud, who is so exact and precise when dealing with this question, has remained very hazy. How, for example, can we give new value to parliament's "influence" or "modernize political forces"? One is struck by the weakness and uncertainty of the proposed remedies in face of the magnitude of the problems.[8]

---

[7] Ibid., p. 126; Moulin: *Res publica,* publ. by the Belgian Association of Political Science (1962), pp. 42 *ff.*

[8] J. Meynaud: *La Technocratie,* pp. 264 *ff.* True, he frequently stresses (pp. 178 *ff.*) that technological development reduces and sometimes eliminates all possibility of control, but states that, on the other hand, it stabilizes political situations and increases secret and hidden political activities at the expense of free political play.

It is very characteristic, for example, that André Hauriou thinks that to reinforce parliament's role it is necessary to give it technical competence. But he thinks that such technical competence can exist only on the mathematical plane. Yet many other technical elements are involved here, and, moreover, by judging things on a mathematical basis one excludes choices. Hauriou's answer to this objection—that the choices are made before the technical study—is lame, for if it were so the role of Parliament would not have declined, as Hauriou himself insists.

This decline of the power of choice is confirmed by an analysis produced by Maurice Merleau-Ponty in *Humanism et Terreur*. As long as political man lives in a world of ambiguity, as long as he makes unnecessary choices, as long as political men have their own perspective (which is nothing more than a perspective based on a particular reason or a particular passion) and stake their lives on it, then politics is Terror. When the course of history is undetermined and a great number of equally likely possibilities exists, one cannot eliminate the need for decisions (but he who makes them must then force the future to implement them) or the expression of truth (but he who thinks he possesses it must also use force to make it triumph). "History is Terror because there is only one contingency": from the moment at which a political act represents a commitment resting on a choice (if that choice is neither arbitrary nor absurd), that act belongs in the category of force.

The alternative is not really to know whether there is a rigorous and predetermined course of history, and even less to jump at a mystique of the proletariat existing by itself as the incarnation of history's rationality. The true alternative is provided by the creation of a progressively compelling necessity, arising from the increased impact of technology on situations, methods, and analyses. All of these confront the politician with a single final possibility if he wants to cope with reality. That the politician is faced with decision-making in areas that are more and more intrinsically technical is not the work of evil technicians. These areas in which the politician operates demand methods of analysis and action which are specifically technological. Yet this is ignored by Merleau-Ponty. This invalidates his analysis of Stalin, for the important point regarding Stalin was precisely his acceptance of technology, his part in the subordination of history and Marxism to technology, which was recognized as a necessity. But we must realize even more clearly that the development of technology progressively eliminates the proletariat itself, both in its present condition and in its metahistorical reality, so that the proletariat changes its nature and can no longer play the role assigned to it by the philosophers of history.[9]

2. *The Ephemeral*

At the opposite end of the spectrum of political decisions we find those that are ephemeral. All the innumerable decisions, the votes, decrees, elections, plans, and fruits of all the political activities discussed above are *ephemeral,* which is the most moving and perhaps the most tragic sign and characteristic of our day.

If we are placed in a period of history and in a society in which necessity becomes ever more exacting, then nothing is truly continuous or durable. Our entire civilization is ephemeral. When one glorifies increased consumption, one must discard machine-made objects in the course of rapid usage. We no longer repair things: we throw them away. Plastics, nylons, are made to be new for an infinitesimal period of time and, as they cost nothing, are destroyed as soon as the gloss of newness is gone. Houses are constructed for the duration of their mortgage; automobiles must be replaced every year. And in the world of art we no longer build cathedrals, but we make moving pictures, which—though real works of art in which man has fully com-

---

[9] The power of words is marvelous. It enables me to present these provocative theses without offending the reader. I could say, for example, in the words of a well-known political scientist: "Bureaucratization and technization of decisions lead to the limitation of arbitrary power, the reduction of discretionary power, and some independence with regard to the political chief"; this would be exactly the same thing, but the reader would be better satisfied than by my formulation.

mitted himself and expressed his most profound message—are forgotten after a few weeks and disappear into movie libraries where only a few connoisseurs can find them again. We bring all our care, all our intelligence to bear on the production of a TV broadcast that will last only twenty minutes and survive only in the spectator's fleeting memory. This is one of the most distressing aspects of contemporary man. Treasures of ingenuity, immense amounts of work, the passions of men believing in what they are doing, end in ephemeral objects—in all spheres of activity—of which nothing will remain. Today's newspaper effaces yesterday's (it does not provide continuity in the mind of the reader), just as a new technique blots out an older one. History is accelerating while at the same time all that could make our presence endure scatters like ashes. Man, who has always worked to leave behind some eternal work that would mark his passage on earth, is driven by a strange renunciation and works for the most futile and volatile ends. And our new huge dams, these cathedrals of modern times? We know that they are built to last for centuries, but the production of electricity by new processes will make them useless, and they will remain incomprehensible, crumbling monuments in stone. We will not leave a single straight furrow behind us.

In this realm of the ephemeral, politics takes place in all its multiple forms. We must unfortunately include here all that agitates us so much and weakens those passionately given to politics, whether it be contemporary fascism (which proved so inane in France), Gaullism (this epiphenomenon without sequence), elections, the importance of parties—questions that, like some decoy or bait, distract men from real problems in the actual political world.

This ephemerality has several aspects and several causes. A general symptom is the often heard formula: This does not commit me to anything. We know well that a political party's program does not commit a man to anything. He can make promises, give his word, sign posters: tomorrow all will be forgotten, and only a few troublesome people will be disagreeable enough to recall the formulas. All these are nothing but weathercocks. If a man criticizes this, he is given the facile answer we know only too well: "What! You don't take thought into account? And change? You want to prevent a man from changing? Or the times? You want to feel tied down by what you have said yesterday? That is a completely outmoded conception of man, contrary to scientific anthropology—don't you know the personality is discontinuous! If you remind me of declarations I made yesterday on communism or some other subject, when I say the opposite today, you simply deny LIFE. Only the senile no longer move; you are just intellectually paralyzed."

As long as we remain on this level of talk, the situation is not too grave. Such talk only gives to political men and intellectuals some wonderful means for self-justification. De Gaulle can claim without blushing that from 1958 to 1962 he followed consistent policies. I fail to understand how Sartre and his friends can accuse de Gaulle of anything at all in this connection, as they are the ones who ceaselessly justified this type of explanation for their own gyrations. But even though de Gaulle claimed that politicians of the Fourth Republic had all been wrong, he simply pursued Guy Mollet's policies. Similarly Pierre Mendès-France, de Gaulle's violent opponent, proclaimed that Algeria was ineluctably French and that only a traitor would let her go. A thousand twists and turns by political men can only show their weakness and vanity. That is without much significance. One might also say it is a peculiarly French phenomenon to gobble up one constitution after another. That the eternal text, laid down in order to build a stable political structure, to bring constancy to political practices, should change with every wind, and that we should have had between fourteen and eighteen consitutions in two centuries, depending on the computations of various specialists, could merely be evidence of French political instability and the versatility of our character, and nothing more.

However, what is more serious in my estimation is the view that, *in principle*, changes in law and political decisions are justified. If I were told: "Contrary to all we wanted, we had to give in," I could not protest; I would recognize indeed an inevitable development.

But let us take Leninism, which, while serving the notion of a legal superstructure (the superstructure of an exploiting regime), moves on from the capitalist situation to the socialist regime. After that the law, like just any regime or political decision, retains not the slightest continuity in itself and must purely and simply align itself with the given socio-economic facts in the situation. The law must be flexible, and if it resists it interferes with progress, inhibits evolution, and is therefore bad. We know, on the other hand, how difficult it was for the Soviet regime to explain the continued existence of all law after the revolution, when by Marxist rules it ought to have disappeared as a by-product of capitalist divisions and relationships. But the law that was retained has been more than ever subjected to the chance of circumstances. It was only a momentary expression, one temporary shape of a certain complex of socio-economic relations. There was no question that these rules would disappear once circumstances changed. This doctrine is remarkably similar to Hitler's doctrine of law and treaties. An agreement has value only as long as things remain unchanged. When given facts change, the agreement becomes by its very nature defunct, without the interested parties having to spell out the mode of its demise.

We find ourselves here in the presence of a fundamental mutation of the laws which means that in the one case as in the other we are in reality dealing with a doctrine based on interest. What is done in the interest of the proletariat, Lenin said, is well done. What is done in the interest of the Aryan race, replied Hitler, is well done. And this formula is quickly extended in two directions: the proletariat assimilates itself quickly to the U.S.S.R., the Aryan race to the Third Reich. Then what is useful becomes just, and the just becomes law. Consequently, what is in conformity with the law is in the interest of the U.S.S.R. or the Third Reich. A treaty endures only on the basis of this conformity, and interests change when circumstances change. There can be no stability of contracts or institutions in this case, no legal norms or references to real values. The law is one instrument among others for political decisions; there are no longer rules of the game; there is only the incoherence of facts that one obeys after having discerned them. Sartre's philosophy inadvertently joins Hitler's conception of the law by its refusal of norms and its doctrines of discontinuity. And if a great man told us the other day: "Things are what they are," it is still more of the same general orientation—the facts are the law. If for a long time people tended to consider only the law, the norm, to consider it as definite in itself and disregard its historical context, we have now collectively rushed to the other extreme.

I have taken up such different thoughts to demonstrate that what is believed to be doctrine in one camp or another is, in reality, only the expression of a trend present in our situation itself. And when I spoke of the law, I spoke of one of the highest expressions of political decisions—the creation of the law. That could be extended in many directions. Nowadays we consider it the highest form of wisdom to adapt ourselves to circumstances. Far be it from me to say that one must not take them into consideration. It would be absurd not to. I simply say that an excessive orientation to circumstances is the negation of what man heretofore has called law or politics—the creation of a stabilized universe, an artificial universe (artificial in the sense that it is made by the skill of man), in which man recognizes forms and objects, assigns names and places, and creates a continuity with the help of (but also against) the fluidity of the universe. That was the highest mark of man's sovereignty. We sacrificed it in favor of a game of interests and an acceptance of things taking their autonomous course. Only in it could we rediscover the independence, the "personality" of the political decision. On the level of that sacrifice we find the committees, bureaus, posters, cells; on that level we find all the vacuousness, emptiness, and futility. One must have no illusions that freedom can be established along that road, for what we are really dealing with here is submission to events.

Undoubtedly the most important element in the ephemeral nature of contemporary politics is "current events." Man in our day is assailed by what is current, actual, new. What has happened last is in his eyes necessarily most important. This man is the politician who depends on daily information. But it is also the citizen, whose participation and weight in political decisions I do not deny. This citizen only knows what happened yesterday, excites himself only over the latest events, and demands that the politician should take a position on it. All the rest matters little to him. And the politician knows well, in turn, that he will have to respond accordingly. He is therefore led to keep himself tuned continuously to this level of current events.

Why is this great influence being exercised by the news, why this great receptiveness to it, so clearly reflected in everybody's passion for the latest news bulletin? A multiplicity of factors converges to create a complex situation. Material factors meet psychological factors. There is, on the one hand, the immense development of the mass media. It is quite obvious that without that infrastructure the news would have no more importance in our day than in the Middle Ages. Obviously there is no primary need to be fully informed on all political events. It goes without saying that intellectuals should have felt the need to promulgate their opinions and write on current events. Yet it cannot be said that, from the beginning, the reader—the king's subject—desired information except out of curiosity far removed from political considerations. But from the moment when the machinery was created—when in the general process of opinion formation political news came to be of possible concern to everybody, a subject on which every person had to take sides, and, even more, a matter each could influence by his action—at that moment the need for information arose. It spread like lightning, like an avalanche, and not only ever more information but also ever more recent information was needed. But, again, this was a function of the economic and technological infrastructure.

Moreover, in our day this trend mingles with psychological factors that are totally different, but tend in the same direction. Superficially speaking, modern man desires to be informed of the latest news because it is an undeniable source of prestige in his group, enabling him to tell others what they do not know, to become the legendary personage, the bearer of news—to be superior by being better informed. It is even more exciting to be privy to a secret that one can transmit to others, to wait for their reaction, their surprise, and by one's superior knowledge undermine the standing of those who are not "in the know"— what mastery! In a world like ours, avid for news, to be the one who is "in the know" and transmits what he knows is to participate in the ruling power; that is why modern man tries to be the first to be informed.

In a society largely penetrated by collective currents, to partake of the news is also an essential means of participation. And the more spectacular the news, the more its bearers and recipients will feel as though they have participated in their society. Alfred Sauvy, for example, thinks it unnecessary for people to participate in depth. In reality, the more superficial, unimportant, and spectacular the information, the more people will be interested in it. Moreover, it is under such conditions that man will not refuse to act. But it is necessary that such action be part of a highly emotional situation in which man sees clearly what is taking place. He will then consent to make an intense and glorious but brief effort; brief as news itself. It is therefore necessary that the latter rejuvenate itself ceaselessly. It must rise again from the ashes in order to regenerate man's opportunity for action in the present surrounding him. Finally, there is the well-known phenomenon that public opinion revolves only around problems of the immediate present. Opinion shapes itself only on matters that seem important to people *today,* and only on matters by which they feel touched (on this subject see the studies of Jean Stoetzel and Gordon Allport). This alone shows that politics is necessarily tied to up-to-dateness. If everybody is in agreement that nowadays the exercise of authority is solely based on public opinion; if the ruling powers draw their splendid existence from public opinion; if, on the other hand, it is true that opinion must come from the outside, never being self-generated; if, finally, this opinion never exists except in connection with a news event—then we will understand both the influence of the news phenomenon and the ephemeral character that it necessarily imposes on political affairs.

I will posit it as a sort of principle that the predominance of news produces a fundamental political incapacity in the individual, be he a leader or just a citizen.

The first effect of insistence on news is dispersion. The newspapers bring us everyday news coming from everywhere, and TV allows us to witness events over the entire world. Imposing a classical view of man would see him as a self-contained individual who merely has been placed before an array of news and information and, in some fashion, absorbs his dosage of information, swallows it, digesting and utilizing this mixed food for his greater benefit and becomes, as a result, somehow more intelligent, better informed, and more able to be a good citizen. But this view of man does not stand up under analysis. In reality this man does not have complete control over environmental stimuli. He is a changing, susceptible being, subjected to influences that divide him. He has discontinuous consciousness and the first effect of news on him is not to make him more capable of being a citizen but to disperse his attention, to absorb it and present to him an excessive amount of information that he will not be able to absorb, information too diverse to serve him in any way whatever, and pure facts that will not enter his consciousness and help him to reflect.

At the same time as the news evaporates—mostly in the course of the same day—it also disperses in time. The very character of the news is to change from one day to the next and never to be based on anything except what exists at the moment. What happened yesterday is of no interest today. News must always be new. But this means that one set of current events necessarily replaces the next. Man will not carefully retain what he learned yesterday. This would require qualities that man does not possess.[1] In order not to drown in this incessant flow, man is forced to forget. The profound significance of this obliteration from his memory will be examined elsewhere. Let us note here only that it is an inevitable result of the news. Here we find ourselves at the most superficial level of politics, at the level of the bait and decoys already mentioned, a level on which not only ordinary people but also some of our best political scientists

---

[1] See Jacques Ellul: "Propagande et Information," *Diogène* (1957).

operate. But this is further aggravated by the fact that the two dispersions of which we have spoken—into space and into time —actually combine. As a result, a truly stupefying lack of continuity is created, for if one information item merely effaces the other on the *same* subject, it would not be so bad; but a continuous flow of information on a specific question, showing a problem's origin, growth, crisis, and dénouement is very rare. Most frequently my attention, attracted today by Turkey, will be absorbed tomorrow by a financial crisis in New York, and the day after tomorrow by parachutists in Sumatra. In the midst of all this, how can a man not specially trained perceive the slightest continuity, experience the slightest political continuity, how, finally, can he understand? He can literally only *react* to the news.[2] But, once more, let us be careful not to draw a false portrait of our citizen. If he were a man with a solid, well-informed political doctrine, a set of political thoughts enabling him to judge, certain information items would be useful to him. But, at least in non-totalitarian countries, this is not the case. Politically, man lives on certain connotative stereotypes without doctrinal content (democracy, republic, fascism, social justice, and so on) which cannot help him understand or interpret events. Therefore, he can only react in the same way as Hales's famous frog. The citizen will have purely visceral "opinions" springing from his prejudices or his milieu, his interests, or some propaganda.

It is often said that there were always prejudices, the influence of one's milieu, etc. This is true, but the new rage for up-to-dateness adds two dimensions. The first is ceaselessly renewed incitement. When few political problems were brought to the citizen's attention, the citizen experienced only rare waves of political agitation and excitement. Conversely, modern information produces an incessant renewal of stimuli provoking constant reactions, intensifying prejudices, hardening groups, and

---

[2] On this subject, see Daniel Bell's excellent comment (*Arguments* [1962]) on the "Eclipse of Distance": the elimination of all psychological, social, or aesthetic distance that leads to "the individual being captured by the object. . . ." According to Freud, "maturity consists in the capacity to introduce the time element into events . . . but the intention of modern culture appears as a breaking and crushing of time."

so on, and we know what finally happens to the frog's muscles: they become rigid. This is not very conducive to political maturity, and it seems that in authoritarian countries, where the citizen's political education is practiced and a ready-made doctrine replaces the democratic citizen's political vacuity, there is practically no current news; information, distilled by specialists, is first made to conform to doctrine. There rigidity is avoided and hypnosis attained.

The second new dimension produced by the flow of news is man's incapacity to integrate in an orderly way the information he receives because he lacks time for it. In another age it was possible to combat prejudices or milieu influences by voluntary and personal reflection. But today the flow of news prevents man from reflecting seriously on political affairs. A striking example of this incoherence was a French opinion survey of May, 1964, which showed the majority of Frenchmen rejecting President De Gaulle's social and economic policies, but voting for him.

A prior poll had also showed that the majority of Frenchmen *simultaneously* approved the president's foreign policy *and* European integration—to which his foreign policy was openly hostile.

It seems evident that from four points of view there is a fundamental contradiction between immediate concerns and political thought:

(1) Even the educated and trained person is becoming increasingly incapable of grasping a political or economic entity. For example, there are, on the one hand, some general views on the USSR in circulation and, on the other, innumerable isolated facts without common denominator or seemingly of no significance. This leads to the embarrassing situation that works written on a precise question with the help of extensive documentation are often very quickly contradicted by subsequent events.

Clement Lefort[3] furnishes a remarkable analysis of the importance of "events" with regard to political thought—in this case Sartre's. Lefort demonstrates that people find it inacceptable

---

[3] Clement Lefort: "La Pensée de la politique," *Lettres nouvelles* (1963).

to "abandon themselves entirely to the truth of what happens here and now," but want "to find refuge in a system with the laws of history laid down once and for all." Surely, one or another event can be symbolic and permit us to "discern the truth in our day." But it is impossible to impart the event, and it is not possible to understand it except from a certain distance and after some lapse of time. Involvement in an event's immediateness and the subordination of all thought to that immediateness can be no more conducive to "discerning the truth of the times" than the external application of a dogmatic framework to the march of events. Too many multicolored and infinitesimal touches overload the picture to leave us truly able, I do not say to understand, but to grasp the whole.[4] And news is piled up on more news, and details multiply infinitely. But if people cannot even grasp political affairs, how much less can they reflect upon them properly? First of all, they have no time. Moreover, in order to reflect, one must come to a halt and suspend time.

(2) One must reflect on the sum of known events within a particular framework, interpret them in relation to a pattern of concepts (and I do not believe this is arbitrary, it is the only method by which scientific inquiry proceeds, the known, straight fact having no importance if it is not integrated into a conceptual framework and then interpreted.) While a physicist can be sure that the object of his study will not get away from him, this is not so in the realm of political reflection. As we are steeped in the news and our good citizen is imbued with the passion for news, he cannot believe, accept, or consider anything important that does not relate to the latest facts and events. All political reflection is discounted beforehand because it relates to the news of the day before yesterday, and neces-

---

[4] An illustration of the incapacity to "grasp political affairs" when a man is plunged into the news and becomes a specialist is William Shirer and his book on the Third Reich. Shirer operated consistently from inside the news as he found it in the archives, and did prodigious work in unraveling events—to arrive at precisely nothing. Limited by being a diplomatic journalist, he was not able to retrace anything but the diplomatic elements; limited by his concern with news, he remained at the most superficial level. In reality, he understood nothing of Hitler's Revolution, its economic components, or its nature. All we learn from him is that on June 16, 1938, at 21 hours 2 minutes, Hitler, wearing a pair of gray trousers, said such and such. And the book was a bestseller.

sarily (at least in appearance), does not take account of or explain the news of this morning. To be accepted by the ordinary citizen, political reflection must be as instantaneous as news; to be accepted by the ordinary citizen, it must take the form of the "editorial" and therefore not be true reflection; it, too, is on the order of a mere—though a more elaborate—reaction in that it is the work of a specialist.

(3) The immersion in the news also produces ignorance with regard to the various levels of political affairs and an incapacity to distinguish them. Under the rushing surface of daily events there are currents, and on a deeper level still, those depths which do not change except with the slowness of madrepores. But only the news interests and impassions us; and our attention span and political acumen are riveted on the latest bomb exploded somewhere. If a man speaks at such a moment of a deeper level, he appears out of tune with his time, uncommitted; although only by digging more deeply can political thought be formed and the present be eventually explained. But who is looking for an explanation? Because he is riveted to the news, the citizen rejects the truly fundamental problems, remaining attached exclusively to perfectly outmoded and useless terms and images such as "Right and Left," "capitalism and communism," and really believes that the fundamental political problems are located.

(4) This citizen steeped in the news also orients himself by false problems,[5] i.e., those imposed on him by the sources of information which are part of the "political spectacle." Increasingly, contemporary political affairs take the form of spectacle, a spectacle for the citizen offered by politicians to entertain their clientele: the spectacle of Nazi or Soviet parades, the

---

[5] I agree with J. Schumpeter's evaluation of the average citizen's attitude with respect to political problems: "Knowledge of facts and logic no longer play the part attributed to them by the classic doctrine [of democracy]. I am particularly struck by the almost complete disappearance of the sense of reality. For the average citizen, the great political problems are grouped among the distractions reserved for his leisure hours. They are not even on the level of fads, and exist only as subjects of idle conversation. To him, these problems seem far distant . . . basically, the citizen has the impression of living in an imaginary world." (*Capitalism, Socialism, Democracy*, Chap. xxi.)

spectacle of elections and referenda, the spectacle of televised parliamentiary sessions—all are spectacles consonant with the emphasis on immediacy in political affairs. Is it not exciting to participate personally via TV in the birth of a great political decision; and is it not a matter of great import to see directly all these great personages agitated over such great problems? Such problems are evidently the most interesting; the limelight of the news illuminates them, dramatizes and exalts them, and digs up each of their details. This is the nature of modern man's passionate approach to politics; he can abandon himself intensely to the political spectacle (but such abandon is mostly passive). These are false political problems because they are always appearances only, visible consequences, manifestations of deeper and more decisive problems from which the citizen living in the news turns away because they are not as exciting as the latest speech. Undoubtedly most remarkable in this situation is that if you try to attract the citizen's attention to true problems and basic phenomena, he will accuse you of trying to turn him away from what is real, to engage in a diversionary maneuver. These are the aspects under which I see the contradiction between our obsession with current events and true political capabilities.

One must try to go still deeper. The man who lives in the news, we have said, is a man without memory. Experimentally this can be verified a thousand times over. The news that excited his passion and agitated the deepest corners of his soul simply disappears. He is ready for some other agitation, and what excited him yesterday does not stay with him. This means that the man living in the news no longer has freedom, no longer has the capacity of foresight, no longer has any reference to truth. Lequier has said that "memory is free man's action when he turns to his past acts in order to retrieve them." Memory in a personality is the function that attests to the capacity of acting voluntarily and creatively; personality is built on memory, and conversely memory lends authority to personality. "One only remembers oneself, which means that one must already be self, capable of creating oneself in order to remember." And, still from this personal perspective, one can also say that only memory permits us to turn to the future—that there is a relationship between imagination and memory.

An analogous relationship exists in the perspective of the political man and the political activity of the citizen. José Ortega y Gasset is entirely right in pointing to the decisive role of memory in political affairs. There is no politics where there is no grasp of the past, where there is no continuity (let us remember Dupont White's remarkable statement: "Continuity is a human right"), where there is no analysis of errors or capacity to understand the present through that analysis and in that continuity. But current events obscure everything, even for the specialists. Current news pre-empts the sense of continuity, prevents the use of memory, and leads to a constant falsification of past events when they are evoked again in the stream of the news.

The process of being steeped in the news also prevents foresight.[6] It is a considerable error of judgment to try to place oneself into the present instant and draw conclusions from it. Even the most minute analysis of news will not permit us to draw conclusions from it: the statistical method, among others, which has no memory, presents false continuities that are never anything but a series of two-dimensional news pictures placed in sequence and compared; the statistical method does not really permit political thought or prediction, despite its involvement in current events and tied as it is, moreover, to the passion for current news. Also, why should the man immersed in current news try to foresee anything? The news will furnish him with his indispensable daily political ration tomorrow anyway, so that he can live in complete security. Political affairs will take care of themselves.

In the meantime, living in this present-day world such a man is very satisfied with himself. He is of "his time," he is at least "*au courant*," convinced that the newest thing is the most im-

---

[6] A good example of the distortion caused by preoccupation with current events, or news, is analyzed by Clement Lefort in his excellent article "La Pensée de la politique," which discusses the behavior of the Left activated by a mythical passion during the Algerian affair. For not having seen the true dimensions of the affair, for having become embroiled in ideology and moralism, they failed at the time to see that the Algerian state was a state like all the others, and because of this "the politics was removed from the facts."

portant. What is more, he is convinced that he lives in freedom precisely *because* he lives in the moment. We see here the curious changes wrought by the vulgarization of a philosophy. To obey the moment seems like freedom. To participate violently in the latest quarrel is the political calling of the freest citizen! What a surprising confusion not to see to what degree obedience to the instant and response to current news are the most radical possible negations of liberty! How can people fail to see that liberty requires integration into a continuity, a genuine basis in reality obtained in very different ways than through "information"? As radical as it may appear, I am not afraid to reverse the proposition mentioned above, and to claim that a man who reads his paper every day is certainly not a politically free person.

Moreover, by his free pseudodecisions the citizen forces the political powers to act and act again, to act without reflection, without delay, for acts must take place in the immediate present. What an outrage it would be to devote three months to reflection, when the news shouts at us from everywhere that the problem is urgent. It is unnecessary to insist that it is urgent; for the problem to be in the news is for it to have urgency. Because the man living in the news is not free or capable of reflection and foresight, he will not tolerate delay. In the stream of current events everything must be done right away. People will say: "There have been ten assassination attempts in Algeria. What! And the government does not do anything? If this continues for another week, if all the guilty are not arrested, if all the conspiratorial networks are not destroyed, it is only because the police do not do anything and the government is in on the conspiracy!" The man living in the news, incidentally, has good reasons of his own for demanding immediate solutions. Perhaps he knows unconsciously that tomorrow he will undoubtedly have forgotten the problem that today arouses his whole ardor, his whole commitment, and his entire uncompromising firmness.[7]

---

[7] J. Schumpeter shows that the characteristics traced in this chapter would still be much more pronounced in a socialist than in a "liberal" democracy. (*Capitalism* . . . , Chap. xxiii.)

It may seem an exaggeration that only the political decisions are ephemeral. And yet, does experience not show how different the durable work done by the technicians is from the uncertainties of political labors always undone and begun again? With technological efforts a cumulative process is at work. Political processes are different. This is not only because of the rapid replacement of government officials who frequently undo what their predecessors have begun; the same also occurs in situations of political stability. All attempts at political transformation by the Vichy Government disappeared very quickly. And we can be certain that on the purely political level little will remain of the de Gaulle government's spectacular decisions. Its laws designed to favor incumbent regimes in elections, its pseudo-presidential system, its government party, its obliteration of Parliament, its international decisions—all this will disappear with the man who inspired them. This impermanence is not a function of the instability of some regimes or governments, but is inherent in the very object of these decisions—in the type of problem that politicians can tackle. One must always remember a double fact: the more serious and important existing problems are considered to be, the more men try to solve them by technical means. As a result, the more one attaches oneself to technology, the more one becomes disinterested in what technology is not: these are two results of public opinion. Let us say that public opinion lends constantly diminishing support to purely political decisions. A political decision that would have had great impact and influenced the course of things a century ago, no longer has the same value simply because the same value is no longer attributed to it. Growing technology devaluates everything outside its realm, and renders ephemeral everything that it has not built.

To be sure, politics continues to exist; political affairs are not simply subordinated to technology. But even with regard to problems that seem exclusively "human" or equivocal and in which, according to Jean Meynaud,[8] "political sense" should retain its place, technology intervenes: for example, men must

---

[8] J. Meynaud: *La Technocratie*, pp. 22 *ff.*

decide between opposite technical opinions, "keep the voters in hand," measure the evolution of opinion. There will always be flux, irrational choices, various games; but does the ordinary politician, as a member of parliament, make the decisive choices? Meynaud is right to say that no one in the government sphere can avoid engaging in politics. But under what conditions does involvement take place? What are the actual aspects of such politics? Are they always decisive; and who exercises the choice? To be sure, there is never a "clear process;" there are always ambiguities, and it is unimaginable that everything could be reduced to calculations and techniques. But even where everything is unclear, will not every effort go in the direction of reducing such ambiguities by technological means and personal decision? The problem is to know in which direction things are moving: which realm or method is in the ascendency, The Political or The Technological? The answer seems clear to me. And my entire analysis flows from this perspective: it is not that political problems are *disappearing*, but, rather, that the free play of traditional political forms is an illusion.

Political affairs now find themselves subject to what is necessary and to what is ephemeral. The relation between these two aspects can take various shapes. And soon the two aspects intermingle, i.e., a decision produced by necessity comes to have only one aspect—an ephemeral aspect and impact—and is but a moment in the fleeting present. Everybody could see that the famous French community was nothing but the result of a necessity about which nobody could do anything, and that, at the same time, it could only be of ridiculously short duration—nothing but a transitory state. It was useful to effect the transition; in fact it was undoubtedly an entirely necessary political decision. But it was perfectly vain to give it such luster and brilliance, the trappings and laboriously worked out judicial structure, as long as on the basis of all evidence it was a construct that must disappear quickly, as soon as it was created.

In other cases we see a rupture inside political activity proper. Certain decisions are durable, but they are the simple fruit of necessity. Others seem voluntary, but they are ephemeral.

Necessity is the root of our great fundamental policies, and all truly serious decisions ultimately are imposed by various types of technicians—at which level propaganda brings public opinion into line with them—while the ephemeral provides the basis for spectacular and superficial decisions in which vagaries of power and public opinion play their part (in the sense described in Chapter III). If, like Alcibiades, one thinks the essential aspect of political affairs is to act and make others act, today's politician is caught in a net of predetermined factors that make his actions futile, his speeches simultaneously effective and lacking in depth.

Are ephemeral decisions freer than others? In appearance, frequently. People generally point to such ephemeral decisions when they say: look at the political men; they make their choices freely. But how often do they make their decisions to please their group, or to obey the pressure of public opinion, and not because of free conviction? If they want to remain independent of public opinion they must hide behind the veil of false information. But then they fall back into the technological necessities that they can no longer escape. Thus the Ephemeral and the Necessary constantly combine to give our political affairs their illusory face—illusion of freedom in some cases, illusion of importance and seriousness in others. Like a stream flowing in its inflexible bed and obeying inflexible rules that shape its meandering course and cross its surface, the political flux, not only at the level of political "action," but also in the entire social body, rolls along without any part being played in it by popular decision, ideology, doctrine, choice, or will. But on the surface of the current there are movements, small waves produced by cross winds, sudden turbulences, permanent thresholds; and therefore the impression of an extraordinary diversity, a multiplicity of ever-changing forms is conveyed. And the cork carried on the surface may well feel it has prodigious possibilities of moving from right to left, or even—for an instant—of traveling upstream as the result of a counter current (which will always ebb away). The cork will not notice that it simply obeys the general flow.

Moreover, we are fascinated by the immediate present, which

fixes our attention, our desires, and our most serious considerations to each minuscule fluctuation of the current scene. Those who attach themselves with all their might to the superficial level, being carried by the current, will not pay the least attention to any opposition against that current, and the idea of turning in another direction will not even occur to them.

I could give no better conclusion to this passage than to cite de Gaulle's famous formula: "We make *'la politique.'* The rest is a matter of indifference to us." What an admirable example of the political illusion. What is durable in de Gaulle's government is purely and simply the application of conclusions established by technicians. Outside of that, the "great" decisions (on the subject of Europe, against England, etc.) are in the domain of ephemeral play, at best able to retard inevitable developments, but destined to disappear without leaving a trace.

CHAPTER

[II]

THE AUTONOMY
OF POLITICS

---

1. The Monopoly of Force

Politics traditionally was classified among the moral sciences.
Nowadays it is classified among the social sciences. But the
illusion that narrow ties exist among morality, religion, and
politics is still maintained. Religion and politics were closely
related in ancient times, and some people still remain convinced
that religion has a political role to play. Almost all people believe
that political affairs are not autonomous, that they are, rather,
subject to some moral law, express or create other forces, and
are subject to value judgments.[1] If a person questions that, the
teachings of Machiavelli will immediately be brought up.

---

[1] All reflection on political morals is at the same time classic; essays like Gilles
Curien's *La Morale en politique* (Paris: Plon; 1962), though interesting as moral
reflections, completely misunderstand the current political world, and are
therefore entirely abstract.

The traditional debate runs like this: "If you admix values to politics, you make politics impossible; if your don't, you deprive it of all meaning. Who was a better man—Isocrates or Demosthenes? In the Athens of 350 B.C., should one have chosen territorial expansion patterned on a Hellenism that had become an empty shell because it lacked freedom, or should one have chosen freedom that was bound to lead to disaster? Similarly, in the France of 1957 was a man to favor French Algeria in disregard of all values of French civilization, or was he to prefer respect for those values at the price of his country's 'definitive' decline?" But this manner of posing the problem is outmoded today; the choice has been made, and politics has taken a different direction.

And here a deplorable misunderstanding occurs. Those holding that politics is subject to morality in effect establish a doctrine and give politics a certain appearance. Because they identify themselves with a certain ethic, they assume that a desirable relation between politics and morality exists; but such an assumption operates merely on the level of desiderata or imperatives. What is always an obstacle with regard to these desiderata is the need to conduct political affairs as they are, concretely, within the framework of the state as it is, or with politicians as they are. People begin their reasoning with a certain idea of the state, and, of course, to the extent that the conduct of politics constantly entails (apparent) choices between numerous (theoretical) possibilities, morality is easily found to be an element. In Machiavelli's teachings there really was no doctrine or, more precisely, only a doctrine of secondary importance. But we are not concerned here with Machiavellianism: the problem is to determine what, in effect, the political situation is in our own century, and what the conditions are under which politics now operates. Machiavelli does in fact conclude that politics is autonomous. Doctrine enters only when he tries to establish general rules and formulate the political courses that he considers the most efficient, having first established efficiency as a value. His point of departure seems excellent, for all political thought must begin with the world's political reality as it exists, the state as it is constituted at a particular moment, the fundamental currents existing at a particular time. But this observation easily leads to the statement of fact (not of value, or hope, or duty) that politics is actually autonomous. Moreover, in contrast to Machiavelli's time, the sole quest for efficiency in our time is no longer a matter of choice, but an intrinsic element in the political situation. In Machiavelli's day there was a semblance of Christian politics; people claimed that they were Christians and followed Christian morality. Machiavelli really demonstrated that the Prince's role, above all, is to be effective. By doing so, he introduced a new perspective, revolutionized his time, introduced efficiency as a value. Today we no longer have the choice: efficiency is regarded as the supreme good by all. It has become the general political rule—not a moral law, but a law recognized by all.

Now it is assumed that all aim at the same ends—and this is true; ends are no longer subject to search or deliberation: the U.S.S.R. pursues precisely the same ends as the U.S., and vice versa.[2] In this search for ends, maximum efficiency is regarded as best.[3] Khrushchev primarily tried to make the U.S.S.R. more efficient than the U.S. This means that efficiency is no longer a doubtful value; it is the necessary form of contemporary politics. Any serious reflection on political affairs will certainly show not merely their autonomous nature, but also the extent of that autonomy, which is not static. I am not trying to establish a general and metaphysical definition of politics here. I only maintain that whatever our intentions—our democratic morality, our liberal or egalitarian humanism, our hopes for socialism as a positive value—may have been in the nineteenth century, for our time (and for the foreseeable future) we have developed a mechanism whereby politics operates independently of any

---

[2] Even though I am in general agreement with Gaston Bouthoul, I do not share his views when he contrasts the ends pursued by the United States (happiness) with those pursued by the U.S.S.R. (power). These notions are relative to one another. The U.S.S.R. seeks power first, in order to assure universal happiness later. And the United States also seeks power in order to protect its happiness. And both have the same concept of happiness (raising of the living standard), and also of power.

[3] *International Situationniste*, No. 8.

such values. In strange and disturbing fashion, our purest political intentions have made politics much more autonomous than before. Socialist hopes that man's position in society would be re-established have produced the most stringent technological dictatorship ever, which still exists despite some appearances to the contrary.

This autonomy of political affairs is essentially the result—as Max Weber said—of the fact that the modern state's principal law is force. And it is precisely in the political sector that force is exercised. The importance of force is clearly evident from the fact that one's political opponent is always accused of using force—and the accusation is legitimate; the Right will accuse the UN of using it against, say, Katanga, and the Left will accuse the United States of using it against Castro.

Here we are in agreement with A. Chatelet [4] when he says that "there is a State from the very moment when a decision-making power instates itself, known by all as having the power to decide for society as a whole what is just or unjust, legal or illegal." But I do not share his truly theological romanticism when he insists that the existence of the state itself implies democracy, that in order to have political life it is necessary to make these two terms coincide (with the subjected individual being at the same time the creative individual), and that "democracy is the essence of any state in the sense that the latter determines a universal domain where everybody's decision is recognized as elemental." We have thus passed from stating a situation of fact to constructing an idealistic superstructure. My personal inclination tends in the direction of such an idealist view, but we must realize that it is only a pious wish and not insist that this really *is* the state's essence and that there is no other form of politics. In the present world the state is taken seriously only when it threatens or defends itself in a fight to the death against some grave danger to its existence. It certainly is virtuous, but politically infantile, to be scandalized if, say, the government of Morocco uses a plot to rid itself of its enemies,

---

[4] A. Chatelet, in *Arguments* (1962).

or if the Algerian government put its enemies in prison, or if all the new African states set themselves up as dictatorships. We are face to face here not with free political choices, but with hard, inescapable necessities.

A very interesting dispute on this subject was precipitated in the United States in October, 1962, by Arthur Sylvester, assistant secretary of Defense (in charge of public affairs at the Pentagon), when he declared that "it is a constant in history that the government has the right to lie in order to save itself. That seems fundamental to me." Sylvester added: "Information is an instrument of power." In this way information and the manipulation of opinion are integrated. On the one hand, the government places itself outside all ethical norms; on the other, information becomes a weapon. Thus Mr. Sylvester very neatly espouses Lenin's theories.

The outstanding fact about the state is that force has become its monopoly. "The modern state is a power group of institutional character seeking to monopolize force within the limits of a territory. . . ." The state prevents other groups from using force: it is no longer acceptable that a party, union, or clan should act by force; it is even less acceptable in the case of an individual—he would simply be a criminal. For a long time the state hesitated with regard to groups. But in our day we see that precisely because groups still try to utilize force, the reaction of the state becomes harder and more relentless. The police have become a decisive and necessarily uncontrolled element. But, it will be objected, the term "force" does not apply in the case of the state; a careful distinction must be made between force and legitimate constraint. For example, the police exists to exercise legitimate restraint and abandons its proper function if force is used, at which point the citizen must protest. Legitimate constraint is exercised by legitimate authorities within the framework of the law, and under the control of the law.

This is a very reassuring form of idealism. But what is legitimate authority? The theologians have failed to tell us, as have the political philosophers of the eighteenth and nineteenth centuries. Quite obviously there are some excellent definitions and satisfactory criteria, but that is as far as it goes. If we consider the practical situation, we will find that powers which are able to maintain themselves are legitimate. Reliance on force does not change this legitimacy in the slightest. Legitimacy is the result of two complementary elements: support by the people and recognition by other states. The first element is purely artificial. The people always give their enthusiastic adherence to any government that asks for it. A plebiscite or referendum in France or Yugoslavia, Communist Hungary or Nazi Germany, Algeria or Fascist Italy, will always yield affirmative votes of from 90 to 99 per cent.[5] This is not necessarily the result of pressure, coercion, or propaganda; the spontaneous movement of public opinion is quite enough. But if necessary, a political regime will use propaganda and bring about the adherence of the people as a whole, thus producing its own legitimacy.[6] On the other hand, a state is legitimate when it is recognized by other states. Here we have, even in the case of states violently antagonistic to each other, a sort of solidarity among regimes, just as in any parliamentary regime, as is well known, representatives of radically opposite parties are nevertheless tied together by a certain camaraderie as deputies, leading them to support jointly certain common interests. Each state, each regime, each government knows well that if one were to search a little, one would find the skeleton. Thus they all accord a measure of recognition to each other. The only condition demanded is continuity. If a new regime "sticks," it is a good regime. For this reason alone, the Soviet Union just as much as Hitler Germany, and Gomulka just as much as Antonescu, are recognized by everybody. The greatest shame today is that Communist China is not recognized by everybody. But to have continuity a state must use constraint, and sometimes force. Has the legitimacy of the Communist regime in Hungary or in

---

[5] With some powerful propaganda and all organizations turned against the government, the government still obtained 60 per cent of the votes, as we saw in 1962.

[6] Jacques Ellul: *Propaganda* (New York: Alfred A. Knopf; 1966).

East Germany been challenged? Or that of Nasser's regime?
It follows that force is legitimate state, and the state is legitimate
when it can maintain itself, even by force.

Let us now look at the law. That force is the opposite of law
is a tenuous argument. The law is subject to the fluctuation of
circumstances, and everybody accepts this. The law varies depending on the case and the pressures exercised. Even in
France many jurists have abandoned as useless and obsolete the
idea that the law is normative; they now consider it pure fact.
But from the moment it is regarded as such, the law can no
longer be considered a barrier, a limit to facts, and still less a
criterion of legitimacy. If the facts collide with the laws, we
change the laws. How can it be agreed then that the observance
of the law turns force into legitimate constraint? [7]

We must go farther. It is now a well-established tradition of
government to observe the law when nothing is happening; but
if something happens, a state of emergency is declared during
which special laws will be in force. This happens precisely at
the moment when some group tries to use force for its own ends.
At that moment the state's reaction is pitiless: it abandons the
framework of the law and engages in a contest of force with the
group in question until it has quelled the rebellious group and
made it reenter the ranks. Put differently, when the state is led
by circumstances to employ force, it never observes the law,
and we find ourselves in the presence of naked violence.[8] The
state is ready, of course, subsequently, to legitimize the use of
such violence. We hardly need to point out how simple-minded
the distinction made by one of our philosophers is between a
"police" (internal), which would be legitimate as a means of
constraint, and an "army," which would be on the order of
force. In the realm of politics these two elements are identical.
Therefore, the more the law adjusts to "normal" (i.e., rare)
circumstances, the more the regime becomes aggressive when

---

[7] Jacques Ellul: "La Philosophie des réformes actuelles de l'Enseignement du
Droit," in Archives de philosophie du Droit (1960).
[8] Even without wanting to, Bertrand de Jouvenel confirms this: "To have
recourse to juridical methods when the situation demands a political decision is
a grave political error." See De la politique pure (Paris: Calmann-Lévy; 1963),
p. 221.

threatened by the slightest danger,[9] and what the regime calls a disturbance of public order becomes ever smaller, and is interpreted ever more rigorously. A carnival or a student demonstration that sometimes created considerable upheavals in the nineteenth century was not the object of constraint and penalties. In our day we know the brutal reactions to such events. And we are not referring just to the French case. Everywhere we find the same trend. The slightest manifestation of independence is immediately considered as a challenge to the state's power monopoly.

Still, it will be said, the citizen's reaction must be taken into account. It is precisely the citizen's political duty to rise in the name of morality and the law against such attitudes on the part of the state; he must be the effective limit to violence! To this I can only say: but this is the very citizen I described in the preceding chapter as being immersed in the immediate present, disoriented, incapable of true political reflection. This citizen will either not be interested in political problems, in which case he will provide not a limit to the state's violence, but will simply be its object, or this citizen enters the political game, and in our days this immediately makes him more than a citizen; it makes him a partisan and a militant.[1] Is it the same everywhere? I will gladly except, partly, Great Britain and the United States. But these countries should take care, for they are traveling along the same road, and are increasingly becoming what we are. France is a choice place for the exercise of political thought.

---

[9] Let me quote one example out of thousands: the Commissioner of Inquiry for Internment Camps stated on June 29, 1962, that among those detained in the Camp of San Maurice L'Ardoise (in Algeria—Trans.) 64 per cent were not charged with anything in particular, 22 per cent were provisionally detained, and 14 per cent were acquitted (yet still interned). The commission concluded: "It must be accepted that the government, charged with assuring public order and the defense of the nation, can and must in case of public danger facing the nation take all necessary security measures." And that was all.

[1] I have already stated that it is very difficult to believe that there is depoliticization. But what seems particularly important to me is that if the citizen does not intervene directly in the course of political affairs, this is not for any of the reasons generally given; it is neither the high standard of living, nor the development of comforts and leisure, nor the loss of civic spirit that provokes a certain—and moreover little proved—distance from political life. It seems to me that the real reason lies not with the citizen, but in the intrinsic and uncontrollable growth of state power.

Once more it is in the lead, but it is not certain that this means progress. The militant citizen is a case in point. In his view the state has no right to use any constraints against his party, and he will immediately call all constraints force; conversely, the state must, in his view, use force against the opposite party, and if it fails to do so, is grossly negligent. The man of the Left will protest against police brutality, tortures, and internment camps for his comrades, but he will overlook the same measures if applied to the man of the Right or call them legitimate, perhaps in the name of the great principle: no freedom for the enemies of freedom. It goes without saying that the Rightist's attitude is exactly parallel though opposite. Therefore the effort to distinguish between force exercised by the state and legitimate constraint is entirely futile. To be sure, moralists and theologians can deal with all exigencies and construct theories, but while this may satisfy the mind, the principal fault—other than that these theories all conflict with each other—is that none of them is *applicable.* I did not say *applied!* To say that the state should not employ force is simply to say that there should be no state.[2]

It is the same with regard to war. To the extent that the state is charged with ensuring the survival of the social group that it leads and represents, it cannot avoid war. Let us assume that pacifists are right in their demands, and on condition that their international movement exerts pressure on all the states at the same time. Any other attitude is only the negation of the state. And war, like violence, is not "just." It exists—that is all. It is very ingenious, but also very vain, to establish rules of war or to define what constitutes a just war. Regarding the latter, one need only recall that the criteria are extremely variable. A just war according to St. Augustine is not the same as a just war according to Emperor Gratianus. And these definitions in turn obviously have nothing in common with Lenin's definition of a

---

[2] Let me add, without satisfaction, that Mr. Nehru declared on June 17, 1962, that no country was any longer capable of observing the theory of nonviolence. To be sure, he said that one must teach people to think in nonviolent terms. But the political practices of the state cannot take their cue from that; neither can protesting groups within the state: witness the nonviolent movement of Negroes against segregation in the United States which finally erupted in violence in June, 1963.

just war, with which Mao Tse-tung in turn is in considerable disagreement (it is often forgotten that both have written extensively on just wars). A war might be entirely just when measured by Lenin's criteria, but completely unjust for Catholics applying Gratianus' criteria. The rules of war, in turn, are either defined by a superior power imposing them with force (for example by the peace leagues in the Middle Ages) or are the fruits of an agreement—a gentleman's agreement—but their limitations are only too well known; they are applied only to the extent that they do not prevent victory, and those on the losing side will violate such laws without the slightest compunction. The rules of war really are valid only when there is no war. For the sole rule of war is to win. Under such conditions and without entering at length into this argument, I can say that all war is unjust and all force to be condemned. But this is a matter for the moralist or the individual; the state cannot possibly judge in this fashion. It would simply condemn itself to disappear and be replaced by another state that would show less compunction to use force. Marx regarded democracy, as an acceptable regime only because it does not dare to use force, being paralyzed by scruples. Thus, says Marx, it is the easiest state to overthrow.

Let me add, finally, that this force, which for a long time was purely physical, has taken on a new dimension in our day—it has become psychological force or violence. When the state utilizes propaganda—"violates" the masses and insidiously determines the citizen's behavior—it exercises repressive coercion, but on a larger scale. Force is in this way no longer used only by the police; it invades the individual's soul in order to obtain his enthusiastic allegiance, his faithful behavior, his devotion to a cause. But this does not change the basic effect of the force used: the state is still acting autonomously; and this occurs because propaganda escapes all criticism and all moral control. Following the momentum created by such separateness—such autonomy—the state then seeks to eliminate all groups that try to exercise any intellectual or psychological influence which contradicts the legitimized propaganda of the state. Churches and universities have long been neutralized or placed in the service of the state-controlled press and other means of mass communication and, progressively, more recent private movements have been drawn into the state's orbit. The latter establishes its monopoly in this area; none can use the means of psychological pressure except the state—here in fact lies the power that makes it the state. It is always said that the state fights against the freedom of the press; but this struggle is nothing but the modern aspect of the struggle of the state against the feudal barons of the fourteenth and fifteenth century. And so we see the monopoly of force, the autonomy of politics.

This autonomy has yet another source. Let us recall the state's claim that it solves all problems and the concomitant, inveterate belief on the part of most citizens that it is indeed the state's function to solve all problems. This attitude of man toward the state is even more apparent if one considers that man's intentions and desires have changed.[3] He is much less sensitive and receptive to the many problems (over which he could try to exercise some influence); rather he demands the total and complete guarantee of his private existence. He demands assured income and assured consumption. He insists on an existence of complete security, refusing to take any responsibility for himself. But all this, as he well knows, can be assured only by the state organization. As a result, whatever a citizen's "political" opinion may be, his appeals to the state spring from sources much more profound than ideology; they spring from his very participation and place in society. It is no longer true that the better part of all questions facing a society is not political. And even if a question is in no way political it becomes political and looks to the state for an answer. It is wrong to say that politics is everything, but it is a fact that in our society everything has become political, and that the decision, for example, to plant one crop instead of another has become a political matter (see Nikita Khrushchev's speech of December 23, 1961). But it must be understood that such politization

---

[3] Max Frisch: *Évolution de la Démocratie en Europe*, in *Bulletin* s.e.d.e.i.s. (1964); Hetman: *Bien-être et Liberté*, in *Bulletin* s.e.d.e.i.s. (1962).

leads necessarily to a totalitarian state, which in turn inevitably leads to the autonomy of politics wherein values are superceded by expediency. This also presupposes, in effect, that every decision by the state ultimately involves the entire community and that the state effectively represents each citizen in his aspirations and desires. Moreover, this is what we hear and read every day. If Morocco is opposing Mauritania, we learn that it is the deepest wish in the heart of every Moroccan to regain the lost territory, and conversely, that it is the strongest passion of every inhabitant of Mauritania to save his independence. It is more than likely that the vast majority of Moroccans and Mauritanians have only the vaguest notions on the subject. But, bound to the masses, the state is entitled to use such language. To be sure, this means conversely that the state can then demand that all citizens participate, even if ultimately they are not at all concerned. These citizens are involved in a totality that the state takes upon itself. And via this totality the state represents, reaches, and engages everyone.

We are here in the presence of a new alienation that has nothing to do with capitalism and is more deeply rooted in the Soviet Union than elsewhere. From the moment that the state becomes what it is—i.e., charged with all things—who will control it? From the moment the state is bureaucratized, what norms of validity or legitimacy can impose themselves from the outside? From the moment the state charges itself with the whole of a citizen's life, how can politics not be autonomous? It is an illusion to write: "To exorcise the anonymous nature of power . . . we must create new channels between the individual citizen and those who hold political power." [4] From the moment at which all fundamentals are politicized (as in our society) there no longer is an individual citizen. I do not mean to say that the citizens all have the same tastes, the same clothes, the same faces, and are identical. That would be stupid. To be sure, each one will have his own profession and his different loves. But this has no relevance to political affairs. The citizen

---

[4] *L'État et le citoyen*, publ. under the direction of Club Jean Moulin (Paris: Éditions du Seuil; 1961), p. 128.

no longer has any *political* individuality even if he has political "ideas," because the state has entirely absorbed all political particularity. Therefore there can no longer be any real currents, any more than there can be between two electric poles of the same sign. This is an inevitable consequence of general politization. And because there is no current, and cannot be, the entire political exercise is *de facto* autonomous.

It is illusory to point to the spiritual autonomy of man's personality. Besides, even those pointing to it add immediately: "An immense educational effort must be made if man's drive toward spiritual autonomy is to prevail over the standardization of minds." [5] But this is a pious wish; obviously, if spiritual autonomy existed, there would be a possible response to the autonomy of politics. But how can we believe that in a civilization entirely oriented toward the pursuit of comfort and the raising of the material living standard, intent on mobilizing all its powers toward that end while increasingly integrating the individual by systematic means—how can we believe that in such a civilization the state would take the chance of making concessions to spiritual autonomy? Even leisure as it is conceived is contrary to that. And it is very superficial to think that spiritual autonomy can result from some sort of steered orientation or education; on the contrary, it must be the fruit of complete social spontaneity. Besides, who would impart such education? The state, of course. And how can we believe that this state, oriented as it now is, could provide an education aimed at spiritual autonomy? Nothing in the evolution of the last half century permits such an assumption. On the contrary, we see the *need* for technological training and adaptation to modern society impose itself more and more; the entire program of educational reforms consists of nothing else. But to say that is to negate all spiritual autonomy. And we already feel the new step that will be demanded in every quarter: true civic education, and education for civic responsibilities, political seriousness, participation and commitment. In short, training for the

---

[5] Ibid.

virtues that make for good citizens; but this only means that politics will become even more autonomous, for the good citizen will not be able to object on the basis of his individual conscience —in which case he would be regarded as an individualistic and anarchistic villain—but would have to apply the collective social morality, which in the present state of affairs is a product of political autonomy.

Here we touch the last and deepest aspect of this autonomy. I have discussed the phenomenon of the growing means and powers of the state organism. This is today its essential character, whatever doctrines may underlie it. We can establish as a basic principle that *the more power grows, the more values disintegrate.* When I talked about the contradiction between the two orders, I really was discussing the contradiction between power and values. The distinction between ends and means is more and more coming to be recognized as fallacious. It is illusory to think that means of applying power must be increased so that justice, liberty, and truth can be attained and realized. These values can exist only in a situation of flux, in the human being's drive toward attaining them. They never exist in and by themselves; they cannot be set in motion like an object. Anyone believing that they can would live in the illusion that a given social order can encompass such justice, freedom, and truth. That is the myth to which Marxists have abandoned themselves, contrary to Karl Marx, who wanted to eliminate these values entirely. But man cannot do without them. He must re-invent them, and, if he is politicized, join them to the state order. But the growth of power ultimately effaces the sense of such values and the limits set by them. When the state has all power, no boundary remains between what is just and injust, true and false, good and bad. The effective boundary then is between what can and what cannot be done. What the state can do, the state will do, and what it does will *a priori* become just and true.

In stating this fact we are not far from the theory stipulating that the law is what the state decides. It is then up to the state to decide what is just—and, to logically extend the result, what the state decided *is* just. I am not exaggerating; this theory of

law has been supported by numerous philosophers and jurists of
greatly varying political opinions. But the state makes its
decisions not at all on the basis of the fundamental virtues but
on the basis of what it can do, i.e., on the basis of power. And
when it attains a sufficiently large machinery, it is in the sovereign ethical position to *declare* what is good (even if it be
evil), and to declare what is evil (even if it be good). Would
this be a perverted state? No, just a state filled with the spirit
of power—and which can be no different. Only a limited state
can accept opposition from the good and the just outside of
itself and tolerate limits; but the more its power grows, the
more the limits recede and the more all distinctions based on
values vanish from the citizens' minds. An all-powerful state,
whatever its nature or doctrine, has never thus far accepted
external values and the limits they impose. This is a historical
fact, and I do not see how the situation could change; to claim
that tomorrow things will be different is a jump into the absurd
to which we are in no way entitled.

All theories to the effect that a rising living standard will end
in democratization and limitation of the state are illusory, for
there has never been any case of an effective diminution of the
use of power. All examples cited to prove the contrary show only
that in a period of revolutionary tension terror is used; and that
after a longer or shorter lapse of time, when the state has installed itself and is no longer challenged, there is a *détente*. The
living standard is only incidental, not directly causal. But in
this process there is no return to a respect for values; there are
those laid down by the state by decree, and that is all. The
state does not in any way withdraw. It keeps what it has gained
by force and terror, but in a normalized and institutionalized
—i.e., reassuring fashion. Under Khrushchev the state was
certainly not retreating any more than it was under Stalin, but
the normalization of society on statist principles was more advanced—that is all. The contradiction between power and values
leads us to the tragic illusion besetting the men of our time, for
whom all values are finally being realized by political means
at the very time when these means have become destructive of
all individual values and powers.

2. *Objections*

Religious men and moralists do not agree.[6] The former are tempted to formulate, in one way or another, Christian politics. But how would such politics be applied by a non-Christian state? And the past experiences of Christian states, or even their present experiences, are not very encouraging. Their hypocrisy has been denounced for a long time. We find ourselves in a strange situation here: the so-called Christian state claimed that it applied Christian ethics, obeyed God's commandments, and considered its first duty was to promote the church. It was then argued that such a state, which *in fact* practiced nothing of what it preached, conducting its policies without reference to the gospel, was transparently hypocritical. In this dispute men stated in very valid terms what politics was *in reality*. The screen was torn down and the lie denounced. Nowadays people can no longer stand such a situation, can no longer bear that the state should be, openly, what the (Christian) state had been accused of being secretly: animated by the spirit of strength and engaged in the use of force and the abuse of power. It was absolutely necessary to create another screen and set up another image: reality was too brutal. And on the one side, Christians have again taken up their work under different forms, insisting in France that they desire a Christian state, establishing programs for the state to put into operation, or defining a theology of state or, more frequently, issuing manifestos, protests, or proclamations against acts by the state. In any event, this was all useless as an approach to political affairs because it was inapplicable. But Christians have a way of never foreseeing ways and means. And so they dodged responsibility: for these Christians not only had no power of their own, but they did not

---

[6] If by chance a statesman speaks cynically, the whole world is scandalized. Take for example President de Gaulle's statement (1961) to the effect that it was necessary to leave Algeria because in effect "things were what they were" and that it was "in our interest to leave, just as it had been in our interest to install ourselves there." All our pious burghers were aghast.

look for a way to participate in the power that existed—no matter how modestly—maintaining instead the infinitely more comfortable stance of refusal, criticism, and accusation.

Moralists and humanists took another road. In contrast to Christians talking of or to the state, the idealists claim that they represent the rights of man. Unfortunately, recent experiences show that such idealists never proceed on the basis of their ethics or vision of man, but begin at once to make political choices which are instead part and parcel of a completely rigorous autonomy of political affairs. They are Rightists or Leftists, not for reasons or values, but because of some instinct, some basic impulse resulting from social pressures, conformism, and passions. The "moral hemiplegia" afflicting the Left and Right are anterior. And the values, the humanism, and so on are invoked only to ward off free choices, justify our determination, and glorify our positions. This is a complete throwback to Christian hypocrisy. It is not because of the value of man that they are, say, Leftists, but, being Leftists, they invoke the dignity of the human personality—of course from the Leftist point of view. For those opposing them are *only* people who negate this so-called human personality! It is not for reasons of honor that others are Rightists, but, being Rightists, they invoke honor against a Left that knows only how to dishonor, vulgarize, and debase all it touches. If one follows the evolution of thought in our political philosophers, our distinguished humanists, a little more closely, if one compares their writings with the concrete positions they have taken, if one examines their manifestos, and particularly if one pays attention to the *lacunae* in their actions. (Why did they keep silent in such and such a case? Why did they consider only one side of some situation? Why did their doctrine omit some particular aspect of the problem?) One will then see that they are the best examples of the autonomous nature of politics, and will understand how little their philosophies, theologies, and moral tenets have affected their decisions or provided them with a clear understanding of specific situations. One can say, very generally, that any tension between such men and the state has been entirely eliminated and that the autonomy of politics has absorbed their philosophy while they are denying its existence. We must also remember the dogmatic refusal on the part of Marxists who, having adopted a particular interpretation of history, cannot admit that things developed differently from the way they had projected them. They therefore cannot accept that politics should be autonomous and, at the same time, remain immobilized in an absolute idealism (for example, their insistence that war, by its very nature, will disappear together with capitalism, as stated in *Le Drapeau Rouge,* March 4, 1963).

But there is another more directly political argument in the dispute; it comes from democrats. They too, though with a different argument, deny the autonomous course of political affairs. Their concern is to integrate politics into the moral formula that democracy or socialism is meant to be. We see this in the theory of Rousseau, who affirmed that the political body *is* a "moral being" with a will, and that this general will tends always to the conservation and well-being of each party. This means that the good coincides with the general will, which is the political will par excellence. Unfortunately this general will, as we know well today, is hardly to be found and applies even less as the expression of the "moral being." But this attempt to subsume politics within a socialist and therefore moral framework is also seen in the thought of Jean Jaurès, who attempted to demonstrate that socialism would finally succeed in giving society its form, not only because socialism was necessary, but also because it was good. Marx, on the other hand, would have wanted to eliminate all values from his interpretation. Jaurès reintroduced them to show the identity between necessary political evolution and the accomplishment of the good and just, which men know instinctively. But we are far from realizing the anterior conditions for that; we are no longer living at a time when questions are susceptible to solution by simple recourse to nature. We live in a situation (and this goes for all countries except those where unanimity is created by manipulation) produced by democracy, in which citizens do not unanimously adhere to a small number of common values. Yet such unanimity would be the indispensable precondition if politics were to be prevented from following an autonomous course: it would be necessary for the citizens to unanimously accept values that would then be imposed on political affairs. But surely the practice of democracy ruins this unanimity and—by default— gives political affairs their autonomy, while in Machiavelli's view there must be autonomy by conquest. Incidentally, the latter is always assured in dictatorships.

François Bourricaud presents some very pertinent criticism when he shows that the attempt is made ultimately to suppress the autonomy of politics "by dissociation and reduction. The dissociation aims at distinguishing technical problems outside the citizen's competence from political problems on which he has the last word. As regards assimilation, it identifies the political with the moral. . . . Unfortunately," Bourricaud says quite rightly, "the distinction between technology and morality seems very awkward." This entire question needs further study, much like the problem regarding moral choices in political affairs, the latter becoming reduced to "bets of varying degrees of chance," whereas the technological imperative is not clearly the determining factor.

Here we must underline another aspect: the idealist's misconception of the autonomous course of political affairs is not only fallacious, but also dangerous. The gravest political errors, which have caused most of the bloodshed and disorders in the last half-century, were committed by those who, denying the regrettable, detestable, yet irrefutable fact that politics in our day is autonomous, acted as though it was not, and as though it was subject to definite rules and values. (These same political men were incapable of formulating clearly the values in whose name they acted.) On the one hand we have, as a result, the rise of such doctrinaires as Stalin and Hitler, who took this autonomy of political matter as their point of departure,[7] stating clearly and constantly what they intended to do. It was enough to take their statements seriously. But democrats never did that, and therefore were always wrong (except perhaps for Churchill,

---

[7] With Stalin, despite his Marxism, the preponderance of means over ends and the elaboration of tactics and strategies ultimately return to this autonomy, economic and social factors having become pieces on the political checkerboard.

who also ceaselessly affirmed the autonomy of political affairs).
If democratic politicians, socialists, humanists, and Christians
committed one error after another and believed that Hitler's or
Stalin's declarations, like those by the FLN (National Liberation Front), Fidel Castro, or Nasser, were only speeches like
those which they themselves delivered on Sundays, it was the
result of their profound conviction that "all this is not possible—
politics is not independent of morality. It is not possible to have
such ideas, to scoff at the law, not to keep one's word, to engage
in vast conquests, to provoke revolutions, to deport masses of
people in order to acquire living space—all that is not possible,
nor is the establishment of socialism by force and conquest."
When Hitler rose to power, churchmen believed that Germany's
reconstruction in a "spiritual" sense was all to the good, and
they simply *could* not believe what Hitler said regarding his
future projects. Similarly the German financiers helped Hitler
on the assumption that he would win (which turned out to be
correct), that a revolutionary was not such a terrible thing after
all, and that they would domesticate him; but his "value" judgment was incorrect. They had arrived at it because they believed that politics was "reasonable" or that Hitler could not
go where he said he would be going. In reality Hitler dominated
them and forced them to submit, just as he had said he would.
The same error of judgment was committed by the leaders of
Poland's and Czechoslovakia's democratic parties, who estimated that it was necessary to collaborate with the Communists.
This resulted from a certain idealism born in the Resistance
movement, but mainly from the conviction that Communists
obeyed "the same morality as we, as all of us"; that they were
searching for justice and truth and were devoted to the good of
the fatherland, and that one therefore could work with them.
People hoped to be able to *moderate* the Communists, to make
them democratic and receptive to the excellence of ideological
and political liberalism by accepting their socialist economic
planning methods. Unfortunately, as events have shown, all
alliances, concessions, dialogues, and so on have only served
the Communist tactic, which was neither liberal nor pluralist
nor subject to values.

In the face of perfectly autonomous political action, no in-
vocation of value can be of the slightest use. Love of peace, and
particularly the happiness of the people, promised by a political
course not recognized as autonomous, assured Mussolini's victory
in Ethiopia, Franco's in Spain, and Hitler's in Czechoslovakia.
Only at the very last minute do the idealists grab hold of themselves and call a halt, which is then terribly costly and bloody
because none of the measures that a clear understanding of the
autonomy of political matters should have necessitated was
taken in time. To say in our day that war is just when it is truly
the *ultima ratio,* and that it is acceptable only under such conditions, is once more to superimpose on a century without morals
or values an essentially Christian judgment. It is to leave a
considerable margin of action to the most realistic political
course in a world in which politics is antonomous, which simply
means that one accepts the most violent and terrible war in
return for not having acted in the beginning, for having been
held back by scruples. I do not mean to say at all that war is
good, desirable, or just. I reaffirm what I have often written, that
"all war is injust." No state can in good conscience wage war.
But in a world where politics is autonomous, those engaged in
politics must know that war or the threat of war is a normal
political means, and that to deny this particular fact of autonomy is, under the cover of virtue and idealism, to make political
affairs ultimately the most ruinous for the community. In our
day there are no "good guys" who are victors and represent
justice and right or "bad guys" who are politicians and are
finally defeated. If Hitler had won, a trial conducted against the
Soviet Union and the Western nations and based on exact facts
would undoubtedly have ended in death sentences for our politicians.

It must not be thought that the autonomy of political affairs
exists only in dictatorships. It exists in different degrees in the
democracies also. The mistake was to consider dictatorships or
the communist regime as abnormal, exceptional cases, manage-
able in the long run, which could return to their earlier forms.
The error was to believe that political activity regulated by
values and generally respected and accepted law, subject to

morality, or a war subject to laws, was possible. The error was to believe that this was in the ordinary nature of things. It should have been clear that any political order based on values was an infinitely fragile thing, a rather astonishing human achievement, and one that had to be maintained by will-power, sacrifice, and constant renewal. As soon as the tension relaxed, the situation again became what is was: autonomous politics, war without law. The trials we have endured in the last half-century should convince us that even if it does not please us, even if we disapprove, the situation as found in dictatorships and communism has become the normal situation, and that we must reflect on the political problem in relation to what happens there, and not on the basis of some ideal democracy that has no chance whatever of asserting itself. We already know well that the mores of the totalitarian states have gained footholds in the democracies. Police regimes, internment camps, an uncontrolled, all-powerful administration, systematic elimination of dissenting opinions and minorities are some of the signs that, on the level of public opinion stereotypes such as "the course of history" (which is only ideological camouflage for the autonomy of political affairs), "things are as they are," or "work means freedom," or "laws spring from necessity" have been accepted.

If we examine the relationships among political men or political groups in a democracy, we see very quickly that these are relationships determined by force, blackmail, pressure, deals, prestige, careers, complicity—but that there is no moral rule whatsoever, no supremacy of values.[8] Even in groups that are strongly ideological—I am thinking here of groups such as the intellectual Left—relations are often sordid and strikingly manifest this autonomy of the course of political events, even though in their public declarations these groups present themselves as defenders of virtue, humanism, and morality. It must be understood that the vocabulary of moral and non-material

---

[8] J. Schumpeter has well illuminated the nature of such "victory," and of pure efficiency in the democratic system. He shows that for political man a "cause" is a weapon for combat. He recalls Peel's word after his campaign against the government: "Jamaica was a good horse to ride." (See *Capitalism* . . . , Chap. xxii.)

values is retained even in the most autonomous type of politics. Thus Hitler and Khrushchev incessantly invoked God. Similarly, we find the word "social" in currently used ethical justifications of political activity.[9]

An important element confirming the autonomy of the political element is the perversion of the use of moral values by citizens who invoke them. The spectacle in France during the last ten years has been very revealing in this respect. The conflict between the moral problem and the political problem was admirably illustrated by the dispute between a pious Jew, Victor Gollancz, and Father Bruckberger, on the occasion of the Adolf Eichmann trial. Gollancz, representing the spiritual side, insisted that it was futile to kill Eichmann. "What good is it to kill one more man? Would such a measure rend the veil of cruelty and hatred Auschwitz has thrown over humanity? Eichmann belongs to God. Only God can judge him. We must not be guided by the mythical idea of compensatory justice, but by spiritual compensation. The more odious the deed, the greater must be our compassion. Hitler's extreme evil must be compensated with an act of extreme goodness. . . ." Obviously these words expressing the deepest moral and spiritual truth cannot be understood by the state. Politics can in no way apply them. But to pretend that justice and truth are given their due is only a fraud and a form of hypocrisy. Those who claim to do justice by condemning a man to death deserve the same accusation of hypocrisy that Jesus leveled at the Pharisees. What we find here is an ideological construct that man builds to justify his acts: these acts are useful so that society can function and survive. Bruckberger's argument was: If we pardon murderers, our society is done for. It is useful for the survival of a group to eliminate the nonconformists, the fools, the anarchists, the maladjusted, the criminals; and it is legitimate that the group should react in this fashion through its judges, its soldiers, its political men. It is the very role of politics to make this reaction more easily possible, for it is under such conditions that no one individual or group has to bear the responsibility. Let us not,

---

[9] Böhm: "Kapituliert der Staat?" in *Politische Meinung* (1962).

then, confuse things by talking of values, morality, and virtue but, rather, try to effect an honesty that is neither cynical nor skeptical.

Such a situation entails a certain number of consequences that are very disturbing for idealists and humanists. In the first place, to interpret political facts by some spiritual or moral theory is to deal with things in a very facile way. But the man who is neither a cynic nor a skeptic in seeking to establish a relationship between the two conflicting areas of the "is" and the "ought" often reasons in just such a facile way. It is a means of not letting the contradiction burst forth into the open, which is always disturbing. If a citizen without actual political responsibility claims that politics should be guided by a moral canon, and judges the acts of political men according to that canon, he is the very hypocrite that he accuses the politician of being. And if he accepts some tiny political responsibilities—for example, making a speech at a meeting, signing a manifesto, pasting a poster to a wall, and so on—it still is much too facile for him to explain his act in terms of moral motivations: I sign because a pal hands me the paper and because to sign it is an act of solidarity with my pals; I make a speech because someone has been illegally arrested; I rush to the aid of victims of brutality because I have a good heart; I help save a member of the underground because he is in trouble. Ultimately these acts say: I bring moral judgments to bear on the just and the true and in addition, I refuse to consider the purely political significance of the act I commit. It obviously is much easier to follow one's good heart and feelings of decency, to follow one's inclinations and act out of friendship. It is much easier to put the moral, individual question to oneself than to try to see and understand the effective political consequences of the act one performs. If one does not pose the entire ethical question—from which there is no escape—but remains at the personal level, the responses are generally clear. If a man is drowning, I must save him, and if a man is in mortal danger at the hands of an enemy, I must save him.

But all this becomes very complicated when we add political

significance to our action. At that point phenomena becomes ambiguous, situations uncertain. The man I save may be a dangerous killer who, once saved, will commit a series of political murders. Or he may belong to a totalitarian political organization and act for and by order of that organization in concert with all the injustices and murders committed by the party he will continue to serve. One may say: It is necessary to commit the charitable act. Very well, but, one must then also know its political consequences, one of which is that as a result of the act other men will be killed and tortured. Or, I may want to defend liberty and work against all curtailment of freedom of expression or of moral judgment; but, by doing this I may place myself in the service of another power, persecuted at the moment, which openly rejects freedom of expression. I helped that power to advance, to gain control; but once it does so, it will suppress what it demanded for itself, namely freedom of expression, or individual guarantees with regard to law or police, and so on. By my act—committed for moral reasons, but without examination of its political consequences—I will then have accomplished exactly the opposite of what I intended.

Yet, while decisions of this kind can have individual moral significance or individual spiritual motivation, they no longer have communal, collective, or public significance: "I am in disagreement with such a petition, but I shall nevertheless sign it because it is necessary that Christians speak up. I do not like the odious design of a poster, but I will put it on the wall just the same because one must commit oneself—that is where my true freedom lies. . . ." Rather than justifying my actions in this way I must realize that my mental reservations and my personal motives will remain only with me and have no effect in the world of my political act. But my name and affiliation, affixed to some doubtful text, *will* have a political effect.

The over-all effect, therefore, is exclusively political, and the political effect must be considered *first*. The text I sign will reinforce some *political* movement in people's minds and, as such, it is in the sphere of autonomous political activity. When I view my act as the consequence of my personal motivations, it is an act of individual conscience, but precisely because the act *does* have political content, it will ultimately enter the sphere of autonomous political events and will be deprived of the moral or spiritual value—which initially motivated me to commit it— and become merely a naked, political act. I will then have reinforced that very autonomy of political affairs I so condemn. Such is the consequence of the absence of true political judgment and of the misfortune of the individual who bases his political acts on moral grounds.

To sum up: every political stance has *first of all* political significance independent of any personal significance that I may like to attach to it. But this political significance is provided by society as a whole, which judges within the framework of what political affairs are today, that is, within the framework of autonomous political affairs. It would be indulging in a romantic illusion to consider it possible to inject genuine moral values and spiritual significance into political acts by the personal loyalty or action of men who themselves are eminently moral, humanist, Christian. It is not enough for somebody to attribute moral significance to political affairs when political affairs will not accept it. It is not enough to insist that politics must be subjected to values; such insistence will not bring about a reign of values. It is not even enough that the chief of a party or a dictator should make decisions inspired by idealism or non-material attitudes. For the autonomy of political affairs to come to an end, it would be necessary that they be subordinated to common values; that the machinery of parties or the state have no autonomy—that they cease functioning like machines; that acts and decisions inspired by moral reasons be clearly recognizable as such in the eyes of all. But the people's education has been proceeding in exactly the opposite direction; they are too convinced of the corruption and Machiavellian ways of politics not to consider such autonomy inevitable.

This leads to two new conclusions. The situation being what it is, we must analyze political facts and deal with them as they exist, not as we wish they existed.[1] I do not mean to say that it is

[1] Here I agree with Eric Weil's "De la politique" (1956), when he stresses that politics can be understood only from the point of view of those who act, i.e., the government, and that it is vain to address sermons to the government. Politics is

necessary to bend oneself before facts or to accept matters as they are. We are not concerned here with effectiveness. But, for example, I reject the habitual game played by intellectuals in which they project values and spiritual content into political facts. On this point the politicians who do not attribute any significance or consequences—except strictly political consequences—to political reality are right, because they are viewing things the way they are. If a Christian insists on God's absolute demand for some particular act, let him do so; but he ought to know that he is not making a political demand. Herein lies the contradiction and the beginning of conflict; for a man ought to realize that there is no common frame of reference in the alleged demand of God and the execution of a particular political act. If indeed we seek a place to make our fine feelings and our humanism count, let us not participate in politics: it is no longer capable of absorbing human warmth.

If we do commit a political act or commit ourselves to a political enterprise, we must first very seriously examine its actual effects and consequences, devoid of any illusory vocabulary: the insertion of values into the discussion of political acts is never more than just words. Liberty, justice, the right of peoples to self-determination, the dignity of the human person— these are no longer anything but pale justifications for social conformity. I do not say that justice or truth do not exist. I only say that in the realm of political autonomy when these values are invoked today they are reduced to pure sound, they have no access to political decision-making, and no chance of being applied in practice (I see *no* chance, not just a reduced chance). Once invoked, they only serve to support an already existing political design. They become part of the propaganda apparatus, and often they are also used because political men like to delude themselves and give benediction to their actions by attributing values to them.

The other conclusion to be drawn is that a certain distance must be maintained between political facts and the individual.

---

what it is, says Weil, which (regardless of what else he says in his book) is a way of stating its autonomous nature. And he is right when he claims that political acts can be judged only politically.

If we believe—and we firmly believe it—that the individual has a spiritual life, a value, that man cannot realize himself except by the accomplishment of moral acts, then it is evident—and necessary—that there be a distance between political affairs and the individual. I do not agree that the individual cannot fulfill himself except by political endeavor or that politics expresses his personality, i.e., that man does not become himself except by political commitment, that not to participate in politics is to be a person without substance. Man may eventually participate in politics, but on condition that he knows exactly what he is doing. If a man does not maintain a distance—an objectivity—his very person will be absorbed by politics and dissolved in the sphere of political autonomy.

We could go to the opposite extreme of postulating that man is *not* a moral being, does not have an ethical calling, and can therefore, without damage to himself, enter this autonomous sphere of political affairs and play his part there. (Most modern opinions assume just that.) But under such circumstances I would say that it would be of little importance whether a man does or does not engage in politics; it would no longer be of the slightest interest or even make the slightest sense, for in such a case the political organism would function like a machine and man would be limited to serving it. Why should man participate under such conditions? If man is not a moral being, what significance would participation in politics have? To ask man to accept a political commitment is to presuppose that he is endowed with significance. And if man does indeed have moral significance, he must retain some distance from the autonomy of political affairs. The personal dimension of a political act may well exist, but it becomes swallowed up by, rather than superimposed on its collective implication. An individual can participate in political affairs, but cannot claim that in doing so he is expressing or realizing himself to his fullest extent. The opposite actually takes place: the autonomy of the political machinery not only does not permit individual acts to influence its operation, but individual acts and motives become completely submerged within it with the result that the individual, as such, simply ceases to be.

CHAPTER

[III]

POLITICS
IN THE WORLD
OF IMAGES

We have so far arrived at two seemingly contradictory conclusions. On the one hand we have found that the political element is fettered and determined and operates only in a sphere of superficial action. On the other hand I have tried to demonstrate that the political domain has become autonomous, which would appear to give the politician full independence. But these contradictions are not exhaustive; we must now take into account another personage in our drama—public opinion. It is a stereotype nowadays that it is not possible to engage in *any* political action unsupported by public opinion. Political affairs are no longer the game of princes; they require the consent of public opinion. In that respect there is no longer any difference between democratic and other regimes. A dictator is forced to

refer constantly to public opinion and lean on it and to manipulate it in such a fashion as to give everybody the impression
that he never acts except in accordance with the people's demands and desires. In similar fashion, a democratic government
is completely paralyzed if it does not control through propaganda the public opinion on which it depends. It must form
public opinion, orient it, unify it, and crystallize it in such a way
as to keep it from constantly interfering with political work in
progress.

Now that the masses have entered political life and express
themselves through what can be called public opinion, there can
no longer be any question of either pushing the masses out of
political life or of governing against public opinion. This particular piece of evidence must be our point of departure if we
want to understand the profound political transformation
wrought by propaganda.

1. Political Facts

Facts.

We encounter facts in the political world. These facts are
concrete and real; one can have direct knowledge of them
and test them. But, surprising as this may be, political facts
have different characteristics than they had in another day.
Before the nineteenth century two categories of political facts
could be distinguished. On the one hand, there were local
facts of immediate interest which were directly ascertainable:
a local famine, a succession crisis in the local lord's family, a
town councilor's bankruptcy—anyone interested could observe
them directly. Everybody in the interested group could know
them. Secrets were extremely difficult to keep: facts had too
many repercussions in such a limited world. Facts on which decisions were based were known directly by those interested and
always remained local, thus providing a base for the formation
of local positions. There was no global solidarity and little national solidarity. Local politics was only very remotely connected
with major political affairs. On the other hand there were politi-

cal facts of general interest that were not known to the entire population. Moreover, the population was very little concerned with these general facts, which were of concern, really, only to the political elite. Palace revolutions, declarations of war, new alliances, were far removed from the burgher who minded only his personal business. He knew little of these facts, except from ballads and troubadours; he was interested in them as in legends, and except when he was in the midst of a war, he felt the consequences only very remotely. The political elite, on the other hand, knew such facts very directly; they were within its reach.

This situation has changed greatly. Firstly, today, as a result of the global interconnectedness established by a network of communications systems, every economic or political fact concerns every man no matter where he may find himself. A war in Laos, a revolution in Iraq, or an economic crisis in the United States will have direct consequences for the average Frenchmen. The second element in this new situation is that, governments being based on people, the people are called upon to give their opinion on everything; it is therefore necessary that the people know the global facts. How does the public know the facts? Such knowledge can no longer be obtained directly; it is verbal knowledge conveyed by many intermediaries. After a kind of transformation, such information eventually becomes public opinion. But precisely because of public opinion's importance, it can be said that a fact does not become political except to the extent that opinion forms around it and it commands public attention. A fact that does not command attention and does not become a political fact ceases to exist even as a fact, whatever its importance may be. This is the thesis I will try to demonstrate.

Let us begin with an example of the different levels on which a fact is known and transformed into a political fact. Hitler's invasion of Czechoslovakia in March, 1939, was a fact. It was a concrete and real fact for Hitler, for the German generals, for President Hacha, for his ministers; it was *still* a concrete and real fact for German soldiers involved and for Czechs living in the invaded regions, but it was already a different type of fact. It was no longer part of a whole web of other facts; it was not part of an entire political policy or of a political necessity; it was a raw fact. The German soldiers were armed. They traveled along a road. They crossed a frontier. The Czechs, filled with terror and shame, saw the German troops march past. From then on the consequences of the fact fanned out in all directions: Czechs who did not see the actual invasion were arrested, Germans who did not participate in the invasion were sent to Bohemia to colonize it. Here we are still in the presence of concrete and real facts, which, however, for those experiencing them were already somewhat remote; they learned of the German invasion of Czechoslovakia only by deduction. Yet their knowledge was still personal, certain and direct—though deductive and not yet become public opinion. Public opinion took shape only when the French, the English, and others read in their papers the *translation into words* of the fact that had taken place.

There is no public opinion except *outside* the personally experienced fact. By necessity, this experience is always limited and fragmentary. For example, nobody can have experienced the political fact of the war of 1914. One need only listen to veterans; if they are not very well educated, if they are simple soldiers, they report at best some details and have no experience of the war as a whole, of its general character. They are incapable of describing its phases and their interconnection. This is even more true for the soldiers of our wars than for Fabrizio del Dongo. But these soldiers who each knew one of the war's details will never fashion public opinion with their experiences. Knowledge must take on a certain abstract and general character in order for it to become public opinion—for it to arouse concern of the masses and move them to action.

Nowadays a *fact* is what has been translated into words or images; what has been worked over to give it a general character very few people can experience directly; what has been transmitted to a very large number of individuals by means of communication; and to which has been added a coloring that is not necessarily present in the eyes of those who experience it. These qualities combine to form the abstract facts upon which public opinion is based.

Political Facts.

In this transformation of facts and its subsequent transmission as public opinion, several stages must be distinguished. A fact can be political only if its general tenor directly or indirectly affects life in the cities (*polis*). However, even there a remarkable transformation occurs. A fact is a political reality only under two conditions: firstly, if the government or a powerful group decides to take it into account, and secondly, if public opinion considers it a fact, and, at that, a fact of political nature. Thus it is no longer the fact itself, but the fact translated for public consumption which is now called a political fact, because the government must govern on the basis of such public opinion.

A government that makes its decisions on the basis of facts known only to itself, which it would hide from the masses, would immediately become unpopular because it would be completely misunderstood. Such a procedure entails the obliteration of innumerable concrete facts which, though political in nature, will never become political *facts* because no public opinion will form around them. It follows that a fact that is definitely political in nature and is experienced by hundreds or thousands of people will not "exist" if public opinion fails to seize it. The foremost example of a "non-fact" was the Nazi concentration camps. Here we were in the presence of a considerable fact, resting on established, available information, experienced by thousands of people; but even as late as 1939 it was a fact that did not exist. Of course, violent enemies of Nazism spoke of the concentration camps, but what they said was generally attributed to exaggeration—their hatred, and so on. Nobody wanted to believe them, and they themselves failed to distinguish between the camps and ordinary prisons. Admiral Doenitz's diary reveals quite convincingly that in 1945 he still did not know what was really happening in the camps; he learned it only from American documents. Thus, to the extent that today public opinion is a determining power in political affairs, what public opinion does not recognize as a fact has no political existence. Testimony by those who have experienced the fact can neither prevail on public opinion nor form or inform it, for these individuals do not control the means of communication.

Not even the existence of the concentration camps was enough to alert public opinion to the possibility that such camps could exist in the future. As a result, the knowledge of German camps, hidden from public opinion for ten years, has in no way served to enlighten the public regarding Russian camps [1]: people are just as doubtful, the only difference being that present-day opinion knows that such a method of government *is possible* in the twentieth century—that there is a great difference between a prison and a concentration camp.

But, it will be said, such obliteration of facts is possible only in authoritarian, or even totalitarian, countries. Yet the same analysis is entirely valid for the democracies where there are also facts that do not exist, because public opinion is not alerted to them. They are fundamental facts—just as they are in dictatorial regimes—that almost everybody is (implicitly) interested in ignoring. One of these enormous facts was the nature of working conditions in England and France in the nineteenth century and at the beginning of the twentieth century. Public opinion purely and simply did not know of these working class conditions. Child labor, slums, low salaries, disease, inhuman working conditions—all these did not, in effect, exist. Consistency and sometimes violence on the part of labor were necessary to impose on public opinion the existence of such considerable facts, of which 15 to 20 per cent of the nation had had direct experience, of which a simple stroll into the labor quarters could easily have provided the obvious evidence. Nevertheless, despite these circumstances—these facts—public opinion ignored them.

More recently we have seen the same phenomenon with regard to forced labor in the United States. There a population

---

[1] Actually, the concentration camps in the U.S.S.R., so violently denied by Communists, are openly acknowledged by the Soviet government, which admits the story of Ivan Denisovich (*Novy Mir*, October 1962), but cautions against generalizing it (*Literaturnaia Gazeta*, November 1962). But, of course, those were *Stalinist* camps. There is silence on the camps still in existence today, which are pretty much the same. Still, the identity of the information and non-information mechanism regarding Nazi and Soviet concentration camps is essential.

estimated at 500,000 people (wetbacks) is reduced to slavery, and yet public opinion purely and simply ignores the fact, with the result that it does not exist on the political plane. An inquiry by the United Nations was needed to bring it to light, and even then with many protests and limitations. Moreover, publication of a UN report cannot alert public opinion, even less shape it.[2]

In France, the phenomenon of the political concentration camps was equally outside of people's consciousness. Who knew of the existence of a concentration camp in Gurs in 1939, or in Eysses or in Mauzac in 1945? Who knew of the living conditions in these camps? Nobody, or almost nobody. They actually became known only after the camps disappeared—at the moment when they could no longer exist in the realm of public opinion, because a non-current fact can no longer be a political fact. These facts were of course known to the enemies of the regime and denounced in their press. The Gurs camp was denounced in *Humanité*, the Eysses camp in *Époque* (a paper of the Right). But this does not shape public opinion, for such papers cannot convince anyone outside the narrow circle of their partisans. Everybody mistrusts their information because they are regarded as biased. And because of that mistrust, they cannot shake public opinion. Only the party, the clan, is touched, but at that moment the fact has no independent existence, because it is based on an *a priori* conviction that does not even need facts to nourish itself. The false and the true serve it equally well. The fact then has no existence except through a system of predetermined references that affirm as facts, or deny existing facts because they do not square with predetermined opinion.

This disappearance of fact in the absence of public opinion may be illustrated by citing a recommendation by the League of Nations as an example: in 1927 the League recommended that its members abstain from publishing anything that would compromise international peace or the establishment of good relations between peoples. If the recommendation had been ac-

---

[2] The term slavery is used here in its broad sense: more precisely it is the "peonage" type of institution as studied, for example, by Gunnar Myrdal: *An American Dilemma* (New York: Harper & Bros.; 1944).

cepted, a systematic elimination of certain facts would have resulted. The motive may be good, the project praiseworthy, but the phenomenon changes character; facts change—disappear—and will never have access to political life because public opinion will not turn them into political facts. All that we can say is that the recommendation was not accepted, but what we actually see is how, even in a democratic regime, this phenomenon of change and ultimate obliteration of facts *can* take place not only unintentionally but also purposefully and in the name of a "good cause."

As a result, the public only knows appearances; and appearances, through public opinion, are transformed into political facts.

Facts and Information.

But if facts exist only through public opinion, would a good information network not be sufficient to solve the problem? Put differently, if a system of honest information transmittal were to convey the facts—all of them—to the public, would this not make the facts political and arouse a public opinion in consonance with reality? This is only the beautiful dream of those who hope for integration of the mass media and democracy.

There are two obstacles to this. First of all, information is not enough to give the fact it concerns the character of a political fact. When the information is conveyed, the fact is forgotten. It has not become a serious concern. One item of information drives out the other, even if it lives for five or six days. The public not affected by one exposure, which it does not understand very well and to which it does not gear its attention. We have innumerable examples of facts of which the public was informed, but which did not penetrate into public opinion or attitudes. One fact among hundreds will illustrate the point. At the very moment when the Rosenbergs were being executed in the United States, uprisings took place in Berlin. Many arrests took place, and it was learned a few days later that one of the demonstrators, a certain Goettling, had been sentenced for espionage and shot. The two facts were strictly parallel: trial for espionage, unimpressive evidence, execution. But public opinion was greatly excited and profoundly moved by the Rosenberg trial, whereas nobody gave any thought to the Goettling trial. The latter never became a political fact because the information was effaced the very next day from the public's memory by other political facts reaching it from Czechoslovakia, Moscow, facts about strikes or the Beria purge.

The second obstacle is that information never produces public opinion on a subject. A thousand informed people do not constitute a "public opinion." Rather, public opinion obeys mysterious rules, secret motives, and forms and deforms itself irrationally, whereas information is of the order of clear knowledge, lucid consciousness, reason and the pure intellect.

Information itself has not sufficient duration or intensity to create a public opinion even after having interested the people. Precisely because there is such a great diversity of information, a single item does not suffice to polarize attention. To accomplish that it would be necessary for the great majority of individuals to pay attention at the same moment to the same fact, but that is inconceivable. In any case, the pure fact has no power at all. It must be elaborated with symbols before it can emerge and be recognized as public opinion.[3]

Information cannot therefore make a fact arise in political life or give it the character of a political fact. Only propaganda can. Only propaganda can make a fact arouse public opinion; only propaganda can force the crowd's wandering attention to stop and become fixed on some event; only propaganda can tell us of the foreseeable consequences of some measure. Propaganda can make public opinion coalesce and orient it toward a certain event which then becomes a political fact or a political problem at that very moment. Only propaganda can transform individual experience into public opinion. One could use all great political events to demonstrate the general validity of this process.

---

[3] Writers who examine the conditions under which information is effective, i.e., under which it reaches and modifies public opinion, usually describe propaganda (Alfred Sauvy: *La Nature sociale* [Paris: A. Colin; 1957]). Some of them are actually aware of it; see Leonard W. Doob's article in Daniel Katz *et al.*: *Public Opinion and Propaganda* (New York: Holt, Rinehart & Winston; 1954), and Maurice Mégret: *L'Action psychologique* (Paris: A. Fayard; 1959), p. 127.

Another question arises: Does the "important fact," important of and by itself, act directly? Hadley Cantril believes this to be the case: "Opinion is very sensitive to important events." [4] But who determines the importance of an event? Hundreds of experiences show that certain very substantial facts leave public opinion entirely unmoved. For example, the Tennessee Valley Authority left American opinion completely cold as long as it restricted itself to honest and non-polemical information; public opinion began to react only when unbridled propaganda was used. When Roland Young says that opinion is only public when it concerns a "public" question, i.e., a question of interest to everybody, he implies that in a given case, public opinion was first made to see that some question was truly of general interest. On his own, the individual will ignore the question, and no public opinion will form around an issue until the moment when propaganda creates the feeling of importance that will *then* make everybody form an opinion on the subject.

American writers, in order to show that facts themselves act on opinion, claim that the kidnapping of Lindbergh's son made public opinion accept the growth of the FBI, or that sulfanilamide poisonings led to the passing of the Copeland Act on pharmaceutical control; but those facts became "active" only through propaganda. For it was not the straight fact that was given to the public, but a fact conditioned so as to make it fit into the prevailing climate of opinion and enter into a debate in which it had a *role* to play.[5] Many other kidnappings of chil-

---

[4] Hadley Cantril: *Gauging Public Opinion* (Princeton, N.J.: Princeton University Press; 1944). Strongly attacked by Alfred Sauvy (see Doob, in Katz *et al.*: *Public Opinion and Propaganda*), Cantril supplemented that law with others: "Events of unusual breadth make public opinion vacillate from one extreme to another"; "public opinion is determined much more by events than words," and so on. His argument was based on and accompanied by analyses, charts, and statistics pertaining to the war of 1914–18. Cantril has been followed by many writers; see, for example, John William Albig: *Modern Public Opinion* (New York: McGraw-Hill; 1956); Carl I. Hovland, Arthur A. Lumsdaine, and Fred D. Sheffield: "Experiments on Mass Communications," *Studies in Social Psychology in World War II* (Princeton, N.J.: Princeton University Press; 1949).

[5] The "important fact" of the consequences of thalidomide did not reach public opinion as long as information remained on the honestly scientific and dispassionate level. Only the scandalous and inciting publicity of the Liège trial created public opinion on a problem which in and by itself *was* important, but of no interest to the average person.

dren, and many other poisonings by drugs did not become historic because they were not the object of propaganda. This is even more evident in connection with situations than it is with regard to simple and limited facts. For example, during the 1952 elections in the United States, a considerable fact that should have played a big role in favor of the Democrats was the country's prosperity. The Democratic Administration had proved excellent, reconversion had been a success, unemployment had declined, and the living standard had risen—those were the general facts, important in themselves, and in plain view of everybody. Yet they played practically no role in the formation of electoral opinion. The fact in itself is nothing. Those facts had little impact because they were not susceptible to propaganda (information yes, propaganda no), because they had no power to excite, and were not easily transformed into images; only a certain category of facts becomes "public-opinion facts," and, objectively, not necessarily the most important category.

It was exactly the same when General de Gaulle reported in March, 1959, on his government's progress during the preceding months. He underlined the importance of the measures taken: the revaluation of the currency accompanied by only slight price increases, the freeing of foreign exchange, balancing of the budget, influx of foreign capital into France, and so on. But, said de Gaulle, these positive facts, objectively important, had not reached the public and did not dispose it favorably toward the government. That was absolutely true. The point was that these facts, important though they were, were not grandly displayed; they had not been imbedded in public opinion by some well-designed, compelling propaganda. Important facts which could effectively change the political or economic structure, are, *in themselves,* neither absorbed nor retained by public opinion. But, because facts are not politically important unless public opinion *does* seize them, there are no longer any facts that are important by themselves in the age of the mass media.[6] A fron-

---

[6] The only problem is to know *how* such a fact is transmitted to public opinion, by whom, through which myths, which patterns: that is the only question. A fact

tier incident, a plane crash, a bombing attack on a nation at peace, is not important unless properly "staged"; neutral and purely objective information does not move public opinion. The latter does not take any written fact seriously unless a campaign is launched in which "values" are injected (peace, justice, life, and so on) and the reader is asked to judge the fact; from that moment on, the reader is concerned, begins to react and form an opinion. At that moment the fact becomes politically important. Eventually, if the campaign continues, the government must make a decision on the problem. But if, after a frontier violation, for example, only the straight diplomatic notes are exchanged, no opinion will form and no reaction will occur.

Still, certain facts strike opinion from the moment of their first publication, seemingly without propaganda. This is rare, but it does happen; when such cases are analyzed, the conclusions that emerge generally show that the event in question collided with a well-established, stereotyped value judgment already imbedded in public opinion. For example, it was learned in July, 1959, in London that a criminal by the name of Podola had been mistreated by the police. This straight information shocked England because British public opinion holds strongly to the idea that the British police do not torture prisoners and that a criminal has a full complement of civil rights—the individual's inviolability being a basic and well-protected value in England. Thus, information running counter to such strongly held public opinion provoked an outburst of emotion. (One might also say that Lindbergh's image was an American stereotype of such import that it elicited the emotion over the Lindbergh kidnapping).[7] But two things must here be observed:

---

no longer has objective importance. The more important a political fact is, the greater its significance, the deeper and more complex its possible interpretation, the more will it be "reworked," given certain colorations, transposed from the realm of facts to that of moral language; see Hans Speier and Margaret Otis: "German Radio Propaganda," in Daniel Lerner (ed.): *Propaganda in War and Crisis* (New York: George W. Stewart; 1951).

[7] Obviously, the Soviet exploits of Sputnik, Lunik, etc., have had such a powerful effect on the United States because they collided with the well-established stereotype of America's superiority in the scientific and technological fields. And at the same time they aroused a certain fear.

these stereotypes themselves are frequently the product of some prior influence exerted on public opinion, some indirect propaganda or education—in any event, some "social training." In the second place, if the same fact occurs a second time, opinion reacts much less strongly; the stereotype no longer has its original freshness, is no longer so set. At that moment, propaganda is needed to revive it and re-create some public opinion around it. To sum up: a fact is of no importance except when it collides with a well-established social stereotype, or when by the use of the mass media, public opinion is led to give it great importance.[8]

But we must go a step further and consider the situation of the informed man—the average reader or listener—who can never personally confirm a fact because he knows only its verbal translation. This man can never be sure of the fact itself—neither of its existence nor of its content. For example: in 1954 a Soviet diplomat's wife in Australia, Madame Petrov, refused to return to the Soviet Union and, having been arrested in Australia by two Kremlin agents, was to be abducted by force when she was saved by the Australian authorities. This was the fact as reported by the Australian press and repeated by the British, American, and French press. But in Russia the fact was presented differently: Madam Petrov *wanted* to return, but was arrested and detained by the Australian police. The *same photo* of the occurrence appeared in the *Manchester Guardian* and the Polish

---

[8] However, after admitting the importance of the fact itself, we must qualify; as Frederick C. Irion says very well (in *Public Opinion and Propaganda* [New York: Thomas Y. Crowell; 1950], p. 533), the information services also must take their public into account. Where little relation exists between the facts and credibility, only "acceptable" facts can be presented. If people hold a stereotype in some area, their first reaction is to reject all facts going against it—such facts are not believable (see J. W. Albig: *Modern Public Opinion*, pp. 81 ff., 324); in these areas credibility rates higher than a fact's reality. That a fact should be exact is insufficient; it is vain to offer an incredible fact (see Martin F. Herz: "Some Lessons from Leaflet Propaganda," in Lerner [ed.]: *Propaganda in War and Crisis*). The more the individual is propagandized, the more he will apply ready-made interpretations, but he will be more responsive to important events. See Irving L. Janis, Arthur A. Lumsdaine, and Arthur I. Gladstone: "Effects of Preparatory Communications on Reactions to a Subsequent News Event" and Leonard W. Doob: "Goebbels' Principles of Propaganda," both in Katz (ed.): *Public Opinion and Propaganda*.

paper *Swiat*; but the latter showed Australian agents arresting Madame Petrov, while the former showed Soviet agents. How can we believe either of the two accounts? Actually, everybody will believe the version that accords with his political inclination. But in neither case can we speak of a fact. There are innumerable examples of this kind. When Khrushchev delivered his famous report to the Twentieth Congress, the French Communist Party's first reaction was that the report was a capitalist invention. What is even more remarkable is that on May 10, 1957, Khrushchev himself said of his own report: "I do not know which speech you are talking about. I understand that in the United States a fabricated text was published by the American intelligence services, purporting to be my report to the Twentieth Congress." Yet, the report's passages, later officially confirmed by Moscow, coincide exactly with the text published in June, 1956.

Of course, facts can also disappear; no information was given in Egypt on Soviet actions in Hungary in 1956. Only thirty months later was the first information given to the Egyptian public.

A careful analysis of the press will show this to be true for almost all facts. However, the problem is not properly defined if one says that different newspapers "present" facts differently, and that the reader's view will depend on which paper he reads. *Before* examining the question of presentation of facts, which varies according to different tendencies, we must ask: What is the fact? But that is almost impossible to determine. Only after long investigation and analysis of all texts, after placing the fact in its political-economic context, and after attaining a sufficient distance can one arrive at certain probabilities with regard to the fact, that is, only when the fact can be seen in historical perspective, no longer bearing the impact of current news, and when public opinion has become indifferent to it.

In the immediate situation no certainty regarding facts can be attained at all. Governments are faced with this difficulty, and are by no means better informed where extraordinary facts are concerned. Certainly the French government was very poorly informed before and after the event at Sakhiet. Bromberger's book,

The Thirteen Plots of the Thirteenth of May, reveals convincingly that the government had no exact knowledge whatsoever of the events. To be sure, this matter concerned the propaganda action in Algeria that had "intoxicated" the French government and produced a psychological victory permitting a reduction of operations—a clear success on the part of French propaganda. But that was possible only to the extent that the actual fact was known after extensive verbal manipulation: and no such manipulation is safe from deliberate or accidental misinterpretation. In the *Thirteen Plots,* the simple publication of exact facts was enough to be in itself a propaganda operation. The authorities are not in a good position to know the facts. Still, when the problem is to prove a political fact, for example in the field of justice, recourse is taken to outstanding political leaders. In the litigation between *Humanité* and *Aurore* in March, 1954, on whether *Humanité* received Russian funds, the matter, impossible to prove, was nevertheless accepted as fact because "it was regarded as such by the highest political and administrative authorities" (from the verdict by the Seine Tribunal). Such are the criteria used for the existence of political facts, for in the "information-propaganda" context it is impossible to determine what is a fact.

How then does the average man react in the face of such "information"?[9] The intellectual will be tempted to be an agnostic. But if the citizen declares that "all these are just tall stories," he still believes them. In other words, his agnosticism is not fundamental. But I now have used a great word: "to believe." Knowledge of a fact comes down to a question of faith.[1] When Algerians declared in Lyons in 1957 that they had been tortured, the Archbishop of Lyons confirmed that torture had

---

[9] He is generally doubtful, mistrusts information, and in particular rejects all information issued by the state, be it ever so accurate. Often the average man will prefer rumors to official information: as they are hidden and come to him through human channels, rumors seem more trustworthy (Albig: *Modern Public Opinion,* p. 363).

[1] Carl I. Hovland and Walter Weiss: "The Influence of Source Credibility on Communication Effectiveness" and Jerome S. Bruner, "The Dimensions of Propaganda: German Short-Wave Broadcasts to America," both in Katz *et al.: Public Opinion and Propaganda,* show that one important factor in propaganda is destruction of faith in customary information sources. When doubt is cast on information sources, there is no more information.

been used. The Minister of Justice claimed that torture had not been used. What were the facts? Actually, we must believe one or the other of two eminent personalities, on his word. In May, 1957, an Algerian by the name of Telidji, in a letter addressed to all authorities and later made public, accused the police of having tortured him. The authorities denied the fact. There is no possible material proof, and after the most objective, nonofficial inquiries, it was concluded that the true circumstances could not be established. Here again a question of faith is involved. Those who believe that the police torture Algerians will believe Telidji and the Archbishop. They will even see complementary proof in the letter. The basic fact serves as proof for those who hold some anterior belief. Those who believe that reports on tortures are Communist propaganda will reject all this. The weight of testimony telling of tortures proves nothing to them. Men above suspicion have testified to the culpability of sixteen doctors in Moscow,[2] and French scientists have affirmed the bacteriological warfare claim;[3] two facts subsequently demolished by the Soviets themselves. In a word, everything comes down to the informed man's "capacity to believe."

But the informed man's beliefs are fruits of anterior propaganda which creates the prejudices that make people accept or reject information. When the prejudice is established and the stereotypes well set, when a mental pattern exists, facts are put into their places accordingly and cannot, by themselves, change anything.[4] If, two years after the event, when a detailed account on the trial of the Hungarian Communist Imre Nagy was published, with all documents, testimony, information, and the most elaborate details, and one finally came close to reality, what could such near-facts do? Who would read this voluminous work, *The Truth About the Nagy Affair*?[5] Certainly public

---

[2] On the occasion of the notorious "Doctor's Plot."—Trans.

[3] The Soviets claimed at one point that American planes had conducted bacteriological warfare against them.—Trans.

[4] Herbert H. Hyman and Paul B. Sheatsley: "The Current Status of American Public Opinion" and "Some Reasons Why Information Campaigns Fail," both in Katz *et al.: Public Opinion and Propaganda*.

[5] There are many examples, such as *The Rayk Trial of 1962, The Life of Tukachevsky*, and so on. But facts in retrospect are no longer of interest.

opinion will not be affected by it. And the facts will in no way affect people's beliefs, or the stereotypes in the mind of the average man, who has lost all interest in the 1956 facts. The over-all pattern of symbols has more power than the straight fact. Those who are filled with propaganda stereotypes can never be reached by logical proof or exact fact. They deny the facts and reject them as "propaganda" because these facts jeopardize prejudices that have become part of their personality.

But are there really no longer any objective facts? Not really. The only counterproof proffered comes from writers like Sauvy, who, insisting—with good reason—on the importance of exact information, keep returning to statistics as examples of objective facts. It is true that only figures can still barely be objective information. But we live in a world in which quantifiable events are definitely in the minority and absolutely cannot, by themselves, take the place of genuine information.

2. The Psychopolitical Universe and Political Problems

This is the nature of the political universe in our day. It is not a real universe, but it is not a universe of lies either. It is first of all a universal subject to psychological reference points and, as far as observable reality is concerned, a fictitious universe. A "new" and relatively independent reality, superimposed on the world of tangible fact is now operative—a reality composed of slogans, black-and-white images, and straight judgments which distract people from observable, experienced reality in order to make them live in a singular universe with its own logic and consistency. It is this universe which is increasingly closing in on people no longer capable of making contact with the tangible world. Yet the contemporary politician must operate in precisely that universe. Political action can no longer be organized according to past principles or even compared with past forms of political action. A decisive factor has been added that must forever be taken into account in connection with any action: the verbal translation of facts operating in a universe of images.

This character of our "uni-verse" distinguishes the situation just described from past historical situations in which the publication of an event rendered the latter durable. Siegfried gives us a humorous example: Leif Erickson discovered America but nobody in the West knew it. Conversely, everybody knew that Columbus had discovered America. And yet the country was not named after him because Amerigo Vespucci, on his part, wrote a book about his journey; his publicity was better organized and would therefore lend his name to the new world. There are many other examples, but until the advent of our age one could not postulate an entire *illusory universe* concerning important facts, and people did not live in such an illusory universe. The whole nature of contemporary "facts" has changed everything; there is no common referent point between that universe and individual observable facts such as can be found throughout history.

What we now have is a universe in which everything is translated into images, in which everything *is* image.[6] Not just the individual fact but the whole fabric of things is translated or transformed into images. For man in traditional society, facts transformed into images by some collective mechanism were rare and secondary. Troubadours brought their fellow men songs on historical themes, merchants brought news from a faraway world; but they did not really concern the listener, who remained aloof from these stories—such things were only distractions, not part of the setting in which he lived. Conversely, as a result of the mass media, these verbal or visual images constitute the total world in which modern man lives. He now spans the entire globe, but experiences it only indirectly. He lives in a retranslated, edited universe; he no longer has direct relation to any fact. This formula seems exaggerated. Yet, first of all, we notice that even facts concerning conditions of general interest in which the individual may want to participate, or has even

---

[6] Only in this context can W. I. Thomas's "famous" theorem be considered accurate: "If a man considers a situation real, its consequences are real for him." David Krech and Richard S. Crutchfield (*Theories and Problems of Social Psychology* [New York: McGraw-Hill; 1948, 1962], p. 449), are right when they say: "The individual who reads a paper or hears a speech [in our civilization] is submersed in a *real*, but special, world created by words . . . that world is as real as the one created by chairs and tables."

participated, are brought to him by intermediaries: in the newspapers he will find a description of a strike, battle, or accident
in which he personally participated. He will find such events
translated, explained, re-created; and against this collective
image his own experience cannot prevail. He will soon be led
to strike a compromise between his own experience and this
image. In the long run, the image will win out, effacing the
facts as observed or experienced. This is particularly true when
the verbal translation takes place in the framework of stereotypes. Facts as experienced are powerless against interpretation
based on stereotypes. In 1957–58 the translation and interpretation by the Communist Party of the events in Hungary obliterated the impression made by the event itself. Those most
shocked eventually reassured themselves; they returned to their
familiar and reassuring verbal universe.[7] We saw the same phenomenon operate on June 1, 1956, when three hundred Arabs
were massacred at Melouza. On the first day, the F.L.N. claimed
responsibility for it, saying that the dead had been members of
the M.N.A. But in the face of general disapproval, the F.L.N.
soon began to deny that it had killed these men, and F.L.N.
adherents in France began to accept this translation and interpretation. The fact itself evaporated very rapidly. Uncertainty
was introduced. From then on, people preferred not to allude
to the event, either because it was too unsettling or because it
was too uncertain. After several weeks of hesitation, those most
shocked returned to their earlier presuppositions. The fact itself
was obliterated, having dissolved in the psychopolitical universe. As a result of this process, local facts, sometimes secondary, are invested with universal scope; they are disseminated
by collective means and are known by all. But, as said before,
the mass media have a singular character: they reach the *individual inside the mass.* And they produce in the listener an extraordinary confusion between the personal and the collective.[8]

Man caught in the web of press, cinema, and radio can no
longer differentiate between what is of personal concern to him

---

[7] Bellecave: "Évolution de la pensée politique de Jean-Paul Sartre," 1960.
[8] Roger Veillé: *La Radio et les hommes* (Paris: Édition de Minuit; 1952).

and what exists in society outside of himself or, in the category of facts, what is real and what is not. These astonishing media, particularly radio, render the most distant and disparate events immediate and contemporary. At the moment a speaker speaks, or an event takes place, the listener is witness. The whole earth is no longer anything but one point at which everything is within reach. Time is no longer anything but an indefinite extension of "now" for the listener. Radio and the press—just consider the excitement of the public over the "latest edition"—synchronize the varying lengths of events and lives.

To become "true" in the eyes of the crowd, fact must be social—registered and localized in society—not necessarily collective, but social in the sense that everyone can recognize himself in it. The most individual fact, taken from what is most typical, such as, for example, the death of a well-known young hero, is a collective fact if everyone recognizes himself in the act of heroism: the suffering, the combat with death, the dead hero's feeling. The same social identification accounts for the success of melodrama and of the radio and TV serial. The mass media can deal only with this type of fact; and where it is social, but simultaneously takes its seeming reality from being individual, it leads to confusion between the individual fact experienced by the reader or listener and the massive fact transmitted to him by his paper or radio. He no longer can differentiate between what is his own life and what is not.

This explains why an event brought to consciousness by the mass media completely forces out all other facts from the area of perception. The more space and time the former occupies, the less the latter exists. Facts nowadays curiously derive their reality primarily from the communication media—the mechanism translates word into image and creates a fictional universe for man. The individual concrete facts of daily life are downgraded by comparison. What is one's working routine, one's family life, as compared with events seen on television? And man lives so much in this verbal and fictional universe that family life is completely invaded by the mass media. A wife will experience her relationship with her husband much more intensely through the intermediary of popular dramas; popular novels fulfill this translating function on a grand scale. What we have is a universe that swallows up all facts and diminishes and casts out all personal experiences not integrated into it.

It is the same with regard to great men. The legend of our great men is no longer left to the discretion of troubadours and gazeteers. We now have specialists for this type of work. Curtis D. MacDougall shows how the image of John D. Rockefeller was put together. The facts of his life, translated, illuminated, "managed," escaped the categories of true and false, and the illusory man became more real than the closest reality.

It would be absurd to confound the problem of our illusory political universe created by propaganda with the old problem raised by philosophers, who say that we do not know the external world except through the intermediary of our senses and have no guarantee that our senses do not deceive us, or even that the external universe exists, and that, in any event, we can perceive the world only through images. Still, quasi-philosophic lovers of generalizations and of the old adage "there is nothing new," will be tempted to make such a comparison. Yet, the analogy is invalid. There is a world of difference between experimental knowledge of a fact and knowledge of it as filtered through the verbal screen. Diogenes already answered this question.

This universe of images is not a lie; rather, it permits and validates all interpretations and translations. For this very reason all variations of information and twists and turns of propaganda are possible. Because we live in a universe of images, affecting the masses can be reduced to manipulating symbols. If we lived in a microcosm of direct experience, such symbol manipulation would have little effect on us. The importance of these symbols also makes it possible for a writer to change his opinion very rapidly, in accordance with the latest doctrine, event, or image of the events.[9] This universe is all-encompassing

---

[9] This universe also permits everybody taking up a position on a social or political problem to feel that the majority (or even everybody) in the nation is with him, and eventually leads to the spontaneous screening out of news; to efface an actual experience would be very difficult, but in a world where symbols have replaced experience, those symbols easiest to obliterate are those not in accord

and well organized. The totality of events translated into symbols actually forms a complete system, a view of the world. Since all the facts are subjected to the same refraction, and operate within the same basic framework, even different propaganda i.e., propaganda geared to different ends, establishes the same type of illusory universe. This universe is not the result of some individual attitude, nor the result of divergent opinions. It is produced by the collective and massive use of the mass media and not the result of some Machiavellian design or the desire to mislead. It is an invisible but global creation based on the systematic verbal translation of events. Those dispensing information inevitably organize this translation and, as a result, ceaselessly reinforce, develop, make more complex, and shape this universe of images which modern man confuses with reality.

All political problems arise in this universe. When a fact has become a fact of opinion—a political fact—it may produce a political problem. Nowadays propaganda is the creator of almost all political problems. There is hardly a political problem that was not originally created by it; there is hardly one that exists objectively by itself. Most political problems become viable problems only when propaganda creates them.

To be sure, this does not mean that there are no questions to be solved in the normal course of political events. There is the problem of delegating powers, the problem of living space or alcoholism; there are economic organizations that must be dealt with, and so on. But today there never is a crisis, a burning problem, except through the intervention of propaganda; the manipulation of symbols appealing directly to the public's preconceptions and prejudices raises a whole set of events to the rank of problems by creating a public opinion about them. From the moment that public opinion enters into the picture, a question can no longer be ignored, can no longer be given a peace-

---

with our preconceptions and prejudices. See Seymour Martin Lipset: "Opinion Formation in a Crisis Situation" and Herbert H. Hyman and Paul B. Sheatsley: "The Current Status of American Public Opinion," both in Katz *et al.*: *Propaganda and Public Opinion.*

ful compromise solution. An extreme solution then becomes necessary and the problem becomes more pressing as time goes by. It is certain that the rebellion in Algeria was a small affair in the beginning; a very small minority of Arabs was involved. It was propaganda in the two senses that, first of all, mobilized the Arabs and, secondly, aroused French opinion; the problem was thus rendered simultaneously insoluble and extremely urgent.

We are in the habit of thinking that a problem exists in itself, and that information only submits the problem to public opinion. Actual circumstances prove otherwise. There is no public opinion by itself. There is practically no problem by itself in our day. The mechanism "information-propaganda" works as follows: the translated and interpreted facts are disseminated by the mass media; propaganda creates a public opinion around them (public opinion is formed only on some universalized event); public opinion then seizes the facts, reorganizes them in its turn, and endows them with the propensity to elicit strong emotional responses. Propaganda then exploits the predictable spontaneous response to them and at that very moment creates a political problem. Public opinion crystallizes around the problem and demands a solution, and a crisis can no longer be avoided because opinion will not accept gentle and moderate solutions. In this fashion, propaganda can turn anything into dramatic problems; from the moment opinion is aroused, the problem exists even if at the beginning it was wholly insignificant. The Algerian problem was of course very dramatic and crucial, even if almost 75 per cent of it was created by opposite propagandas. Passionate public opinion aroused by propaganda is a reality. There was indeed a social and economic problem of relationships and exploitation, a demographic problem, but there was no problem of national proportion, neither for the Algerian people nor for the French Republic—all this was superimposed, produced by propaganda.

Let us take a less recent question so that we can study it with less passion—the Sudeten Germans. The Germans in Czechoslovakia after 1918 were an ethnic and political minority. On the whole they were not badly treated. Objectively and officially, they were the equals of the other peoples in Czechoslovakia and had equal rights. They did have to suffer some tribulations and unpopularity because they were not loved by the Czechs, but all this never attained large proportions, and if any Sudeten German had reason to complain, it was only on matters troubling any citizen in any state. But Hitler's propaganda seized on these tribulations, these hostile manifestations, and so on, blew them up, particularized them, and grouped them together. This showed the Sudeten Germans how unhappy they were, the Czechs how much they disliked the Sudeten Germans. The Germans in Germany then became aware of their responsibility toward their brothers abroad; a political fact appeared and developed and *from that moment on* demanded a solution.

The same goes for the Jews. True, one can admit to a very limited extent that the Jews constitute a strange body—a strange body rather than a body of strangers—in a nation. In intellectual and financial circles they occupy a place that bothers some people. It is true that one can accuse them of certain faults . . . but not more than non-Jews! However, old traditions have established a reservoir of mistrust and hostility toward them. But in Germany, France, or in America, there is no objective Jewish problem. Only propaganda will seize at some point on what can be blamed on the Jews. It will use actual facts, but interpret them, present them in a particular way, and so on. At that moment, public opinion will take shape, and Jews will become a political problem. If Sartre and Curtis Mac-Dougall insist that the key to the Jewish problem is not in the Jews but in the anti-Semite's psychology, they are partially right but do not go far enough. They take into account only the confirmed anti-Semite, who is at the phenomenon's point of origin; but the confirmed anti-Semite is of importance only if and when followed by public opinion. If anti-Semitism remained a mere attitude on the part of some individuals, not much would happen. But propaganda turns this opinion into an element of public attitude. At that moment only can it be said that a Jewish problem arises, and the sudden growth of the anti-Semitic feelings will be based simultaneously on some hidden and inchoate natural tendencies toward prejudice and on some actual (though not unique) shortcomings on the part of the Jews.

The aggressive element given by propaganda to a political fact results from the wide dissemination; once a Jewish problem has been established, it reveals itself not only in Nazi Germany but also in the United States and in the Soviet Union; it becomes invested with a force of expansion because it has become a *problem*. We could make the same analysis with respect to the Berlin situation since 1950 or the Israel-Egypt dispute.

The masses are invited to take part, to take sides, i.e., to assume an attitude. Before such a propaganda operation, the masses were amorphous. Only propaganda will focus their attitudes. At the moment when propaganda sets in, political facts become political problems, which implies they must be solved (even if in reality they are not even problems) in order to give satisfaction, not to those directly interested, but to those aroused and disturbed by public opinion. The government then can no longer ignore the demands of that public opinion. It must respond to what the ordinary man considers to be a problem. For political reality exists there and nowhere else.

If facts have no relation to public opinion unless the information enjoys a certain continuity and is carried along by propaganda, then a country upon which a news blackout is imposed will no longer have real political problems. There was no Goettling problem, only a Rosenberg problem. There is no problem today of Vietnamese massacred and tortured in North Vietnam, nor of Chinese massacred and tortured in the first years of the present Peking regime, but there was, in France, the problem of torture being used in Algeria. There is no anti-Semitic problem in the Soviet Union in the eyes of Frenchmen, but there is the problem of American and South African racism. What is the situation of the Tibetans annexed by Communist China? Or of the Cubans under Castro's dictatorship? When information is obliterated in a country, political problems no longer arouse public opinion—they have reality only for the enemies of the regime, and are promulgated by unorganized individuals. Put differently, public opinion, if not aroused by propaganda, can only have an effect on democratic regimes; it cannot be brought to bear against authoritarian regimes that obliterate facts and problems. This accounts for the extreme ease with which it can be shown that opinions leveled against the injustices of democracies are based on fact, while opinions hostile to totalitarian regimes are only the result of propaganda—and, to a large extent, these claims are true.

That there were fully justified campaigns against torture in France during the Algerian war proved that democracy was still functioning. But this was at the same time evidence of the democratic regime's greatest weakness. Public opinion exercised over such scandals will turn against a prevailing regime and demand another, which will then *necessarily* be a dictatorship in which all facts will be destroyed. From then on everything will go well. But, can a democratic regime permit itself to be led to the slaughter by democratic public opinion in the name of democracy? Will it not be tempted to defend itself? Need a regime be like a religious martyr?

The feeling that a political problem exists is further increased in the process of public opinion formation when two contradictory propagandas are at work. It often seems as though in democracies two conflicting propagandas destroy the mechanism described above, but in reality that is not the case. When differences arise concerning fact, the proper attitude is agnosticism: It is impossible to know anything about it. In this fashion, on the one hand, the purely fictional character of political fact is confirmed. Such an attitude often develops in countries where two propagandas of equal force oppose each other and are accompanied by a certain lack of popular interest in political life. Politics then appears as a game, of which public opinion tires and from which it eventually withdraws altogether. This may well be one of the important facts concerning French political life since 1948. But, on the other hand, public opinion, in the face of contradictory claims, usually will divide along lines that have nothing to do with the facts. We accept some statements not because we have by experience learned that they are true, but because they correspond to our prejudices, our milieu, and so on (all the irrational factors that determine public opinion), or because one propaganda was superior to the other.

But even if there is doubt or hesitation regarding the facts, public opinion as a whole, faced with contradictory propaganda claims, comes to feel that a serious "problem" exists; therefore anti-Semitism created a Jewish problem not just for anti-Semites, but for everyone. The problem arises even for those who reject it; and by the mere fact that public opinion is divided, the problem becomes solidified and exists on an even larger scale. From the very moment at which two segments of opinion, responding to two different propagandas, confront each other, the *division* of opinion and the polemics and hatred they engender become the political problem: unilateral and bilateral propaganda arrive at exactly the same result via completely different routes. And in fact the "aloof" people become much more aware of political problems in the case of two contradictory propagandas, and can much less protect themselves against infection.

Not only does propaganda transform concrete facts into political facts and then into political problems, but it can also use as its point of departure some illusory, non-existent facts, even if a large part of the public knows that the facts do not exist. Let us take just one example among many:

Under Stalin's rule, Communist peace propaganda in no way corresponded objectively to Soviet policies. Between 1948 and 1952 Stalin did not take a single concrete step in favor of peace or an international *détente*. What the Soviet Union proposed turned out to be completely unworkable. During the same period, it increased its army and stepped up its military preparations. Yet, despite an utter absence of facts, the propaganda issued by the peace fighters, by defining the problem of peace in Communist terms, obliterated all non-Communist peace movements and was able to persuade world public opinion of the United States' desire for war. It monopolized the word "peace" for the Soviet Union and communism and made it symbolic of Communist language and attitudes. We are not speaking here with believing sympathizers, or crypto- or para-Communists; this propaganda affected everybody. Even anti-Communists were forced to consider the peace problem in the way propaganda had posed it. From that moment on, every man who fought for peace was suspect of communism, and public opinion

as a whole was convinced that nobody did anything for peace
except the Communists.[1]

Thus we sometimes witness between adversaries and partisans a debate based on a fact that is perhaps illusory or, in any
case, unverifiable. Curtis MacDougall has analyzed the impossibility of defending oneself against an illusory fact. Let us take
incidents in conjunction with a strike, reported by only one
newspaper. Irrefutable (but invented) testimony is presented in
its columns. Because the labor press cannot possibly prove the
opposite, it will seek to explain and excuse the fact—and it certainly is amazing to see a debate arise over the interpretation of
a non-existent fact. If, after long examination, it is found that the
fact does not exist, the public is in no way affected by a retrac-
tion; it has forgotten the fact, but has retained a general impression of the affair and the debate.

The making of something out of nothing—the creation of political problems out of nothing—is one of propaganda's most
astonishing capabilities. Khrushchev's propaganda campaign of
November, 1957, is an example: the Turks, he claimed, were preparing to invade Syria; a detailed plan of the plot was in the
hands of the Soviet General Staff, the date of the operation was
known, and NATO maneuvers in the Mediterranean supported
Turkey. This was an insult for Menderes and a threat to Turkey.
As a result, troops were massed. There was a suggestion of
general war. Yet, as far as can be learned, there was absolutely
no basis in fact for any of this. Moreover, only one month later,
Khrushchev proclaimed that there was no danger whatsoever
and that things were now in a state of *détente,* even though no
more trace of a *détente* could be found than of the earlier alleged danger. Whatever the aim of his campaign may have been
(probably to tie Syria closer to the U.S.S.R.), it was apparently
created out of nothing; for two weeks people were overexcited,

---

[1] The contradiction matters little; a Chinese text of 1956 said literally: "China is
the foremost buildler of peace. We are ready to make war on Formosa in order
to make peace." (Albig: *Modern Public Opinion,* p. 308). A student insisted
that Khrushchev's belligerent speeches at the UN in October 1960 had been a
pacifist act, as had been his constant threats to shower with bombs all those who
failed to agree with him.

others terrorized, by nothing. Exactly the same was true of the Berlin crisis of February, 1959.

The magician, with a wave of his wand, creates a problem, or makes it disappear. But the problem, once evoked—even if it is based on nothing—lives on, because public opinion believes it exists, and forms and divides over it. Does public opinion really function this way? Concrete experiences show that it does, and the little, well-known game of launching trial balloons (experimentally creating an opinion on nothing) always succeeds. A case in point is the famous poll undertaken by *Tide* in 1947 on the subject of the "Metallic Metals Act." Americans were polled on this "act." Seventy per cent of those polled gave an opinion, 30 per cent did not. Of those having an opinion, 21.4 per cent thought the act was of benefit to the United States ; 58.6 per cent felt the matter should be determined from case to case; 15.7 per cent believed that such arrangements were possibly of benefit abroad, but not in the U.S.; and 4.3 per cent said the act had no value. But the most remarkable thing was that there had never been such a thing as the Metallic Metals Act. Yet, there was a public opinion on the subject.[2]

3. Political Action

But what is the nature of political action? The first principle, evidently, is that political man will act in relation to political facts as public opinion knows them.

A cabinet member may have precise information from direct sources, but consider it preferable not to mention the facts that he alone knows. All secret decisions by the state *whose effects run the risk of becoming public as a result of propaganda*, will be condemned. If a government acts on the basis of information that it alone possesses, public opinion will soon be aroused and, faced with incomprehensible facts, will stiffen. In our day, the man in the street, convinced of his political intelligence and the

---

[2] Cf. Frederick C. Irion: *Public Opinion and Propaganda*, p. 698, and Chap. vii.

value of democracy, will not permit himself to be excluded.[3] He is ready to accept scandals or injustices committed by his government, but he will not tolerate living in a politically incomprehensible universe or not having any influence.

As a result, the government faces the following choices: (1) it can give the public all its sources of information, and all the facts it has, on the basis of which it makes its decisions. But that creates many difficulties. There are, first of all, the difficulties of informing the public.[4] Then there is the fact that it is obviously impossible for the government to give its secrets to the public. Often facts are involved that it would be disastrous to disclose, not only in the military or diplomatic realm, but also in the economic area. Some have insisted there are no such secrets, and there is reason to believe that governments have a tendency to exaggerate them, but common sense can tell us that, for example, bringing a monetary reform in preparation to the knowledge of the public would have disastrous consequences.

(2) The government can resign itself not to disclose facts that it alone possesses. Here we find a possible criticism of Sauvy's theses. He believes that it would be madness on the government's part not to act on the basis of facts emerging from economic analysis, primarily statistics. On the surface his reasoning is irrefutable. But it collides with the fact that a public opinion exists that *cannot* be correctly informed, that considers itself the ultimate source of political wisdom—and that is the fact on which the politician must act. Such a politician will follow public opinion, not carefully analyzed facts. And in following it, he will neglect in his decisions the precise documentation at his disposal. In so doing he will perhaps "stack" the facts against himself, but in *the short run* that is much less of a chance to take than to "stack" public opinion against himself.

(3) Finally, the government can act on the basis of its private information, and at the same time launch a propaganda operation justifying that action, explaining it, transforming it into a

---

[3] Cf. Maurice Mégret: *L'Action psychologique* (Paris: A. Fayard; 1959), pp. 80, 81.

[4] Jacques Ellul: "Information et propagande," *Diogène* (1957).

political fact, and giving it valid reasons in the eyes of public opinion. We postulate here that the reasons given to the public are not those the government keeps secret. If they were, we would not really be dealing with propaganda, but with managing of information. The Soviet attitudes in this area have always been very typical. As late as November 1962, when de-Stalinization was being emphasized again, the party was instructed to select for dissemination information that would serve de-Stalinization. (Thus the essential nature of Khrushchev's propaganda system in no way differed from that of Stalin.) Ilya Ehrenburg produced a remarkable formula (*Mémoires*, 1935–41): "When I was still a naïve man, I believed that genuine information is an asset in political activity. But the opposite turned out to be true. Information is needed to confirm that a chosen political course is right."

As a result, a fragmented political world is created in which opinion constitutes and installs itself. But for such an orientation to be possible, unilateral propaganda is necessary; an authoritarian government is necessary which will ban all other propaganda. Only in that way can the many divergent kinds of propaganda in a democracy exercise a profound influence.

One can say, roughly, that of the three solutions, democratic governments select the second.

Moreover, the politician not only must take into account all facts known to public opinion, but must also take the latter into account as *public opinion proper,* as he understands and interprets it. In this context, propaganda plays a major part: anyone undertaking a political action must first manipulate public opinion in such fashion that it will provide true or false reasons for such action; propaganda must manipulate both the political act itself and its rationale. Dictators know how to create public opinion on a decision and then, making the decision, they create an atmosphere in which the decision seems to follow the popular will. It is also the task of public relations to create a certain ambiance around an enterprise or government, and in the same fashion lay the groundwork for an economic or political measure. After that, the manipulator selects the facts that are to be given political life, and then transforms them into political problems, so that public opinion will demand a solution—or at least accept one. The political game is thus based on the facts that are selected to be brought to life in this fashion. This is simple in authoritarian systems, but very complex in democracies, where the opposition brings to life facts contradicting the government's actions.

In many cases, censorship is justified because some panic animates public opinion, or because absurd interpretations of some fact make reasonable decisions impossible. Eisenhower's *first* decision during the attack on Bastogne was to forbid all public information on the subject. He feared that morale would collapse or fall into a state of fruitless perturbation that would hinder necessary decisions.[5]

At that point the political game tends to become increasingly abstract, as the facts selected and spread in both camps are picked from the point of view of their probable repercussions on public opinion: it must not be thought that the opposition reveals the truth that the government hides; that, for example, a Communist party will reveal the truth as a move against a bourgeois regime; it only reveals the negative aspects of facts of which the government reveals the positive aspects. The fact itself is rendered volatile. At that moment, the political game tends to become a manipulation of illusions. The statesman must then act in accord with both the kind of knowledge the public can have of the facts and the meaning of that knowledge.

What is essential is to obtain an "impression," a "feeling." To make the people feel that they live in a democracy and make the government appear democratic in the eyes of public opinion is obviously essential. Some very democratic governments give the impression of being authoritarian, and conversely, some dictatorial governments know how to create the kind of public opinion they need so as to be *felt* as democracies—the People's Democracies, for example.[6]

---

[5] John Toland: *Battle: The Story of the Bulge* (New York: Random House; 1959).
[6] Lambert, in *L'Opinion publique* (Oeuvrage collectif; 1957).

But, if we take this influence of public opinion into account, what kind of political action does it demand?

First of all, any action must conform to the set of facts known to public opinion. It must be of the same order as the facts spread by propaganda, must correspond to them in the eyes of the masses. Even though sociologists correctly insist on the illogical character of mass opinions and inclinations, the masses need to find some seeming logic in the acts of their rulers. A legislative measure will be applied only if it fits into a previous context of opinion based on knowledge of the underlying political fact and the conviction that this fact is a political problem.

Consequently, those who create public opinion limit the government's action and force it to move in certain directions. Seen from this angle, only those need to be taken into account who control the instruments capable of reaching public opinion. Those lacking the means of influencing the presentation of facts do not exist in the world of politics. Wine growers setting up road blocks or teachers on strike at examination time only pursue the aim of involving public opinion. Of course, their method is the most elementary and simple, and therefore the least effective; still, they do not expect any political action except after such an effort. Only the power of modifying political demands gives a group the chance to participate in the political game. The rest may be real, but legitimate, just, political action will not be touched by it. A political act's effectiveness depends entirely on previous efforts aimed at public opinion.

In any event, the state must know that its action takes place inside a verbal universe and that opinions have primarily a verbal character. Therefore, political action must obey a double principle: it must be translated into a flow of images and stereotypes and must not contrast real facts with such images.

According to Walter Lippmann's analysis, the images through which modern man sees the world are schemas, stereotypes. The schemas have two aspects: first, they stand between ourselves and reality. We do not see reality, we do not absorb the facts; we understand our milieu only through the veil of these stereotypes. Any political action must therefore be conceived with the distorting glasses always worn by public opinion in mind. One must know a group's stereotypes to know how the group will interpret some action which, like all other objective reality, has no meaning in itself; it has no impact, coloration, or value except that lent it by stereotypes.

As a result, these patterns have more power than reality itself.[7] Man's ability to interpret facts and turn them to his advantage is as well known as his ability to forget and repress facts that conflict with his convictions or stereotypes. Facts have never convinced anyone or modified anyone's view of the world. The striking silence that Communists have observed on the Rajk trial, or the Russo-German pact, or the Berlin rebellion of June 1953 is not unusual. There is no sense in opposing the "reality of facts" to propaganda's presentations. A political action cannot base itself on such objective and intangible reality. It cannot oppose stereotypes with facts; nothing can be gained thereby. Everything comes down to a series of psychological manipulations aimed at modifying the schemas and stereotypes themselves by methods that are becoming increasingly well known.

We are now coming to the major law imposed by propaganda on political action. The latter must actually have a double character. In bygone days, political decisions were calculated in terms of factual consequences as they applied to some situation or government, and in view of their economic or other consequences. Normally, the action was undertaken in order to succeed. As a result, political decisions affected things and situations. Besides, that conception of political action still prevails in most democracies, and particularly in France. The French government's prodigious paralysis after 1950 was primarily the result of an obsolete conception of political actions and decisions.

Today political action must be calculated with two objectives

---

[7] I have often stated that the raw "information fact" has no power against stereotypes rampant in public opinion. It is known that slandered people can never fully rehabilitate themselves. Cf., for example, Lipset; Hyman and Sheatsley; Janis, Lumsdaine, and Gladstone; and Eunice Cooper and Marie Jahoda: "The Evasion of Propaganda: How Prejudiced People Respond to Anti-Prejudice Propaganda"—all in Katz *et al: Propaganda and Public Opinion.*

in mind: (1) the precise object to be attained in the military, administrative, or economic sphere (as in the past), and (2) the propaganda possibilities offered by such action.[8] With regard to the second objective, one further step is needed. Thus far I have only shown the necessity to take into account existing —spontaneous or prepared—public opinion in order to obtain some result; this consideration is the foremost objective of any action. But public opinion may again be felt in reaction to the political act. We must therefore ask the following questions:

(1) Will the decision have spectacular consequences or tangible results likely to reach public opinion?

(2) Does the decision carry in itself an element of propaganda, and can the fact's interpretation by public opinion be permitted to develop spontaneously? Will opinion respond favorably?

(3) Can the action serve as a springboard for further propaganda?

Raw facts serve propaganda, and political acts are raw facts. They can thus be a springboard for a campaign or a stimulus for the renewal of a conditioned response, or can provide a stronger coloration for some myth. This is not in conflict with my description of the universe of images; I said that this universe is largely based on raw facts. The question the politician must ask himself is whether his act is suited to enter this universe.

Today, political decisions have become more important because of the effect thay may have on opinion than because of their practical and objective significance. The same is true of political facts. Take the extraordinary shock produced by Sputnik. To be sure, space satellites have some practical value, and the feat showed Soviet superiority with regard to missiles, and thus proved some military superiority. But all this was nothing as compared with the psychological shock. We were witnessing a propaganda triump. We saw a crisis in American

---

[8] Leonard W. Doob shows that every political action must be viewed with regard to its psychological effects ("Goebbels' Principles of Propaganda," in Katz *et al: Propaganda and Public Opinion*). This justifies Mégret's position that propaganda must remain in the hands of the political powers and not be entrusted to the army (*L'Action psychologique,* p. 142).

public opinion, a reinforcement of various myths on the subject of Soviet society, increased Soviet prestige among underdeveloped peoples, and new interest in the Soviets on the part of the neutralists. In all these domains the psychological repercussions were immense and the Soviets understood how to exploit the fact with extreme cleverness in their propaganda, thus transforming the scientific fact into a political fact that fitted into an over-all program of political action.

Every political decision must be judged in relation to its propagandistic repercussions. This presupposes a certain continuity of propaganda and a particular orientation of all decisions. It is no longer possible to accept economic measures as the function of economic facts only; they must also correspond to prevailing propaganda. Only the Communists have so far attained full mastery of this combination. At the core of this mastery is the aforementioned continuity, which rests on a rigorous scheme and program of political action.

But today's political art must go still farther. Political actions, whatever their actual effect, will be undertaken primarily as springboards of propaganda; this is the most subtle element of all. If a decision yields good and anticipated results, it is proper to enlarge on it through public opinion. But this is now the only aspect considered. A victorious Roman general would celebrate his triumph. But the total employment of propaganda means has changed all this; if a decision was wrong, if the enemy wins, if the expected results are not obtained, the action's meaning must serve propaganda, even in failure. The point is not to hide a failure, or explain away an error with nebulous comments and call a route a strategic retreat; everybody is aware nowadays of such tricks and nobody would fall for such misrepresentation. What we have here is an action calculated, *from the beginning,* as follows: either it succeeds, and the concrete, desired results are obtained, or it fails, and the failure itself will still be an excellent vehicle for the cause, whatever that cause may be. In this kind of calculation the Communists have proved themselves masters. They always confront their opponents with a dilemma, in which both horns favor them. If the Communist Party introduces a bill on trade unions or salary scales, it is impossible to know whether the aim is the demanded reform or its failure, either of which can then be exploited in propaganda against the government; the factual and propaganda elements are so closely interwoven in all political Communist actions that they cannot be distinguished: all Communist political action has both actual and propaganda aims. If a sliding wage scale is adopted, the capitalist system will be placed into somewhat greater jeopardy, economic difficulties will be created, and positive propaganda provided for the Communist Party which proposed the reform. And the government cannot take credit in the eyes of the people—the Communist Party will. If the measure is rejected, violent propaganda will be launched against the bourgeois regime hostile to the labor class and accentuate the split between the classes.

Most Soviet proposals on the international plane are of this kind. Every Soviet proposal is clad in a psychological appearance favorable in the eyes of the average man. Examined objectively, the proposal will seem reasonable—it will be one for a summit meeting, one for thermonuclear weapons control, one for the withdrawal of occupation troops, or one for Poland's neutralization proposal. If these proposals are accepted, the psychological glory redounds to the Russians, and the concrete effects benefit the Soviet Union; if they are rejected, those who reject them can be called warmongers or enemies of collaboration and coexistence. Generally, the method of joining several elements into a single project is very effective (Bulganin's speech of January 1, 1958, for example).

In 1962, the Soviet Union engaged in such a policy when establishing missile bases in Cuba: either the United States would not dare to say anything, in which case a threatening weapon against them would have been installed nearby; or the United States would respond in kind, which, from the propaganda point of view, would have produced a remarkable sequence, i.e., the United States showing its imperialism by attacking a weak opponent, world public opinion being shocked by intervention in the affairs of another country, and so on. Unfortunately for him, the Western powers prevented him from exploiting the second possibility.

This double possibility of exploitation allows the maintenance of a very intransigent attitude. One can afford not to give in to an opponent at any point, for if the opponent refuses to give in it will work against him. It is not important to reach a real goal. A typical example was the armistice negotiations at Panmunjon. If from the Communist point of view they had succeeded, so much the better; but no concessions were made, for they could succeed only if the NATO allies went all the way and acceded to all Chinese wishes. If they failed, better still; this would then be the fault of the NATO allies, who would have shown their wish for war, which would aid the peace campaign. In either case the opponent is made to lose face when presented with seemingly reasonable yet inacceptable demands.

The only American example of such a combined operation was the food packages sent to the East German population in 1954: if the distribution of food took place, it would be splendid propaganda for the West (not to mention the important result of feeding some starving people)! If it was barred, what splendid propaganda against the Communist regime! Such propaganda is so evident that it does not even need to be "made"; it makes itself. The reaction against the Communist regime would be automatic, and it would not be necessary to orchestrate a whole propaganda campaign; it would be enough to let psychological consequences evolve spontaneously from the facts themselves. Here, we are fact to face with a subtle form of propaganda in which the action itself produces the desired propaganda.

Political action undertaken under such conditions permits the saving of a great deal of political effort, be it by obtaining through voluntary action and good will what otherwise would have had to be obtained by force, be it be reducing the enemy's resistance, be it by making war less costly. For example, propaganda that develops fear of a fifth column, or poisons an atmosphere or a government, or reduces an opponent to passivity is a specific political means. Such political action can also be used to avoid war; Goebbels's propaganda made Austria and Czechoslovakia yield, Stalin's propaganda beamed to Czechoslovakia and Khrushchev's propaganda beamed to Cuba are cases in point: the results obtained in these countries could have been obtained only by force in another day.

All this shows that political action must no longer be undertaken unless it works toward this dual result. It matters little whether the action is truly useful; its utilization in this ambiguous way is what matters. Every political course must have and present this character. Any other approach is the result of outmoded idealism or incoherent, short-term policy. The politician operates in a world of images that constitute people's opinions, but he can also create such images and modify them by his means of information and propaganda. Conversely, public opinion, thriving in this universe, determines the politician's course; he cannot govern without it. But if everything takes place in a universe of images (including the inaccurate image the government has of public opinion), results are neither automatic nor predetermined. The government does not "make" opinion; the latter clings to its stereotypes and prejudices, which are hard to combat. And public opinion in no way forces the government, as it cannot specifically express itself. In reality we have a double paralysis rather than a double effectiveness. The government is paralyzed by the weight of this inchoate opinion, against which it cannot govern and which constantly impedes efficiency. And the paralysis also besets public opinion, which cannot really express itself, and to the extent it does express itself, does so only under the pressure of propaganda, which alone can activate public opinion.

It follows that these two political elements are factitious. They mutually reduce each other to appearances: each seems to control and govern the other, but in reality each has only factitious power, not so much because it is dependent on the other as because both, jointly, can no longer deal with real problems or hold real power. There is a third player in this game: he who controls the means of action. In the universe of images, he is the one who dispenses information and makes propaganda. But if, as it seems, he obeys the orders of the politicians, he occupies the post of autonomous technician. If, in appearance, he represents in a liberal democracy the "expression of freedom of information," he is in reality a technician with very little concern for the citizens, being rather a representative of political or economic powers in whose interest he will shape opinion. In these terms, and with respect to this world of images, the political illusion develops, the illusion in the mind of those who believe that they can modify reality itself in our day by the exercise of *political* power. The same illusion is held, though conversely, by those who think they can master and control the state by participating in the political game.

CHAPTER

[IV]

THE POLITICAL
ILLUSION:
CONTROL
OF THE STATE

———————————————————

———————————————————

Today's standard reaction to the growth of the state's size and power and the autonomous nature of political affairs is that the citizen must come to exercise effective control over the state. The citizen must be made to shed his passivity by various ways and means, and succeed in again taking the situation in hand. Many feel that this is difficult, but not impossible. Mostly, this is thought of as an effective control over political figures, the new significance added to universal suffrage, or new importance added to the deliberative process, or as a particular organization of democracy, what is called, for example, organized democracy. Generally, the assumption is that everything depends on the citizen's ability and political involvement. The greatest evil, which would permit the state to run rampant, would, according to this way of thinking, be the citizen's apolitical attitude. It is believed that the citizen, if educated and endowed with knowledge of his rights and duties, could ultimately impose his rule upon the state.[1]

This, I think, rests on an idealist view of man, and an old view of the state.[2] I will not discuss here the problem of man's general capacity, so often advanced first, but only the outstanding problem of our times: how can modern man exercise effective control over the power of the state as long as people would not really have the time to inform themselves on all questions even if they were given all the necessary information. To exercise effective control over the state means to be fully available. To be a citizen under such conditions would be a full-time occupation. The Greeks and Romans understood this perfectly. That political affairs should become the free man's principal function in our anticipated new civilization based on leisure is very desirable indeed. But this civilization of leisure is not around the corner, and besides we may experience great disappointments in that area. Even if the promise of leisure should be fulfilled, this man of good will with time on his hands may not be able to reverse the current that has progressively established itself in the political domain. These things are not as malleable as we would like. The citizen's belief in his ability to control the political machinery is a result of unrealistic views or lack of experience with state power.

When it is a question of controlling the state, we quickly see

---

[1] This is different from what was examined in the preceding pages, which was the idea that the individual can be a *limiting* factor in the state's autonomy. Here it is a question of the citizen *controlling* the state. The many articles on the problem of controlling state power, which appeared in France from July to September 1962, prior to the Referendum, mostly contained the old ideas of control over the Chief Executive by Parliament; the safeguarding of liberty by keeping legislative powers in the hands of the assembly; and so on. Few things said on that occasion showed real comprehension of the modern state.

[2] J. Schumpeter shows clearly in his critique of democracy's traditional doctrine that the people cannot control the state (see *Capitalism, Socialism, Democracy* [New York: Harper & Bros.; 1950], Chap. xx).

that man's view of political powers is old: he still attributes great importance to structures and constitutions, the search for juridical processes, the proper placing of authority and control. All these things are of course of some importance, but they can never lead to true change. Even less can they affect the state's evolution. This does not mean that a modern democratic state is the same thing as an authoritarian state. The rule of law *is* of importance. Some proposed reforms *are* of interest. But all that I have read or heard on control of political power by the citizen is based on a completely obsolete view of the state: we are presented here with an illusion that, like all illusions, is a mortal danger.

1. The Bureaucracy

The idea that the citizen should control the state rests on the assumption that, within the state, Parliament effectively directs the political body, the administrative organs, and the technicians. But this is a plain illusion.[3] Böhm has demonstrated very well that the organs of representative democracy no longer have any other purpose than to endorse decisions prepared by experts and pressure groups.[4] In the same vein, Giovanni Sartori,[5] in his extraordinary study of parliamentary functions, has demonstrated parliament's incapacity to fulfill the functions with which the democratic ideology has invested it, and on which still rests our naïve conviction that control by the citizen is possible. In particular, Sartori shows that parliament's actual place at the center of the government, and its identification with the government, radically modifies the foundations on which the parliamentary state was built, to wit: the idea of representation, the idea of control, the need for protection by

---

[3] No value judgment is being made here. I do not say that bureaucracy is good or bad. Bureaucracy corresponds to the direction in which our whole society is traveling and is therefore inevitable. Nor do I see the problem as a conflict between bureaucracy and democracy (see Michels: *Les Partis politiques* [1913]), but rather as a pre-empting of political affairs by the bureaucracy.
[4] Böhm: "Kapitulirt der Staat?" in *Politische Meinung* (1962).
[5] Giovanni Sartori: "L'Avenir des Parlements," in *Bulletin* s.e.d.e.i.s. (1964).

the law. His is one of the most lucid studies on the failure of the principle of representation, which has been caused by— among other factors—the politicians' professionalization and the filtering out of candidates in political parties, with the men sent to parliament tending to become a representative projection of the party itself. Sartori concludes that our parliaments are "atypical" with regard to the nation as a whole. No special attention will be devoted to his analyses, however, as the problem of parliamentarianism is only secondary.

The state is always described as an organ of decision, relatively simple, with decisions being taken according to established, regular, and controlled procedures. But the object of decisions has radically changed, and is no longer concerned with exciting political questions on which the masses' attention is riveted. Similarly, the process of decision is no longer a simple system of clear judicial procedures as established in a constitution. These procedures still exist, but they are no longer significant. The decision-making process consists of a complex mixture of personal judgments, traditions, conflicts among the state's many organs, and pressures from outside groups. Proliferation of decision-making centers has become the rule inside the political organism. This organism is not at all simple. When we talk of a president, ministers, or an assembly, we have not yet said anything, for the state has become a vast body, dealing with everything, possessing a multitude of centers, bureaus, services, and establishments.

All this is perfectly well known to political scientists.[6] Many detailed and realistic studies have been made of the structure and process of decision-making. But here we encounter a peculiar psychological problem. When these same political scientists, who are perfectly aware of these problems, write a political article or take a position on some current problem, they completely forget their painstaking analyses and fall back into the

---

[6] Of course, I do not claim to be examining the entire problem of bureaucracy here. Besides Max Weber's and Robert K. Merton's well-known works, see *Arguments,* No. 17 (1960); Mathiot: *Bureaucratie et Démocratie* (Études et Documents; 1961); Schnur: "Tendances de la Bureaucratie," in *Bulletin* s.e.d.e.i.s. (1962); Michel Crozier: *Le Phénomène bureaucratique* (Paris: Éditions du Seuil; 1964).

antiquated concept of the state; surprisingly, we then find them once again discussing the presidential regime or electoral procedures as though the political future were dependent on these illusory forms. As yet no connection exists between concrete studies on the true nature of the state and basic thought on actual political problems in the modern world. Particularly with regard to the control of power, there is a manifest contradiction between our knowledge of what the modern state is and the constant affirmation that the citizen can control the state.[7]

---

[7] A difference must be made between the influence of technicians and experts in the political domain and the bureaucratic organization. These two phenomena are often insufficiently distinguished. Even Michel Crozier, in *Le Phénomène bureaucratique,* is not always aware of the difference. He sometimes stumbles upon it, as on page 183: " . . . the leaders of this conservative and bureaucratic organization profess a philosophy of change, whereas the technicians are at bottom systematically conservative in their conception of organizational problems." This is really very characteristic of the two positions. Similarly, Crozier sees clearly, on page 219, the difference between "the *power of the expert,* i.e., the power an individual holds through his personal capacity to control some factors affecting the functioning of an organization, and the *functional hierarchical power,* which is the real bureaucratic power, i.e., the power certain individuals hold through their function in the organization." But the latter cannot control the power of the experts or substitute for it. This is true when the expert is part of the bureaucracy and part of the system; but the experts' relationship with the governmental machinery must also be considered; the pattern will then emerge differently. I disagree with Crozier on the experts' "true" influence and future role. Underestimating their role, Crozier makes certain errors: for example, that change in France is almost impossible because of "bureaucracy's omnipotent powers on the level of routine and its helplessness with regard to the problem of change." He overlooks the problems facing the technicians, who provoke, in their ranks, changes that have repercussions in the bureaucracy. What should have been analyzed is the development of the bureaucratic system in direct or indirect relationship with technicians. There is rather extensive change in sectors responding to the demands of the technicians; the latter, rather than the politicians of the "deliberative sub-system," provoke changes. In fact, contrary to what Crozier believes, politicians are incapable of producing bureaucratic changes.

The shortcomings of Crozier's analysis become very clear when he shows (on pages 377 *ff.*) that in a system where there is economic planning and "the future unfolds more rationally," administrative rigidity must come to an end; a new form of rationality must then appear, leading to the disintegration of the traditional model. Crozier gives as an example the Soviet Planning Commission—but this is precisely what I mean by the role of technicians and technical administrations. These administrations "of the new type" correspond to different needs and have different functions and different modes of action. This does not jeopardize automatically the traditional bureaucratic administrations, which have other functions to fulfill.

Meynaud (in *La Technocratie* [Paris: Payot; 1964], p. 59) clearly shows the differences and points of contact between bureaucracy and the technicians' influence; that technocracy's range exceeds bureaucracy's, and so on. We are here face to face with the blending of the two forms inside every apparatus. We

A modern state is *not* primarily a centralized organ of decision, a set of political organs. It is primarily an enormous machinery of bureaus. It is composed of two contradictory elements: on the one hand, political personnel, assemblies, and councils, and, on the other, administrative personnel in the bureaus—whose distinction, incidentally, is becoming less and less clear. Tradition accords great importance to deliberative bodies, councils, votes, and the designation of political leaders. Political thought revolves around this; from the point of view of democracy, the people's sovereignty operates here. This goes hand in hand with the well-known pattern, the classical and reassuring schema of administration; administrative personnel are named by the politicians: such personnel therefore depend entirely on them. It constitutes the ranks of government employees, who have no latitude whatever with regard to the state as, in another day, the officer corps had. At best they have freedom to look after their professional interests. The administration exists in order to execute the decisions of the political leaders—that is its only role. It is activated by the decisions of its central brain. Thus the vast administrative body is nothing without the political center, which is everything. Against this administration, the citizen can be and is being effectively protected: he can have recourse to channels. But more than that, the citizens are the masters, thanks to elections, councils and assemblies. They can act upon the state's decisions and therefore upon the administration. The latter is nothing but a relay mechanism, a transmission belt.

This very simple and classic view includes, without being aware of it, both the Hegelian concept of administration as a relay between the state and society, and the Marxian concept of administration as a means of the state. This also explains the insufficient importance most people attribute to the study of the administration proper (except for administrative law). There are very few sociological studies on government administration.

---

then have, in Meynaud's words, a "techno-bureaucracy" because the technicians can exert their weight on the bureaucratic machine and manipulate its elements, which does not always happen.

Finally, one must look at efforts made everywhere to define the bureaucratic body and the technicians' role. The two complement each other, but are still, in most cases, opposed to or unaware of each other.

Even a book such as *L'État et le citoyen* contains only one insignificant paragraph on administration. Yet, in reality, the state is gradually being absorbed by the administration. A façade or appearance of political power still clings to some man or council; but it is only a façade, even in authoritarian regimes. The true political problems, those concerning the daily lives of the nation and affecting the relationship between citizen and public power are in the hands of the bureaus. In them resides the reality of the modern state.[8]

First, governmental administration has acquired considerable weight and complexity. It is all well and good to claim that the corps of functionaries can be reduced to some simple rules or statutes, the administration to some general structure. That takes no account of reality. On the contrary, one would have to penetrate into the endless mass of bureaus and their competences, the hundreds of services under a cabinet member, the divisions, the hierarchies, and above all the liaison organs. Relations among administrative sectors have become incredibly complicated, so much so that liaison organs had to be created. A dossier must go through five, ten, twenty services, with each adding something and attesting to having taken note of it. As those services are subject to different chiefs, and even belong to different ministeries, the channels are not clear. The liaison organs know the proper channels, and put one bureau in touch with the other. We must not condemn bureaucracy's expansion —its complexity is the mirror image of the nation's complexity and the diverse tasks entrusted to the state.[9] Nobody can have exact knowledge of this vast machinery, and, to my knowledge, no organizational chart detailing the various interrelationships exists. Even if there were a chart for one minister's department, it would not amount to much, as it would not indicate the horizontal relations with other departments and administrative

---

[8] For concrete examples, see Gabriel Ardant: *Technique de l'État de la productivité du secteur public* (Paris: Presses Universitaires de France; 1956); the Report of the Central Committee of Inquiry on the Cost and the Efficiency of Public Services (1960); *La Fonction préfectorale et la Réforme administrative* (Study published by the Association of the Prefectorial Corps and of Civil Administrators of the Home Office; 1961).

[9] *La Fonction préfectorale et la Réforme administrative.*

organs. Nobody can grasp the whole, and in reality nobody controls it.

But this bureaucracy penetrates the entire state. A cabinet member amounts to nothing without his bureaucratic infrastructure. A ministry in turn is an enormous administrative organism. The bureaucracy penetrates the top levels of the government, which in turn is reduced to being a bureaucratic complex, except for some personalities whose function is not always clear. It will be objected that the minister makes the decisions, and if he does not know all his bureaus or his department's entire administrative structure, he does know the various section chiefs. These chiefs are well acquainted with their subordinate chiefs, and so on; with the result that as one descends the hierarchy, everyone at each level knows his immediate subordinates and the offices under his command, and the well-regulated machinery ultimately depends on the man at the top. That, too, is an entirely theoretical view of the matter. From the very moment that a general policy decision has been made by the minister, it escapes his control; the matter takes on independent life and circulates in the various services, and all depends eventually on what the bureaus decide to do with it. Possibly, orders will eventually emerge corresponding to the original decision. More frequently, nothing will emerge. The decision will evaporate in the numerous administrative channels and never really see the light of day. Everyone knows of ministerial orders getting nowhere simply because they were blocked—purposely or not—somewhere along the line. We know the even more frequent case in which a basic decision is couched in a one-line decree, with the addendum that another decree for its implementation will follow. These implementation decrees never see the light of day. They depend entirely on the bureaucracy.[1] In France a major and essential order issued in 1945 was never applied. Twice, in 1951 and in 1959, a minister gave orders to implement the decision, but to no avail. Was this simply a question of disorder? Complicity? The chief's inability? The jungle of offices? Laziness? Actually, the phenomenon is much

---

[1] Report of the Audit Office (1959).

more important; the bureaus by now have taken on an independent life; the bureaucratic administration has powers of decision and censure *outside* the elected political powers, and obeys special interests (though it does that at times) and person pressures (which is very rare) much less than inexorable operational laws. What is frequently overlooked is that the administrative machine's complexity precludes any decision by a single center and that the bureaucracy's—inevitable—weight makes it impossible for a chief to activate the whole mechanism transmitting orders.

Does that mean the state is paralyzed, impotent? Not at all. What we see is a transformation of central importance: what used to be a system of transmission has progressively turned into a system of decision; what used to be a ministery (literally, service) has turned into a power. But we do not have here a real range of *diversified* centers of decision-making in opposition to one another; rather we see here a multitude of interrelated decision-making centers, none directly responsible, all included in the same machine. Today, *that* is the state. This emerges even more clearly if we consider that not one, but, every day, at various levels of the various organisms, hundreds, sometimes even thousands of decisions are made. These decisions are not the work of an individual. It cannot even be said that they form even *one* general decision of which the other decisions are only implementations; even when these decisions reach back to fundamental choices taken, these thousands of partial decisions will lend that basic choice its particular coloration, value, efficacy. The basic decision amounts to very little. For example, a treaty such as the Évian agreement amounts to nothing; what turns it into something is the thousands of interpretations, the thousands of decisions taken by various executive organs. One cannot even say that such an agreement sets the general course of action; entirely different general lines of action will affect decisions, pretending to be implementations or justifications and interpretations of theoretical tests. As Clement Lefort has said:

> Whoever may be the director-general, the power of decision has
> necessarily devolved back upon the various services, and in each

service becomes concretized only through a more or less collective participation in the solution of fixed problems. To ask whether the top level is or is not distinct from bureaucracy as a whole is to ask the wrong question. In every organization whose hierarchy eventually delimits the function of top leadership, the latter, in a certain way, operates outside those under its command; *this is no less so even if it remains part of the framework it dominates.*

This is the true problem inherent in political affairs.[2]

This machine nevertheless obeys certain laws, though not those regulating a constitution or parliament or even the established rules of administrative law (though, to be sure, they formally apply, and lead us back to a reassuring universe in which all controls, relationships, and hierarchies are properly established). Rather, they obey laws inherent in existing organizations, sociological tendencies, customs, such as the law of continuity and, stability: the administration remains, the personnel changes. True and false. We throw out administrations and the men representing them when we change regimes (as in France in 1940, 1944, 1958). But the politician who has become deeply anchored in politics, which is his trade, even when he is thrown out of power, remains active nevertheless, through others or through his influence. Therefore, behind the changes in administrative personnel, a constant structure, a continuity of tradition assures the administration's actual power. Change incumbents, even regulations, and you will change very little; after some search for new bearings and some floundering, during which efficiency will be reduced, there will be a quick return to old procedures that did not develop merely from arbitrariness, routine, or bureaucratic stupidity. Most of these procedures are simply best suited to obtain the desired results.[3] Obviously the average citizen does not feel that way, but that is another matter.

Another well-known law applies to the administrative struc-

---

[2] Crozier (in *Le Phénomène bureaucratique*) is perfectly right in stating that bureaucracy is necessary, not only from the point of view of the state, but also from that of man. "One of the basic reasons for the development of the bureaucratic system is the desire to eliminate relationships of power and dependence and the desire to administer things rather than govern men."
[3] Rueff-Armand Report on the obstacles to economic expansion (1960).

ture: specialization and rationalization. The specialization of tasks and division of functions for the purpose of arriving at a maximum competence and efficiency in all domains is one of the basic causes of bureaucracy's proliferation and increasing complexity. It also accounts for considerable precision in the work done, unambiguous decisions and executions, and also, contrary to general feelings and appearances, the speed of operations. Talk of administrative slowness is a *leitmotif*. But if one considers how complicated the problems are, how enormous the tasks, how colossal the amount of information received and disseminated [4]—not by choice, but because the means of information simply permit the assemblage and use of constantly growing documentation—one realizes that in reality transmission and execution have been speeded up tremendously, without a concommitant growth of personnel. Efficiency is, after all, the machine's fundamental law. This imperative really aligns the machine with the technological world and ideology. The bureaucracy has nothing whatever to do with values. It does not know social justice or political liberty. It is there to function, to make a political-economic-social body function, to make it advance as a whole. It does not seek to promote verities. It cannot consider individuals. It obeys the sole rule of efficiency. Yes, it will be said, this machinery operates in order to attain an aim set by politics, and that aim incorporates value! Not at all. If a political aim is set, it becomes diluted in the machine and soon has no more content. The administration no more obeys central leadership than it knows values. Everybody is merely concerned that his political-economic-social sector should function well, without crisis or stoppage; everyone has his sector and fails to know the whole.

But it should not be thought, either, that a superior political power is pulling the whole together. Only a certain amount of coordination is established among the various sectors (whose only concern is efficiency); some interrelations between hierarchies exist. But these hierarchies are not those envisaged by the law or by administrative statutes. For many, and often very

---

[4] *La Fonction préfectorale et la Réforme administrative.*

subtle, reasons deriving from the social body itself, for reasons of state, or of an organ's greater or lesser efficiency, the various administrative branches assume different weight and values. For example, finances once were the key to all the rest. This is no longer entirely so. Depending on the country, propaganda, the police, or scientific and technological research may assume the greatest weight in decisions. In France, on the local level, the Administration of Highways and Bridges is all-powerful; its decisions are unassailable, and all other administrative bodies of allegedly equal rank must bow before it. This is only to indicate that the body has its own particular structural and evolving principles, motivations independent from pure politics. But, as has been said, this bureaucracy, precisely because of its stability, tends toward certain fixed ways of doing things and develops a certain rigidity.

G. Lapassade has said: "Administrations spread an ideological orthodoxy whose dogmatic rigidity is the reflection of this power system." To be sure, administration—except for propaganda—is not an agent for the dissemination of an ideology. But, unconsciously and involuntarily, it creates this rigidity in the social body. Today's clearest example is the development of public relations aiming only at assuring greater efficiency on the part of the administration by the social body's complete psychic and moral adjustment to that administration.

Finally, there are two other important laws: anonymity and secrecy.[5] The decisions taken are anonymous. This was clearly revealed in connection with the great Nazi war crime trials after the war. Nobody had ever made a decision. This happened again in the Eichmann trial. We must not say: "This is a lawyer's argument, a lie." On the contrary, it was the exact image of all that takes place in the modern state. All a chief can do is to give a general directive, ordinarily not incorporating concrete decisions, and therefore not entailing true responsibility for the concrete acts emerging at the other end. New decisions taken at every level are necessarily the anonymous fruits of several

---

[5] Gabriel Ardant: *Technique de l'État* and Robert Catherine: *Le Fonctionnaire français* (Paris: A. Colin; 1961).

bureaus, technicians, and circumstances. Ultimately, every decision becomes independent of all individuals. And just as every decision is anonymous, the criteria of judgment, the processes, the methods of action employed by each service or each bureaucratic element are completely secret. Here one must distinguish between official public juridical forms and rules known only to interested parties—which, even if they were made public, would still be known only to the interested parties, as they are too numerous and technical—and decisive customs that remain absolutely secret. This derives from the fact that, ultimately, bureaucracy knows no law except necessity.

There cannot exist, at any time, for any of the administration members or for the administrative organs themselves, any true freedom of choice. They can only make decisions dictated by necessity, which best illustrates what was said in the first chapter. Nor can the overall decisions be taken at the so-called political level, precisely because of the state's bureaucratic structure. By way of illustration, the conflict between a liberal state and an imperial administration is well known. Freedom can in no way enter into the bureaucratic order.

2. *Administration and Men*

Sociologists object:

An administration is not an organism; it does not obey its laws, or function in accordance with known rules. That is an abstraction. In reality, an administration consists of people, is subject to people's foibles, disorders, and personal inclinations, and also to their impulses and personal decisions. Some officials have greater influence; there are "informal" channels of organization and communication, purely human habits, applied or contested value systems, and a psychological and moral element much more important than any automatism. There are professional conflicts between officials, and their work ultimately depends on promotions or the maintenance of somebody's personal status; bureaucracy lives altogether by such rivalries and personal situations. It includes class struggles, with the classes often divided along political or labor lines. And when great political changes take place, the capture of important administration posts is equivalent to sharing the booty; the political element regains all its authority at that point.[6]

In reality, all this is secondary.[7] In order to justify it, one may have metaphysical reasons to affirm man's freedom, but in so doing will hide the systematic nature of the whole. It is a typical case of not being able to see the forest for the trees. Trying too hard to "observe the official in his setting," one forgets bureaucracy itself. The facts mentioned earlier are correct, but they are merely *inside of* and *dependent upon* the system described

---

[6] Crozier (in *Le Phénomène bureaucratique*) has analyzed the effects of the human element in the bureaucratic process, showing how it creates vicious circles and in the end reinforces the bureaucratic process.

[7] Crozier (in *Le Phénomène bureaucratique*), in his minute analysis, in no way modifies the Weberian concept of the bureaucratic system's impact in and on the state. Crozier properly shows the importance of power relations *in* the bureaucratic organization; but that does not change the fact that the bureaucratic system ultimately eliminates all political powers extrinsic to it. Crozier has demonstrated how, proceeding from Weber's analysis, the relationship between bureaucracy's efficient, rational character and its "dysfunctions" (routine, oppressiveness) must be examined, as well as the relationship between the system and the people constituting it. But he neglects the "macro-sociological" aspect. When he states that "bureaucratic" traits were more pronounced in organizations of the old type than they are in those of today, he disregards the fact that in the old bureaucracies the system was more pragmatic and partial, whereas the universalization of the bureaucratic system is the hallmark of our modern state and society. When bureaucracy becomes universal, some of its more rigid characteristics may "soften." The more bureaucratized the society becomes, the more flexible the bureaucracy, while remaining just as rational, anonymous, hierarchized and so on, will be because, as a result of its spread, its "dysfunctions" are much less felt in view of the all-encompassing increase in "security."

For this reason I doubt whether the contrast shown by Crozier between the French and American bureaucratic systems is valid. American bureaucratic oppression is different. It is more internalized and acts more through external psychological means, because it is even more all-encompassing and deeply integrated into life. Centralization is less visible, but the effort to press everybody into the bureaucratic system with methods such as Human Relations compensates for that. Impersonal rule is on the increase there, too, and when Crozier contrasts impersonal rules defining the work (French type) with rules providing procedures for conflict-resolution (American type), this is not a genuine contrast, but the pattern of bureaucratic evolution, and we in France are in the process of arriving at the American type. Incidentally, that is what Crozier himself seems to suggest when concluding that bureaucracy is forced to change its form and methods under the pressures of a rapidly growing industrialized society. But he stops at a fragmentary view of bureaucracy.

I think Joseph Bensman and Bernard Rosenberg understand much better than Crozier that bureaucracy is not an element one can study in isolation. They are right in insisting that we are dealing here with a new form of society as a whole. (See *Mass, Class and Bureaucracy* [Englewood Cliffs, N.J.: Prentice-Hall; 1963].)

before. Only with the help of traits extrinsic to bureaucracy does the bureaucrat attain a small degree of freedom, advancement, and competition. There is no contradiction here, not even compensation. We must also remember that the "human" elements reported above are generally in disfavor with public opinion; the latter demands that the administration function like a machine, with the precision, objectivity, and rapidity. Public opinion does not understand the internal power struggles in this game and is quick to anger over it, regarding such things as signs of corruption and poor team spirit. And public opinion obviously effectively imposes the model of what bureaucracy should be. The state itself also seeks to prevent such clique influences and to normalize and regulate the machine's functioning. To be sure, we will never arrive at a purely mechanical level, and the vagaries of the human element will remain inevitable, but they will be reduced to a very small margin of uncertainty—very important only for each individual bureaucrat, but without real influence on the characteristics of bureaucracy as a whole.[8]

What can a politician, a minister, a deputy, or a parliament do against that? The politician is generally not competent with regard to the problems that are his to solve, particularly if, as it is now inevitable, he has become a specialist in political affairs. But we must distinguish, for we are faced here with a strange confusion of terms concerning the word politics. Yet it is well known what "to engage in politics" means: there is always some methodical action aimed at obtaining power; this aim need not be pursued for careerist reasons, or for the sake of personal success, or to make more money—the simple taste for power is sufficient. Neither are there any differences in this connection between capitalist and communist countries. Nikita Khrushchev

---

[8] I am not judging these facts, but want to call attention to Joseph A. Schumpeter, who thinks that the administration is a power with its own specialty, one whose prerogatives cannot be subject to interference by politicians. Only the administration is efficient, and democracy, in an industrial society, is remarkably inefficient. Moreover, those who reject Schumpeter's ideas and want to democratize the executive branch always agree that this is not possible with regard to economic affairs. (See *Capitalism, Socialism, Democracy* [New York: Harper & Bros.; 1950], Chap. xxiii.)

was a clever politician in his methodical pursuit of the top position, just as Tardieu or Laval or Hitler was. The methods may vary slightly; the essence is the same. Rivals must be eliminated, a "clientele" built up, access routes and strategic positions held, and so on. Politics takes place inside parties, before men arrive at top positions. This is the war to the knife against party "comrades." Once at the top, one must maintain oneself there. At the same time, it is necessary to help the party to gain more importance, friends, or voters. The party's fate is tied to the leader's fate, and vice versa; and if a man attains power, his principal concern is to defend it and protect it against every constitutional, juridical, half-criminal, or purely political ambush or trap.

The political leader must be a politician by trade, which means to be a clever technician in the capture and defense of positions. The situation is the same in a dictatorship. Hitler was an ingenious tactician, but had to guard during his entire rule against ambush from his own friends. Clearly, we are a far cry from a noble and idealist sense of politics: "The common good, search for just institutions, good organization of cities, and so on." Between the two, desire for power clearly has priority, not because the professional politician is a dishonest or overambitious intriguer, but because he cannot undertake just and desirable reforms or guard the common good unless he *first* obtains power and keeps it. This then must be his prime concern. And even when he has obtained the power, it still remains the principal concern to which he must subordinate all constructive political pursuits.

In fact, the two forms of politics are incompatible. They demand radically different personal qualities and contrary preoccupations. To be a clever maneuverer in arriving at the summit is no qualification for perceiving the common good, making just decisions, being politically enlightened, or mastering economic problems. Conversely, to have the moral qualities and intellectual competence to be capable of genuine thought and of eventually putting a genuine political program into operation in no way ensures having the equipment needed to reach the top. The specialist in how to make a political career is not and never will become a boon to civilization or even a good custodian for the commonwealth (even if he were to apply himself to the task, for which he would have very little time). This is not a general evaluation of political careerism, but only an observation on what it is in the modern state, i.e., in the face of the large and complex political "machines," parties, or administrations. This has no longer much in common with political life in the Greek city-state. And Pericles' example would help us little.[9]

Therefore, the very fact that the politician, no matter in which regime, is forced to play this game renders him incapable of thinking about true political affairs. He will never be anything but an amateur, hastily trained, hastily informed, never having the time to reflect on political matters.

From an entirely different point of view—if we recall the bureaucratic problem—it is very clear that the politician carries no weight with regard to the bureaucracy.[1] He does not know its branches well, He has few means of forcing them to obey him, except that of staffing them with his own men. He does retain a purely theoretical power of decision, all the more theoretical because he is technically not very competent as the bureaucracy knows perfectly well. He cannot even use the feudal system of attaching vassals to himself. If he does, a scandal will soon develop. Adherence to the same political party is his only possible guarantee of his subordinates' loyalty as they pursue their own personal careers. Yet, he must place his faith in the bureaucracy, as all he will say in the assembly or in public, and all the decrees he will sign originate with it. Moreover, the politician, every day, signs several hundred papers he literally has no time to read. But his signature is affixed to them. This compounds the situation: the politician accepts responsibility for acts and decisions that he has not really taken and for which he cannot really answer because he does not know them or knows them only slightly. And yet, in the eyes of parliament and public opinion, he is responsible. Ultimately, a politician opposed

---

[9] Schumpeter is right when he stresses this aspect of the politician's career.
[1] Waline (in *Rapports des Scissions politiques* [1961]) has well analyzed the administration's power vis-à-vis the political power, and its capacity of engaging in technical resistance.

to the rule of bureaucracy would be nothing but a scapegoat, a role that would hardly be to his taste.[2]

But, the larger the bureaucratic machine becomes, the more impossible it becomes for the politician to have effective knowledge of it or effective power over it—to really direct it. Even if he can make some personnel changes, that really changes nothing, as we have seen. The weight of the administrative structure is much too heavy.[3]

If by chance major changes are made and the structure is modified, great disorder ensues but does not significantly change the disequilibrium between politician and bureaucrat. For a brief instant, the former will have the illusion of freedom and domination, but only at the price of efficiency in the country's administration. One way out seems to remain: the politician can improve administrative methods, adjust administrative organs, improve channels, strengthen controls, improve coordination; he certainly can give bureaucracy certain impulses: we constantly see this in the Soviet Union. But these impulses can never go in any but one direction: to make the organization more effective and to perfect the bureaucracy and contribute to its progressive autonomy. In other words, all reforms undertaken by the politician can only make the administration more self-contained, and further reduce the effect of political decisions.

Can any particular development be discerned under these circumstances? Could bureaucracy have reached its summit and be about to decline? The state's "withering away" promised by communism only opened the way for a triumphant and total bureaucracy. But here we find a disturbing mystery. To the extent that the bureaucracy, in every country, penetrates the

---

[2] Crozier's remark (in *Le Phénomène bureaucratique*, p. 72) applies here: "Decisions are inevitably made by people who have direct knowledge neither of the area in which they take place nor of the variables that may affect the resulting action. Because of the lack of such direct knowledge, those responsible must rely on information furnished them by subordinates in whose interest it is to hide the truth from them. . . . Those who have the necessary knowledge have no power to decide. Those who have the power to decide are refused information that they need." Therefore, those who have the information, i.e., the bureaucrats, inevitably end up by assuming power over decisions.
[3] Cf. Jean Meynaud: *Les Groupes de pression de France* (Paris: A. Colin; 1958).

political machine and "corners" all power of decision, it actually becomes the state. To say that the bureaucracy survives is to say only that the state's form changes more quickly—but not differently—in the Soviet Union than every place else, though fundamentally it remains what it is. The objection will be on the one hand: for bureaucracy to become smaller, freer access to all resources, greater social mobility, a wide distribution of power would be needed, and a contest among different powerful and articulate political groups for the conquest of power would be necessary (S. Dasso). Well and good, but our societies certainly are not developing in that direction.[4] Conversely, we are told that bureaucratic growth is tied to the development of industrial labor, the specialization of services in our society, the increase of delegated authority at all levels, the growth of state authority. Is our society not traveling precisely in that direction, spontaneously and entirely? The more authoritarian the state becomes, the more functions it assumes; and, in doing so it swells its bureaucratic system. Society's spontaneous movements and the state's constant, tolerated growth work in that direction. And yet, modern revolutionary governments still believe that they can liquidate the bureaucracy and the system of government officials.

All dictators inflating bureaucracy do it with the cry: "Down with bureaucracy!" This was one of Hitler's major lines, a subject of his most biting sarcasms against the bourgeois democracies. Then Stalin (at least ten times between 1947 and 1953), Khrushchev, and Nasser attacked bureaucracy, making it the scapegoat for all that was wrong. After them, as any good dictator must, Fidel Castro took up the same facile explanation in August 1963: "The government's branches are full of people who do nothing . . . When these people find that their salary

---

[4] I do not entirely share Crozier's optimism in Le Phénomène bureaucratique when he sees the bureaucratic system as one protecting individuals against a certain society, and when he says that the centralizing process goes only so far. He seems to neglect the effects any growing and nationalizing state has when it produces a certain type of bureaucracy. On the other hand, he has not fully understood the system of decentralization which permits the extension of centralization beyond limits that would otherwise be imposed on it by the growing weight of its functions.

is secure, they no longer feel any urge to serve the public . . . our comrades at the Institute for Agrarian Reform should resign. . . ."

But all these leaders wisely returned to the road of bureaucratic organization because they had to. A state that wants to do everything and change everything, can do so only with the help of an enormous bureaucracy. Anti-bureaucratic litanies are on the order of magic incantations, and absolutely no genuine modification of bureaucratic autonomy can ensue from them. Rather, according to reports recently received from the Soviet Union, bureaucracy enjoys an unbelievable rate of growth there. And one must not forget that Khrushchev won the top post because he was supported by the chiefs of the bureaucratic machine who ultimately abandoned him. As the barons used to be the king-makers, the bureaucrats now make the politicians.

Still, there is the well-known argument of parallel hierarchies and state parties. During the 1789 revolution in France, mission representatives or popular societies were in control, making and unmaking administrations. But France never experienced an equal administrative paralysis and, despite the terror, the government was prodigiously impotent. Still, the elements of choice are clear: a government taking on responsibilities for the whole range of national life will build up an administration that will eventually take all power away from it; or, rejecting bureaucracy, it will employ terror. But today control by the state party has taken on other aspects. Organizations like the Nazi or Communist party are great propelling agents and great control agencies; they inject political mystique into bureaucracy's bottom layer and subject everything to the state's political impulses. They are political counterweights to bureaucratic administration. Not the well-known dangers of the one-party system, but two other aspects will be discussed here: first of all, such a party does not change the interplay between political organs and bureaucracy when top-level decisions are made. There, at the summit, the situation is the same as in all other states: the party chiefs are always the highest officials. And very soon they begin to act like high officials. The party's role as promoter and controller is effective only at lower levels. In the second place, by a strange turn of events, the *party itself* becomes more bureaucratized! [5] The party that promised to fight against the state's bureaucratization can do so only if it has a strong structure, a rigorously established hierarchy and, at the same time, an independent decision-making capacity at all levels. In fact, a hierarchy in which lower levels are overdependent on the top is not at all incompatible with considerable decision-making powers at all levels, contrary to theory. An authoritarian party needs considerable controls, particularly if it is large, and a strong structure if it wants to be militant; it must obey precise rules of organization, which, precisely, make it a bureaucratic machine. One need not stress the point: everybody knows that the Nazi Party, the Soviet Communist Party, the Communist parties in the People's Democracies—and also in France—just like all labor unions, have become enormous bureaucracies.

We often find two bureaucracies battling one another and thereby reducing their respective efficiency, but that does not prevent the state's bureaucratization.

The modern state being what it is, one aspect of the political illusion is plain to see.[6] If the unreflecting citizen, comes into conflict with the bureaucracy, he will react according to his temperament, either finding it silly or, getting angry, talking of bureaucratic trickery and disorder in the machinery. If he reflects on it, he will regard the machine as profoundly absurd, an impenetrable mystery, and feel himself the helpless object

---

[5] The reform carried out in the U.S.S.R. in December, 1962, gave the party a larger share in the administration. This touches on a central point in my study: as a result of the struggle against bureaucratization, an administration may be replaced by a formerly political organization that is itself becoming increasingly bureaucratized, and which now begins to implement administrative tasks that it only influenced or inspired before.

[6] Bensman and Rosenberg have shown in *Mass, Class and Bureaucracy* that the system of officials is no longer merely a method of employing people, but has become a way of life. In a society become officialdom, the individual's functions are strictly organized, not only on the professional level, but also in his life. Social relations become functions which replace personality, which becomes a social component. This must never be forgotten when one thinks about contemporary political life. This phenomenon has also been treated by William H. Whyte, Jr.: *The Organization Man* (New York: Simon and Schuster; 1956).

of some incomprehensible fate whose decisions, affecting his entire life, are as impenetrable as predestination itself. This would be the Kafkaesque interpretation. Let us not forget that *The Trial* and *The Castle* are concerned, not with the state, but with bureaucracy; the citizen comes into contact with the state only via the bureaucracy. And vice versa. All descriptions of citizen-state relations are abstract, theoretical, and metaphysical; the contact is not established by votes, but only by the bureaucracy. And in the citizen's eyes, when he tries to act on the real and non-ideological contact point, the parliamentarian's job is to deal with taxes, customs, the police, and so on; and the citizen's pragmatic view is correct. Conversely, in the Kafkaesque vision, two contradictory aspects need to be considered: the vision surely is accurate if one places oneself in the shoes of the citizen who does not really understand what is asked of him, who fails to see why his request or complaint is rejected, who always feels that the machine is arbitrary and slow. But the same decision, viewed from bureaucracy's vantage point—if we leave aside the increasingly rare instances of malfeasance and abuse—is generally fully justified by explanatory circulars, based on a series of micro-decisions, and is part of some general practice that makes it fully explicable and legitimate. Yet the citizen cannot understand it at all, just because the system is so complex; and the greater and more numerous the problems confronting the bureaucracy become, the more complex the system will be. The citizen therefore feels that it is absurd for him to think that he can play a meaningful role in the system and the impression that the bureaucracy is omnipotent is further strengthened.

But the bureaucracy really *is* omnipotent. Omnipotence lies in behemothic size and functional complexity much more than in the intentions or statements by statesmen, or in constitutional provisions. The postulate that power should be "personal" or "democratic," is a nice enough propaganda slogan, but has practically no real meaning. For the state's truly authoritarian face is not modified by one or the other decision. A bureaucratic administration cannot be anything but authoritarian, even if it has no intention of being so. It is simply necessary that the rules be applied, that the machine turn, the uncomprehending citizens obey; the public order must be maintained and public works carried out.[7] Those protesting most against police excesses will, once they become police officers themselves, exercise the greatest repression—as happened in France in 1848 and twice after 1944—in order to maintain order: an administration cannot have another point of view. As Max Weber said, bureaucracy functions without regard for individuals; it executes impersonal rules.[8] It would go against the entire progress of modern states and administrations to run things and pay attention to individuals, i.e., follow personal interests and subjective judgments; instead, administration is objective and cannot budge before individual complaints or needs.

But the crux of the problem is that this bureaucracy, which cannot, by its very nature, have any regard for the individual, has become the very point at which objective norms are applied to the individual; for the bureaucracy is the point at which the political idea, the legal rule and the individual—the "administratee"—come into contact. In this context, even if individual bureaucrats are friendly, understanding, and human, the individual is delivered hand and foot to the authorities.[9] He can never protest against a bureaucratic decision because he cannot possibly know the rules underlying that decision. There is no real recourse. Cases in which administrative recourse is taken

---

[7] This seems to remain true even when one takes into account what Meynaud has said on collaboration between interested parties and officials and the contractual relation between the administration and the administrees, i.e., an infinite number of citizens. (*Les Groupes* . . . , p. 258.)

[8] "The administration is often accused of functioning for itself rather than for the people, of losing sight of its objectives and of substituting its own views for them. . . . In order not to fall into that situation, the administration must react. The principle of all administrative reform rests on the constant struggle against this natural inclination, on a constant concern with services rendered, a search for wasted energies. . . ." (Gabriel Ardant: *Technique de L'État*.)

[9] Theodore Caplow has put it very well (in *Arguments* [1962]): "Gradually all family life, communication, education, and the arts are being subjected to bureaucracy's norms and controls." Each day, a growing segment of human activity is placed inside that great organization. And, agreeing with William Whyte, Caplow shows that man's integration into that organization effectively solves most of his problems, even those of conscience. "The individual no longer needs internal motivations to choose between good and evil. He need not struggle with his conscience or with temptation as long as his allegiance to the organization is sincere."

to higher echelons presuppose unusual importance and availability of various means not within reach of 99 per cent of the "administratees." Even if some decision was improper, and was reversed after two or three years of contest, the important point is that the decision was made, and the damage (such as the seizing of newspaper issues) cannot be repaired. Could it be otherwise? Absolutely not, unless the citizen had the right to disobey the administration openly or even to have the respective bureaucrat brought before a partisan political tribunal; but in such a case, an administration or, for that matter, a state would no longer exist. In that case the majority of citizens would soon be complaining of the "disorder"; moreover, to be able to have a functionary convicted under the revolutionary situation I posited, a man would have to belong to a privileged group. The people whose food-ration cards were revoked in Hungary in 1955 by an unjustifiable decision on the part of their administration were always free to lodge a complaint!

This omnipotence of the administrative machine is in the nature of the state. The state is authoritarian neither because some major political decision so ordained it, nor because it is headed by a Führer with absolute powers, but because (in France) every day ten or twenty thousand little administrative decisions are taken against which the "administratee" has neither recourse nor protection. Moreover, these decisions are mostly routine and deal with such unimportant questions that it would not be worthwhile to precipitate a rebellion, which, moreover, would only reinforce the administration.

But there is a means to reduce the impression of arbitrariness and omnipotence created by the state. The application of "public relations" by the administration aims at making the citizen understand the "why" of the decisions taken and even to collaborate actively with the administration: specialized services are placed at the disposal of those being administered in order to show them how the services function, what rules are being applied, why some decisions are being taken and not others, why something should be done in a particular way, and so on. As a result, the feeling of anxiety abates; the individual finds himself in a comprehensible universe in which acts are rational rather than absurd. He then enters into the system. Decisions that once shocked him now become completely acceptable in his eyes. Police behavior that shocked him before becomes completely understandable when he places himself in the shoes of the police. Thus, "PR" is a method of psychologically integrating the administratee into the administration, of making him accept in good grace the acts committed and sympathize with their reasons. Put differently, the aim is to reduce conflict, to create good relations—good relations not based on the fact that the administration is of service to the administree (which is impossible), but based on the fact that the administree, having caught on, no longer balks. As in all other domains, Public Relations is a mechanism to reify conformity—which only accentuates, rather than alleviates, the authority and omipotence of the administration.

But it is precisely here that the political illusion resides—to believe that the citizen, through political channels, can master or control or change this state. Lalumière has admirably demonstrated this helplessness on a specific point: the publication of a certain court report in connection with a public scandal had no effect because it rested on the assumption that "public exposure of a scandal will lead the administration to make amends" under the pressure of public opinion. But "public opinion does not exercise sufficient social pressure to force public services to change their methods." [1] How could it be different? To the same extent that politicians can do nothing without the administration, and practically nothing in opposition to it, the citizen's control over the choice of politicians serves no purpose because our genuine political problem is this particular state structure, and not, for example, the war in Algeria or the *force de frappe*. The antinomy between bureaucracy and democracy is well known and has been extensively studied. The illusion is to believe that bureaucracy can be controlled democracy.

Yet, new notions of popular democracy coincide well with those of totalitarian bureaucracy; democracy is no longer actu-

---

[1] *Le Monde,* July 14, 1964.

ally a means of controlling state power, but of organizing the masses. The error lies in believing that "democratic control" really works; "democratic control" is impotent with respect to the administrative state. But it is simple to change a word's content and make the masses accept a new stereotype. (Once democracy becomes the device for controlling the "demos," there is complete harmony, for this control will be effected by the intermediary of state and party administration.) But back to the "democratic control." How can one hope to control the state? Certainly not by universal suffrage. True, we no longer accept the simple beliefs of 1789 or 1848, according to which such suffrage expressed the national will and permitted the designation of true popular representatives, controlled the government's acts and decisions, was the fairest method of se-lecting rulers, and so on. All this has been progressively aban-doned, if not in popular methods and beliefs, at least in the minds of those reflecting on political problems. Experience has well shown that the right to vote does not create power—in no way affords true control; that the uncertainty of public opinion on all questions is such that falling back upon its formal ex-pression to solve a political question is meaningless. To be sure, it is still held that the vote symbolizes the citizen's participation in public life, and permits him—though in inadequate fashion— to express his opinions on some questions. But these are illusory manifestations, for this is a participation in what is no longer real power and the expression of opinions on matters that are spectacular but unreal most of the time.

Finally: TV's effect on politics is being much discussed. The televised transmission of parliamentary sessions, the direct ex-posure of politicians, the possibility a statesman has to show his face to everybody when making a speech—all this, it is argued, provides some sort of direct democracy.

As we have noted, however, this entirely passive role of the citizen has nothing to do with a working democracy. Such TV transmissions illuminate precisely the division discussed above: on the one hand, there is the political spectacle, on the other, the reality of power. TV accentuates the spectacle, and makes it all the more special because it gives the individual the impression of life itself, of reality directly seized. He will say: "Political affairs? Of course. I've seen this important debate in the Assembly, where everybody played his role so seriously. The State? Of course. General de Gaulle or Mendès-France talked to me yesterday over the TV." All that is just a spectacle, appearance without root, a game. And precisely because all this is only a game, such a telecast is possible. The real political mechanism—the state structure—remains completely hidden, outside of all control; all the more so as the flickering little screen fixes the individual's attention on the spectacle, and prevents him from searching deeper, and asking himself questions on the true nature of power.[2]

Finally, Giovanni Sartori's excellent study demonstrates clearly how political people, and particularly the members of parliament, cannot play the role of controller. He rightly adduces the fact that they are forever overburdened and lack time. Members of parliament suffer from chronic overwork and are forced "to avoid basic choices." Sartori explains well how in any conflict between the "parliamentary and political state" and the "bureaucratic state" (they are not two separate entities but a blend) the problem of knowing "who wields the power" or "who controls whom" in the democratic structure is only a minor "family quarrel." "Whether we ask if parliament controls the government, or the parties control parliament, or a presidential system is needed, the fact remains that essential sectors and entire spheres of power escape all control; the fact is that the very size of the object to be controlled threatens to overwhelm the controller, and that the bureaucratic state's elephantinism escapes the control of the democratic state more and more merely by virtue of its dimensions." But the solutions proposed by Sartori to give true control to parliament seem to me inapplicable.

---

[2] Focusing on deeper causes also completely escapes doctrinaire Communists, who are convinced that they have a simple, coherent, and universal explanation when they reduce the entire state problem to the concept of the class struggle.

[V]

THE POLITICAL ILLUSION: PARTICIPATION

Another aspect of the political illusion is to believe that the citizen *can* effectively participate in political life. In considering the problem of competence, we are told, for example, that it is not necessary to be an expert in order to reach an over-all judgment on the atomic bomb or some other international problem. This is a fallacy. Even to pose questions in simplified form, in which they demand merely an over-all judgment, is an error. The citizen following his inclination will always say he does not want war—never. Egotism, comfort, tranquillity are his criteria. But the citizen lacks the imagination to foresee where that attitude will lead him. He is forever startled by the results, by the fact that a Munich pact in 1938 leads to a war in 1940.[1] Simone

---

[1] Justice Holmes: "I do not know the truth, or the meaning of the universe. But in the midst of doubt, in the crumbling of beliefs, there is one thing I do not

de Beauvoir tells us that an individual needs not the least competence, or even information, to participate in democracy; the vote
is a matter of feeling and instinct.

Very impressive on this subject are Sartre's statements. In the
political domain he holds the same opinion he expressed in a
debate on dialectics in November, 1961, when he said to a phy-
sician: "Be quiet! Only we philosophers understand this matter." This formula explains his constant mixing in political
affairs of which, by his own judgment, he knows nothing. Even
if he does not really mean it, his avowed incompetence in
political affairs [2] must be taken seriously, all the more as it is
reflected in his constant, mistaken assertions.[3] . . . Such
admission of incompetence emerges more frequently in involun-
tary ways,[4] as in the recantations and superficial judgments expressed in all of Sartre's political articles.[5] Yet this man, who
declared himself incompetent, and really was, and still is,
formulated at the same time watchwords for the young and
insisted that positions must be taken and that every intellectual
worthy of the name must commit himself. All that is simply
ridiculous. On the commitment of these "incompetent intellectuals" the reader is referred to an excellent analysis by Georges
Lavau,[6] and particularly to the very characteristic example of
Olivier de Magny: the latter describes the contemporary intellectual's situation as one in which knowledge of the world and
men is impossible. For the intellectual, says Magny, everything
is false nowadays—"the order of society, liberty, justice, our psy-

---

doubt—that there is something admirable and true in the faith that makes a
soldier obediently risk his life, accepting his duty blindly for a cause he does not
comprehend, in a campaign of which he has not the slightest understanding, and
according to tactics whose purpose is obscure to him."

And Nietzsche: "Every time a war breaks out in our era, there also breaks
out—particularly among our people's noblest sons—a secret desire: they expose
themselves to the new threat to life, because in their sacrifice for their country
they believe they have found, finally, permission to pursue what they never
ceased to seek, to escape their human destiny. For them war is an easier form
of suicide, it permits them to commit suicide with a clear conscience."

[2] *Les Temps modernes*, No. 184, pp. 320, 324, 349.
[3] Ibid., pp. 313, 314, 325, 328, 347.
[4] Ibid., pp. 330, 334, 338 *ff*.
[5] Bellecave: "Évolution de la pensée politique de Jean-Paul Sartre," 1960.
[6] See the article by Georges Lavau in Georges Vedel (ed.): *La Dépolitisation:
Mythe ou réalité* (Paris: A. Colin; 1962), pp. 183, 189.

chological knowledge of beings, even our language," which did not keep Magny from signing some important political manifestos. This is the perfectly irrational jump into the absurd, but, alas, with all the necessary war paint of good feelings, virtues, and values. Our committed incompetent intellectuals are precisely at the level of the *Credo quia absurdum*. What we are offered here is, in reality, a propaganda-democracy in which the citizens decide nothing because they are organized in a rigidly structured mass, manipulated by propaganda, and limited to endorsing with enthusiasm all decisions taken in their names or to pronouncing with authority all that has been suggested to them. We know, after all, that Simone de Beauvoir considers the Castro regime a democracy.

I am not repeating the traditional criticism of democracy which comes from the Right or authoritarian parties. On the contrary, I shall deal only with opinions held by people in sympathy with democracy. It is significant that Tibor Mende—an avowed democrat—should be able to say on the subject of India: "On the one hand, democracy is valuable as an educational process in shaping a national feeling and reducing particularism, and commanding international prestige and respectability [he apparently thinks that democracy as a regime has no value in itself!]; on the other hand, democracy is doomed in India, in the face of its techno-economic problems."[7]

This evaluation is shared by a large number of recent works on Africa, so much so that the following analysis does not apply to any one country, no matter how much it may be influenced by the French model. For example, a report by the Stanford Research Institute[8] shows that the same problems exist in the countries of the *tiers monde*.

In a democracy in which state propaganda is limited, citizens who believe in democracy and cherish their rights believe that they share in state power. There are elections, referenda, articles, petitions, motions by associations, or group discussions in which they participate. As a result, they believe themselves to be fa-

---

[7] Tibor Mende: "Les Élections indiennes," *Le Monde,* March 8, 1962.
[8] "Évolution du progrès scientifique et politique étrangère des U.S.A.," in *Bulletin* s.e.d.e.i.s. (1962).

miliar with their political problems. They believe that they can participate in politics, and what they propose can be seen in the letters to the newspapers, for example; these are not subjective "opinions," but solutions claimed to be well documented, convincing, and thought out. But for that the citizen would have to be well informed. The doctrine relating democracy and information is well known. This doctrine is surely accurate from the general and theoretical point of view, but as I said in Chapter III the illusory character, not only of information, but of politics inside this new universe of mental images—the only one in which the modern citizen resides—renders this doctrine illusory.

It must also be asked whether the citizen *desires* to participate. This is a problem different than that of depolitization. It is a cultural problem. It seems that the citizen of today wants to assume the least possible responsibility for the state. To be sure, he wants to express his views on all great questions, and he demands to be taken seriously, but he refuses at the same time to be an active and constructive participant in the power structure or to consider himself responsible for political actions and events.[9] He debates and protests, but takes on nothing. This absence of any desire to participate is partly caused by the displacement of contemporary man's centers of interest. Less fervent now with regard to the great democratic demands of the past, less animated by the requirements of social justice—progress having been made in that area—the citizen is now much more occupied with his job, his security. And, whereas he expects such security from the state, he fails to see what his responsibility to the state is. Results of polls on depolitization are therefore quite misleading; the citizen will always say that he *is* interested in politics, but there is a wide gulf between that interest and active participation.

In this connection a problem of considerable magnitude must be considered, and I will not claim to do more than just raise the issue. It is the current conception—accepted as entirely

---

[9] Max Frisch: "Évolution de la Démocratie en Europe," in *Bulletin* S.E.D.E.I.S. (1964).

natural—that as the state becomes more structured, stronger and more encompassing—with the whole structure tied to a democratic concept of power—the more the citizens participate and come politically of age; as though the growth of the state's political function were reflected in those participating in that function, i.e., the citizens, and thus given validity. Following from this, it is regarded as obvious that the more the living standard rises and the more liberal the form of government becomes, the more the citizens are able to exercise their political function. These are two premises of a general view according to which citizens come more and more of age politically. But these two points do not seem at all certain or demonstrable. Men have reached a high degree of political maturity without participating in a state organism or attaining a high living standard, as for example the Bantus of the sixteenth century, the French anarcho-syndicalists, the Ukrainians in the nineteenth century, the Irish, and the Spanish anarchists. Rather, it seems that the more organized the state becomes, the more its institutions become streamlined and its economy planned, the more it becomes necessary to eliminate the politically mature citizen who is independent and thoughtful and acts on his own. Actually, he is asked to demonstrate *another political maturity*, i.e., participation and allegiance; and, at best, he is granted some right to political resistance within limits and in fields set by the technicians or the state. But there can no longer be specific political maturity that entails radical disagreement.

It seems, on the contrary, that the growing state (even the democratic state) can do nothing with such genuine dissenters except eliminate them. Inevitably such people deal with politics at the direct level of man and his experience and reject generalizations and abstractions. They will not let themselves be trapped in choices established by technical organisms. They interfere with the power game. Precisely because they are mature, they tend to become obstacles to good political organization; the state feels the need to eliminate them because they can be neither used nor integrated. For that reason, anarcho-syndicalists *and* Ukrainians were eliminated. Let us recall that for the latter, history is particularly edifying: the Ukrainians, after having violently opposed the tsarist regime and then the Austro-German occupants, also rejected a totalitarian national-ist government, fought against Denikin's and Wrangel's White Armies, and finally against the Red Army trying to absorb them. Here was an example of very strong political organization and genuine participation, not on a nationalist basis, but on the basis of generally shared political values. They resumed strug-gling against the Nazi troops in 1942, contrary to what has often been said, and, after 1944, against the Soviet troops. A modern government cannot tolerate the survival of such strong political autonomy, based on the group members' political maturity: such maturity inevitably leads to the search for some degree of independence from the state.

Yet, it will be said, the citizen can effectively participate through the intermediary of political parties. But in this connec-tion many modern political scientists are skeptical, not only because of the internal transformation of parties or the almost universal failure of new parties in almost all countries, even if they are energetic and try to think in political terms, but also because the function of political parties has changed; in the democratic game, parties are nowadays only groups maneuver-ing for the purpose of capturing political power for some team.[1] There no longer is a living force for political judgment or in-spiration; inside the party, there is no longer true thought. Old positions are preserved, obsolete thoughts remain what they were, and teams brought to power by different parties really follow the same policies because they are conditioned by ele-ments and means that have nothing to do with doctrines. The great choices are outside of party reach. The citizen who thinks that he is participating in political life because he shares in the

---

[1] This change is unmistakable. André Philip (in *Pour un socialisme humaniste*) describes this decline very well as far as the quality, number, and devotion of militant party members is concerned. He stresses that public meetings are poorly attended. He shows what keeps the parties going: the "machine," organization, the *apparat*. A small handful of cadres is invested *a priori* with general confidence. But it must be considered that participation in elections depends on group membership. The group exercises pressure upon the members to vote; see Seymour M. Lipset: *Political Man* (Garden City, N.Y.: Doubleday; 1960), Chap. iv. This pressure is felt increasingly as the vote loses its significance.

activities of some party committee or attends some meeting gives in to the most pitiful illusion; he confounds party activity with participation in real political affairs.

This raises questions about the entire problem of being politically committed. It is understandable and honorable that average citizens of one political inclination or another should join a party and then think themselves engaged in politics while their illusion is fed by the press, politicians' speeches, and their sincere attachment to democracy. The reasoning is: "Democracy is good. To have democracy, the citizen must participate; thus, what I am doing is my form of participation; it is real. Not to do it would be to despair of everything. . . ". That is normal, and an individual easily succumbs to this temptation if he has democratic inclinations. But the fact that intellectuals reinforce this spontaneous response with their theory of political engagement and avoid reality in truly amazing fashion can be understood only at least to some extent, when viewed as a result of the marginal role played by the philosopher in our times —and also as a compensation and justification for the satisfaction of psychological needs. Sartre proclaims his theory of political commitment only to vent his personal complexes, without reference to political reality; this also is, without doubt, one of the important reasons for the success of his invitation to political engagement, which is a means of fleeing reality in the name of a pseudo-reality.

A strange process of obliteration is in progress today among the existentialists and phenomenologists. They set up general theories that they claim apply to man's concrete situation in the world, but end up by saying precisely the opposite of what sciences designed to perceive reality can possibly conclude. It is remarkable that speeches by these philosophers on the subject of history never are based on historical science or what it can teach us about historical events. The modern philosopher does not speak to us of what happened in the past or constituted the course of history. He seeks a key to the understanding of history, and to that purpose constructs an historical idea, or, rather, a myth. This myth then provides him with the key! When producing their philosophy of history, Hegel and Marx, like Montesquieu, took as their points of departure the given historical facts as they were known in their time. But that method now is regarded as too tenuous; known facts are increasingly contested and replaced. It is obviously safer and easier to disregard facts altogether and abandon oneself to historical romanticism; that approach has assumed increasing power and meaning and in the modern philosopher's metaphysics almost occupies the role of the ancient gods. In our day, at the very moment when the impact of psychological and sociological findings—similar to the impact of the physical and biological findings of the nineteenth century—make us think that man is rather rigorously determined by his milieu, existentialism posits man as free—not in conflict with the necessity of these findings—but rather, endowed with a freedom that disregards the results of such factual studies and derives from the purely arbitrary and theoretical process of denial of the discernible facts. One cannot help thinking that such mental pirouettes, claiming to relate to what is real in man and inviting him to commit himself to what is real, are nothing but methods of escaping reality by the artificial creation of pseudo-reality. But it is along these lines that the entire process of existential political engagement proceeds.

A study of Sartre's and other texts thus reveals an entirely abstract approach to politics; these texts view political action without considering the state's reality or the actual political problems of our time. Such thoughts undoubtedly serve as a point of departure for a philosophy concerned with the need for free men to commit themselves in reality, but the reality is tailor-made to provide a good conscience on the one hand and prove man's freedom on the other. But Sartre's writings, particularly his palinodes, reveal something entirely different than even the slightest liberty. This very clever obscurantism is accepted by many young people because, politics being what it is in our day, they *need* to engage in politics, and *need* to find a meaning there.

But commitment, particularly to a party, rests not only on a philosophical impulse but also on two additional elements; first of all, on a framework of uncritical, unexamined, and uncontrolled presuppositions; it is assumed that parties have real influence on political affairs and can truly influence historical decisions. That is why, when the government, pushed by plain necessity, acts in one way or another, some party will glorify itself by saying: " . . . We have done this." When President de Gaulle signed the peace treaty for Algeria, the Communist Party took credit for it. People assume that their own party's actions are on the whole good in themselves, for parties are becoming increasingly intolerant and true discussion usually leads to schism. People therefore insist, as do the militant members in the lower ranks, that the party's actions are good; they assume, moreover, that their party will come to power and then exert its good influence. People believe, finally, that once their party has come to power, militant members in the lower echelons will be able to dictate their will to deputies and cabinet members, and through them make important decisions. How absurd!

The second aspect of commitment to a party is the personal, psychological aspect: the individual's need to find security and clear, ready-made judgments, i.e., a need to surrender. It cannot be stressed enough that commitment to a political movement or party entails the surrender of personal responsibility and freedom of judgment. To commit oneself is to indenture oneself. The citizen indentures himself, loses his freedom of action and his authenticity; he can then expect only to be in a creditor's clutches, and will lose the last ounce of his liberty. To join the army, for example, is sign and symbol of all commitment, i.e., to be entirely indentured. It means the integration of an individual into a well-oiled organized mechanism that can function only if fed with human flesh—the army is nothing without soldiers, the party nothing without militants; *Perinde ac cadaver* is the formula for those who are committed. But in the case of the Jesuits, with whom the formula originated, it was the result of a hard and ascetic exercise, of a break with nature; in the case of our political militants or soldiers, it is the result of their surrender as individuals. To be sure, this surrender coincides entirely with a great devotion and great mystique, with meetings every night until 2 A.M., pasting posters on walls, and fighting if necessary. But all that is only a bromide for the conscience, a means of fleeing from the true problems of politics by engaging in much activity and experiencing the illusory prestige acquired by belonging to a group. This false commitment is probably one of the most striking results of the political illusion.

This illusion is reappearing under a different form in the recent theory that if the universal suffrage fails to correspond to old ideas and doctrines, it at least permits a dialogue with the state: the governments must talk to the citizens who command votes. The talk, complaints, promises, slogans, and announced programs produce a dialogue. In this fashion—according to the theory—universal suffrage can become a means of decision when these decisions relate to simple choices—which is rather rare. Much could be said on the fallacious character of such dialogue, and such simple decisions are generally not in the cards. Only two observations need to be made: first, such dialogue would require a continuity of public opinion and an identity between that opinion and its expression at the polls, which is not at all the case, according to most public opinion specialists. Secondly, any such dialogue and the questions with which it would deal are exactly on the order of what is either necessary or ephemeral, as analyzed in the first chapter. We are here in the presence of plain illusion.

Finally, in the general contemporary effort to return to democracy some of its sense and value, there is an important trend among political scientists, ever since Schumpeter, which considers democracy not a choice among programs, ideas, or objectives, but only one among ruling groups, men charged with leading the game. First of all, that is diametrically opposed to the concept according to which the people themselves are to select the nation's broad objectives. But one must also ask: if the leaders are tied down by goals that have already been accepted and by their experts who dictate the means, is there really any sense in debating issues? Can the people really discern the technical and economic skills that will make one man the best person to implement a plan? This seems even more idealistic to me than the alleged choice people have regarding ideas, doctrines, or programs.

The future, it is said, will bring organized democracy. It will be said: Of course, the citizen alone can do nothing, his voice has no reach, he cannot stand up against the administration, he cannot make political choices, he is exposed to all the influences of propaganda, and at election time he allows his head to be turned by some clever speaker. . . But, must democracy be individualist? Is the popular will truly the sum of perfectly single individual voices? Must we not rather conceive of a democratic infrastructure, somewhat on the pattern of the old intermediary groups in society before 1789 in France—such as unions, political parties, youth movements; or the formation of a democratic administration and some very different pressure groups? The citizen would then express himself through and with the help of these intermediary groups. As these groups are powerful, they really can exert some influence upon the state. The latter, incidentally, asks for nothing better than to agree with people through such machines—with the more representative labor unions, for example. These groups, composed of smaller cells, are channels for popular support, which then reaches a higher level and, far from being lost, really exerts an influence. And a body organized in this fashion will select election candidates, as in the American political-party mechanism. This obviates upsets at election time which might otherwise be produced by some skillful speaker or negative local influence. This would then be "mediated choice" (as distinguished from the way in which Maurice Duverger first used that term). Through a whole series of steps, the choices made at the lower echelons—which are genuine choices, because effected in small groups after many sessions of information-dissemination and discussion—would reach the summit, and that national "summit" could then speak with authority, not only because it would be supported by large numbers, but also because it would represent the true will of the people. A genuine fusion of individual ideas would take place, a sort of amalgam of all impulses is obtained, providing the closest approximation of a group's will in the electoral body. In this fashion, democracy fulfills itself; the citizen is really and permanently consulted, and his demand is really heard. Such grass-roots groups can truly exercise their influence upon the state.

Does this idyllic picture correspond to reality? Is that the ideal that must be reached, the channel through which men must commit themselves? Why change the ideal, and why is the formulation of the general will by and through the sum of individual wills in the most individualistic fashion not equally good? It will be said that events have shown this ideal to be unattainable. But the facts already clearly show that organized democracy is no more democratic than individualist democracy, probably less so. Organized democracy is a theoretical vision whose real development reveals itself very clearly.

First of all, organized democracy can function only if the elements are in balance, and none tries to paralyze the others, as was the case with the Communist Party in Poland, Czechoslovakia, or Hungary, not to mention the American party machines that smother all opposition, or the mechanism of democratic centralism in the Communist parties, or of Soviet planning. All these are outside the people's reach, as everyone knows.

The concept of organized democracy neglects an anterior question of the greatest importance. René Rémond's study [2] shows very well how new groups enter upon the political plane and become political. But in this politization process the tendency seems to be that these essentially democratic groups are absorbed by previously established (and therefore autonomous) political activities rather established as independent bodies influencing politics from their own perspective. I am not convinced of what André Touraine's study of unions [3] calls a "countervailing power" and "anti-power" control. In reality, the growing integration of unions into the state mechanism makes them increasingly an element of state power, and their tendency is to reinforce that power; at that moment a union becomes a mechanism of organizing the laboring masses for the benefit of the state. It is not by itself a "counter-power"; it could be that only if it maintained its anarcho-syndicalist character.

Leaving the general problem aside and considering concrete examples, what do we see? [4] Take first the rank-and-file party

---

[2] In Vedel (ed.): *La Dépolitisation.*
[3] André Touraine: "Le Syndicalisme de controle," *Cahiers internationaux de Sociologie* (1960).

member and sections. Even in Communist Party cells there is considerable absenteeism at meetings. Is that the members' fault? Generally they fail to attend because they have contempt for such meetings, during which they cannot express themselves. They do not want to go so far as to leave their union or party, but they realize that participation is useless and fictitious. Actually, these meetings are supplied with information coming from the top, controlled by the local delegate's authority, and often by central directives. Those comprising an insistent opposition are ill received, and the leaders must either neutralize their objections or utilize their resistance.[5] I have yet to see in any group a true debate starting at point zero and taking all opinions into account. As it is, the motions that carry are always those made by the local delegates. An exceptional crisis is needed for things to be different. Another means of neutralizing the rank-and-file member is to plunge him into action. Most of the time he asks for nothing more. But from the moment he is sticking posters on walls, distributing pamphlets, or collecting signatures on a door-to-door basis he no longer thinks of debate or of assuming a dissident point of view.

At a higher level inside organized democracy, we see the national congresses held by such groups.[6] The convening of such congresses—the number of adherents and the relative importance of various local sections—rests on dubious factors to begin with. There is padding of membership lists, falsification of statistics, competition among sections, even in the best organized

---

[4] Contrary to current opinion, I believe that in France the political parties, even the traditional ones, are still powers with a real base. They have not been "broken," and will reappear immediately after de Gaulle. Anyone who saw the resurgence of the parties of the Third Republic in 1944–5 will be convinced of it. Cf. François Goguel: "La Vie politique dans la Vᵉ République," *Revue Française de Sciences Politiques,* Vol. xiii; cf. also M. Frisch: "Évolution de la Démocratie en Europe," in *Bulletin* s.e.d.e.i.s. (1964).

[5] Michels's analysis seems to be correct (*Les Partis politiques* [1913]).

[6] According to Joseph Schumpeter (in *Capitalism, Socialism, Democracy* [New York: Harper & Bros.; 1950], Chap. xxii), political parties in a democracy are only instruments in the competitive struggle for power: "If that were not so, it would be impossible for different parties to adopt the same program. The existence of parties makes it impossible for the mass of voters to act differently than Panurge's sheep, and represents an attempt at regularizing the modalities of political competition."

parties, such as the Communist Party. Moreover, when a congress meets, false procedures predominate. Even in the best parties and unions these procedural modes are nothing less than fraternal or amicable. This is probably a basic shortcoming of all organized democracy: the relationships among the men of the same party or union are fundamentally those of competition, defiance, mistrust, and war to the hilt (for either personal or doctrinal reasons). There is no basic reason why these men should control their spontaneous feelings or desire for power; their adherence to the same ideology will not have that effect. Sympathizers with the Communist Party—in which alleged fraternal feelings are greater than elsewhere—have all been shocked by seeing these comrades, so united at one moment, denounce, ostracize, and insult each other as though human feeling did not exist per se, but was merely a function of allegiance to some ideology.

Everybody knows the methods and techniques practiced at national congresses to prevent the opposition from expressing itself: drowning them out, passing motions when nobody is in the hall, pushing votes through by surprise, obtaining decisions giving a free hand to headquarters, publishing texts at a time when the congress is not yet over, and so on. No national party or union congress reflects the will of the rank and file, and all use the classic tricks, now further refined by the knowledge of group dynamics.

Added to this is the bureaucratization of unions, parties, movements—even such volatile movements as student organizations. The cadres become specialists; they are separated both from the grass-roots militants and the professions they represent; they are then hierarchized and appointed labor or political professionals: they make a career. Why should they permit themselves to be ousted or replaced by grass-roots movements? They master the rank and file rather well and generally receive new votes of confidence from them. They supervise recruitment and distribute posts and other plums to their faithful followers. The more they are consulted by administrations or governments, the greater their capacity to exert pressure upon their adherents will be. Practically, they are undisplaceable.

At the top, we see a phenomenon reminiscent of bureaucracy, though much less stabilized. But the top of a party or union is as undemocratic as any true bureaucracy, though in a different way, because of its habit of speaking on political problems in the names of all, although actually nobody has been consulted. At periodic intervals we see some proclamation in the newspapers according to which some party or union, speaking in the name of all shoemakers, or intellectuals, or Europeans, takes a position on torture in Algeria, or the defense of the West, or some other subject. Such declarations have rarely been submitted in advance to those concerned, and when they are, it always is much too late for them to respond. Still less do they reflect the real desire of the individuals they allegedly represent. Invariably they are ukases concocted in at headquarters by five or six head speakers, members who consider themselves entitled to make decisions.[7] Doing that, they are like deputies who, once elected, often vote for bills by no means desired by their

---

[7] Pierre Mendès-France (in *La République moderne* [Paris: Gallimard; 1964], pp. 171 *ff.*), describing the structure of unions, implicitly agreed that they are authoritarian organisms. To be sure, he retained the democratic vocabulary when he said so. But that vocabulary is in contradition with the facts. He states: "A union's efficiency does not depend on the number of workers in its ranks, but on a series of direct and indirect effects. . . ." The latter in no way represent the will of the rank and file, but are the result of its habit of following authoritarian elites. It would be better to recognize the matter frankly, as does Tixier, and stop fooling oneself about "union democracy."

There is no question that as a result of their internal organization, unions resemble not democratic bodies but authoritarian, one-party regimes. Their oligarchical system is not the result of some abuse, but, as Lipset has well demonstrated, a necessity; these are vast organizations that can function only when they have a strong, competent, and rigid bureaucratic structure. They represent collective responsibilities, which is why they must have continuity in political life. The more they are in contact with patronizing state elements, the more they must structure themselves on the latter pattern (S. M. Lipset: *Political Man* [Garden City, N.Y.: Doubleday; 1960], p. 394). Lipset has also shown how information inevitably is held back by union leaders and allowed to filter down only through them, so that members cannot have freedom of opinion. Finally, for ideological and sociological reasons, the leaders must continually reinforce their own power and not leave room for democratic interchange. This is an example of the ever-present choice in our society: either the unions become efficient in their actions, strikes, and participation in economic and political life, in which case they become totalitarian, centralized, and bureaucratic, or they remain democratic and unstructured, in which case they cannot do more than stage a local rebellion or engage in fragmented opposition.

Union discipline increasingly insists that if the union is to be efficient there must be no opposition or minority in it. For that reason, a clergyman counseled his union parishioners to join the majority, as the aim no longer was to express individual opinions, but to achieve efficiency.

electors. But union representatives are much freer than deputies. The latter often encounter resistance from other deputies and are forced to submit their reasons; and the bills on which they vote, being only partially of their making, are the products of amendments and log rolling, whereas papers signed by party or union officers are drawn up completely arbitrarily and without any counterweight.[8] Finally, deputies risk not being re-elected if they act too often against their constituents' will (though this happens rarely), while union or party members—just because they control the machine—have a very good chance of maintaining themselves in their positions. But, aside from this independence, there is a considerable difference between certain movements, federations, unions and the dputies of parliament. A deputy speaks in the name of the people who, in his party, have embraced a certain ideology, and he speaks only in the name of party members.

But in an organized democracy the normal way for a citizen to express himself is through his group. Each citizen must belong to one or even several groups; he can act more consistently that way than through sporadic elections. The party then becomes an instrument for organizing the masses through meetings and petitions, and not just for winning elections.[9] In such a case, the group will feel entitled to speak in the name of a much larger category of citizens than it actually represents. To take a fictitious example, posit that the union of metal workers comprises only 10 or 25 per cent of all metal workers. The organization will claim to represent a social or professional group, but

---

[8] But, the objection will be, these groups hold annual congresses examining the policy followed by their officers and criticizing it. The officers are responsible to the congress. This is true, but experience shows that, first, proclamations by the officers are generally forgotten two or three months later and do not come under discussion; second, that the congress's composition is so modeled by the general secretariat as to produce a sure majority for the head office. Criticism producing change in officers is extremely rare in parties or unions. If the opposition is too strong, it generally provokes a schism.

[9] Giovanni Sartori (in "L'Avenir des Parlements," *Bulletin* s.e.d.e.i.s. [1964]) stresses the party machine's importance in the professionalization of politicians. Which type of politician is becoming predominant? The one who "becomes" professional because he has been re-elected several times, or the one who is "born" that way, and has therefore made a career in his party? In the latter case, which seems the more prevalent, the politician is a party bureaucrat. In that case, the state will be (partly) controlled by political parties, but the citizen will have still less chance to make himself heard.

it is only the movement's boss who declares it to be that unless the state itself attributes some such designation to a union by regarding it as a representative body. From then on, even those who do not belong are publicly assigned opinions that are not theirs. It is agreed [1] that "those who do not belong to a group have only themselves to blame for not being there. They need only join and enter into the debates; they will surely be heard when some resolution is under discussion. Moreover, as membership in a union is a sign of considerable political consciousness, those who speak are really the most capable and intelligent persons. It is therefore valid that they speak in the name of all." The first part of this statement is unacceptable; it presupposes that this type of group is legitimate in itself, that the individual is of no importance at all, and that there is no political activity except in adherence to a group. It also presupposes that in such groups minorities can affect official decisions. The second part of the argument is equally false, primarily in its reference to the past. True, in 1880, a union was the laboring class's most developed, intelligent, active, voluntary, and revolutionary party; at that time political conscience had a positive side. But all that is completely past. Today adherence to such groups and movements is on the order of sociological coagulation. Surely the members are not those with the highest moral and social conscience or the deepest political sense. It is even probable that those with the strongest conscience and the greatest knowledge of political affairs refuse to enter these machines, which fabricate conformism. The same goes for those who are very committed to professional or social activities and are afraid of the enormous amount of time lost in union or party meetings. It

---

[1] I entirely disagree with Goguel and Grosser (*La Politique en France* [Paris: A. Colin; 1964]), when they accord political primacy to that minority which actually belongs to a political party. They think that the militants are better entitled to be heard by the regime than the broader mass of indifferents. This seems tragically dangerous, for the militant is often on a lower level and more narrow-minded than the non-militant; and the passion he has for his "cause" usually prevents him from seeing true political problems. Grosser and Goguel are equally mistaken if they think that the militants, who are in contact with their fellow citizens, are therefore better able to translate their aspirations into deeds; the militants interpret other people's opinions through the colored glasses furnished them by their party. There is no reason to assume that the militants express the political will better than the non-militants, especially if we consider the *actual* reasons for their belonging to a party.

may be said: A man of strong personality will always eventually influence the group and make himself heard; therefore people should commit themselves. To this the answer is: Yes, but at the price of how many compromises and maneuvers? Automatic triumph is not of virtue and truth, but of procedures and techniques. Perhaps something can be done in such an organization, but at the price of how much lost time? After how many years? Eventually, the time spent in such groups prevents a normal life and forces the participant to become a professional. And if he wants no part of that?

In reality organized democracy, nowadays presented as future democracy, is nothing but the establishment of a feudal system, structured differently than a system based on landed estates, but with all the sociological characteristics of traditional feudalism; and the professional organization of parties, unions, and movements perfectly represents the hierarchy of the new lords.

A one-party system is not needed to reach that point. France is reaching it at a rapid rate. One aspect remains—the opposition of various factions. They exist; from time to time some opposition arises, and therefore it will be said that the system is not as closed as I have described it. The answer to that is, first, that the system is not yet fully established—far from it. But the principal point is that ordinarily these oppositions and quarrels do not spring from any initiative at the lower echelons. Wherever factions make their appearance in political parties or trade unions, such opposition arises in the executive organs. Some leader, often for purely personal reasons, comes into conflict with other leaders and submits his resignation. Then there is excitement at the rank-and-file level and the members are confronted with choices whose real causes they generally fail to know; they will then follow the man they like best. Obviously, a deviationist at the top will often claim to act at the instance of members or because he knows their secret aspirations, but those are mostly excuses.[2]

---

[2] The critique I have presented of organized democracy is, I think, in no way disproved by articles devoted to it in *Démocratie aujourd'hui* (1963) or *La Démocratie à refaire* (1963).

There still remains Seymour Martin Lipset's theory: a group of associations of oligarchic character contributes to maintaining democracy. For society to be democratic, it is not necessary that the democratic rule be applied inside the organisms that constitute it. Unions, for example, represent the general interests of their members, who do better by joining unions than by remaining at the mercy of industry (i.e., the worker has the choice between two forms of submission, either to the union boss or to industry); all the associations combined represent the divergent interests of all society; whereas every one of these associations limits the individual's freedom, it gives the leaders a much greater *real* freedom. This conception of democracy is really very touching, for it literally reproduces the description of feudal society. Still, it would be necessary to measure the distance between a regime resting on individual judgments and a regime resting on the interplay of groups authoritatively organized and confronting each other. To be sure, the feudal system can be called a democracy, as that word can be used for just about anything. This is neither more or less absurd than the famous formula of the constitution of the revolutionary year XII: "The government of the republic is entrusted to an emperor." But it is the same thing.

It must be added that the state, with its unlimited technical means and its claim to represent the general interest, necessarily gets the better of *all* these groups. Each of these groups represents limited, special interests. Thus the functioning of democracy, no better assured by such an organization, remains very theoretical. Not too much should be made of the difference between this "organization" of intermediary groups, which are really part of a centralizing social function, and the spontaneous existence of intermediary groups representing countervailing influences limiting state power on the surface. These local and intermediary powers have disappeared, leaving the field open for democratic authoritarianism.

This leads us to a final question: how can anyone fail to see the profound similarity between this "organized democracy" and the older conceptions of the reconstitution of intermediary social bodies, the institutionalization of natural social bodies and live forces? Put differently: between a Vichy system and a

corporate state system? The ideology of organized democracy
may well claim to be to the Left; it strangely resembles the best
in Charles Maurras.[3] The fact that this organization relies on
parties and unions does not change the general sense of the
operation or the over-all conception of the relationship between
state and society. Words have no magic power and cannot hide
reality.

On the subject of organized democracy we often hear talk of
democratic or popular administration. To be sure, no precise
content is ever given to such formulas. In what I have read on the
subject, I have discovered no trace of reality behind the words
that are being bandied about. What do they mean? Of course,
allusions are still made at times to administration directly by the
people themselves. And the grand memories of the Paris Commune and the Terror are evoked. But generally these views have
been abandoned. It is recognized that in reality those experiments were failures and that there simply was no functioning
administration during those periods. The result was administrative arbitrariness, the destruction of regular procedures and
controls, and finally the creation of the local administrative
dictatorships that were much more crushing and senseless than
the orderly administration described so far.

One may also think of control over the administration by an
all-powerful popular party. We have already envisaged such a
case. Others again would consider an administration democratic
if its leaders were recruited from the lower social strata. Napoleon recruited his administration from the bourgeoisie in order to turn it into an authoritarian instrument par excellence;
Marxists consider that every political effort on the part of
the proletariat is broken by an administration recruited from the
bourgeoisie. An administration is, in the view of Marxists, the
result of its class character, and to democratize the recruitment
of its members would solve the problem! That is an entirely
theoretical and abstract view. The machine cannot be modi-

[3] Maurras (1868–1952) was an extreme Rightist who served a prison sentence
for his collaboration with the Vichy government.—Trans.

fied or the bureaucratic system altered in its principles and its characteristics by changing its members.

Three things can be said on this subject: manifestly, in France, since 1945, there has been a very large government recruitment, and "democratization" is accelerated not for doctrinal reasons, but because the number of functionaries is growing so rapidly. But at such a moment the bureaucratic system becomes more and more "itself"! My second remark concerns proletarian administrations: the administrative recruitment in the Soviet Union and the People's Democracies has in no way led to a different type of administration—bureaucracies there are entirely traditional, and even the Soviet authorities confirm this. Thirdly, the attitude of administrative personnel recruited from popular and proletarian milieux changes as soon as they are given a little authority; they become just as, if not more, rigorous and bureaucratic than personnel recruited from any other milieu.[4] Employees of the social security system or post office, sheriffs and customs' officers, are classic examples of bureaucratic authoritarianism. Officials not recruited frm the popular class are more subtle and ready to shed their bureaucratic comportment. It is well known that those who have risen from the ranks are more rigid, like the Africans who, when given some power, treat their brothers as "dirty niggers." The business tycoon who has risen from the laboring class is hardest on his workers.

Finally, the failure of French colonization, for example, is not just the result of capitalist exploitation, but also of the poor quality of the administrative personnel that represented France, though generally these members of an inferior administration had been recruited directly from the people. Absolutely no change in the bureaucratic state can be expected as a result of a change in personnel. The latter is absorbed by the machine and transformed by the structure it enters.

---

[4] This is demonstrated in Lipset's important study (*Political Man*), which shows that popular milieux and the laboring class in particular are pervaded by an authoritarian attitude. The Communist Party's authoritarian structure is neither a deviation nor a historical accident but the expression of a definite tendency of the laboring class, particularly in countries in the process of rapid industrialization.

Eventually, any democratic administration inevitably redis-
covers the idea of administrative decentralization. Of course such
"local freedoms" are desirable; in fact, local autonomy is essential. But, first of all, there is very little likelihood of true
decentralization taking place; it runs counter to the entire course
of our society, and there is not the slightest indication of a
reversal in that respect. Above all, such decentralization could
take effect only in local communities and departments. But
these are only a secondary aspect of an administration. The
great administrative forces such as finances, police, propaganda,
and the administration of science and technology, cannot be
truly decentralized. They demand a carefully worked-out
national organization, not diverse centers free to make
autonomous decisions. An economic plan can include the establishment of decentralized organs, but it does so only within a
perfectly centralized framework. One cannot see, therefore, how
there can be true decentralization if a local organ, except for
certain details and relatively unimportant technical means, is
held to do and execute what has been decided beforehand.
Therefore the term "popular administration" or "democratic
administration" is nothing but a hollow formula with only a
purely emotional content.

[VI]

THE POLITICAL
ILLUSION:
"POLITICAL
SOLUTIONS"

---

1. Politics as General Solution

One more aspect of the political illusion resides in the conviction, anchored in the heart of modern Western man, that ultimately all problems are political, and solvable only along political lines. Without repeating what I have already said on this belief held by modern man, or on the influence of Leninist thinking in this direction, let us just look at one example: We all feel that when a man is "bad," it is "society's fault."

Studies on criminals and other antisocial elements have no

other aim but to demonstrate that "it is not *their* fault." Guilt
and responsibility rest with the milieu, the social body, the par-
ents, housing, the cinema, circumstances. With all of us. We are
all murderers. Conversely, people are convinced that if society
only were what it should be, there would be no criminals or
other antisocial elements. And who, according to the average
modern man, should reorganize society so that it would finally
become what it should be? The state, always the state. In this
fashion the entire problem of morality is thrown back upon the
state, even by non-Marxists. Morality, like values, resides in the
political realm. We want to attain justice, liberty, and even—
through science and information—truth. But what is the average man's attitude toward these goals? In his mind there is no
doubt but that the state can and must accomplish all this.
The state must assure social justice, guarantee truth in information, protect freedom (which leads to Tito's admirable abbrevi-
ation: the more powerful the state, the more freedom). The
state as creator and protector of values—that is the business of
politics.

Yet in all these domains we are facing the most tragic illusion
of our day. It is certain that politics can solve administrative
problems, problems concerning the material development of a
city, or general problems of economic organization—which is a
considerable accomplishment. But politics absolutely cannot
deal with man's personal problems, such as good and evil, or the
meaning of life, or the responsibilities of freedom. Of course we
also know that all these things are of no importance in the eyes
of most people. So be it. But then they should not be discussed,
and our ears should not be continuously assailed with stories
of tortures, the seizure of newspapers, democracy—for all that is
significant only if good and evil, the true and the just, or the
meaning of life and responsibility have personal value. Without
it, the torturer and the tortured are entirely impersonal, and
there is not the slightest sense in protesting, condemning, or
glorifying anything. Those who discuss the use of torture presuppose that it has a personal and not just a collective meaning.
But if that is the case, no solution can be found through political
channels, political action, or a transformation of the state. In

fact, if one disregards the mythological explanations in the post-Marxist style or the unconscious Marxist style, the enthusiasm with which everybody has reached for this convenient solution—existentialist intellectuals, reactionary businessmen, and petty bourgeois radicals—shows one common preoccupation: to escape personal responsibility in such matters. The conviction that the individual's inner conflicts, like the external realization of values, are a collective and social affair and will find their solutions in the political realms is only the mystifying aspect of every man's personal surrender with respect to his own life. Because I am incapable of doing good in my own life, I insist that the state must do it in my place, by proxy. Because I am incapable of discerning the truth, I ask the government to discern it for me; I thus free myself of an onerous task and get my truth ready-made. Because I cannot dispense justice myself, I expect a just organization to exist which I only have to join to safeguard justice.

Paul Johann Feuerbach's perfectly convincing proof of God can today be transferred to the subject that has taken God's place in modern man's conscience, i.e., the state. The motives, the processes, the mysteries that made man accept religion and expect God to accomplish what he was unable to do, lead him nowadays into politics and make him expect those things from the state. "But," it will be said, "in politics man is prompted to act for himself; he commits himself, sacrifices himself, takes his destiny into his own hands." It is easily forgotten that in religion, too, man was by no means passive; he acted a great deal, sacrificed himself even more, and engaged himself to the limit. And, looking at contemporary politics, we already have seen how little man really attains influence over his own destiny through it. In reality, he does not expect to accomplish this from politics, or from any person, but from a mysterious and superior power, invested with indefinable qualities such as sovereignty—a power which, by a sort of magic, transforms the citizen's poor efforts into something efficient, good, and absolute. As prayer will release transcendental forces, the voting ballot will move the sovereign will. But the latter assumption is no more reasonable than the former. We are all agreed that the sovereign will is not

simply a sum of individual wills. This is really a religious phenomenon. Political engagement is thus comparable to a religion.
Moreover, both terms have the same general tenor of "tying the
individual" (*in vadiam, religare*). This becomes a true flight
from oneself, from one's own destiny, one's personal responsibilities. On the one hand, we assume personal, collective, and social responsibilities: but they are never anything but vicarious
and secondary, external, even if the individual completely sub-
merges himself in them. They are never anything but a dis-
traction and are taken seriously only by those concerned with
the behavioral sciences. On the other hand, in the confrontation
with ourselves, we reject, hide, and flee all immediate responsibility vis-à-vis our neighbor. We find here the same mystifica-
tion, but in the reverse sense, as when Marxism rightly said that
personal virtue allowed men to forget their collective responsibilities or that charity allowed them to forget justice. Such
criticism was justified in the nineteenth century. Today this is
no longer the problem, for the same phenomenon takes place
under our eyes, but in reverse. To charge the social organism
with the solution of all one's personal problems and the realization of all one's values is to absent oneself from the problems
of the human condition.

   This mechanism, resulting from politization, presents two
aspects: first of all, it means that nobody is truly responsible or
has any real obligation with respect to justice, truth, or freedom,
which are the affair of organizations—a collective affair. It is not
"I do," but "one does." If our values are not attained, if things
go badly, it means that the organization is bad or that there is
a saboteur, a devil who prevents me from being just, in accord
with society's objective justice. We will then accuse this Enemy,
and also the state power, because state power must provide
all just organization and the elimination of the pernicious
enemy. This strenuous flight from the personal obligation to
accomplish, oneself, what is good and just is often accompanied,
in the case of intellectuals and Christians, by a corollary vice,
that of insisting on universal responsibility. To consider oneself responsible for the tortures in Algeria while actually being a
professor in Bordeaux, or for all hunger in the world, or for

racist excesses in various countries is exactly the same thing as
to reject all responsibility. What characterizes this attitude is
impotence in the face of reality: I really cannot do anything
about these things except sign manifestos and make declarations or claim that I act through political channels and establish a just order with the help of some abstraction. To say that
we are all murderers means, translated, that nobody is individ-
ually a murderer, i.e., that I am not a murderer. To admit that I
am co-responsible for all the evil in the world means to assure a
good conscience for myself even if I do not do the good within
my own reach. To admit that I am a dirty dog because, being
French, I am involved in the acts of all Frenchmen in Algeria,
means to free myself of the slightest effort to cease being a
dirty dog personally and to do so, moreover at the cheapest
price, namely by joining a political party or shouting in the
streets; in addition, I am assured of being on the right side of
those who want "the French" to cease being dirty dogs.
Clearly, the demands made on us by religion were more severe.
and all these proclamations of scruples, bad conscience, and
divided responsibility quickly resolve into the claim that the villain is on the other side—in the F.L.N., or the O.A.S., or the
Communist Party. And the same people proclaim both, without
seeing the contradiction. This contradiction reveals that we are
dealing here with a myth.

The second mythic element inherent in the politization of
problems and values springs from the facility with which all
things are relegated to tomorrow or the day after tomorrow. Because justice is a political matter, and will eventually be
brought about as a result of some new organization, why not
wait until tomorrow? People say: "Today we are only in a state
of preparation, in search of means; we are following tortuous
roads, but the direction is surely right. Injustices happen, but
only pending the achievement of greater justice. We are destroy-
ing freedoms, but we are preparing the ultimate freedom. We
are asking you, today, right now, you, the militant, to lie, kill,
jail; but you will be absolved of your deed by the grandiose
results.

You yourself will never see those results, as one, or two, or three generations must be sacrificed, but be reassured, your sacrifice will not have been in vain, your injustice will be compensated by the great justice to come." Here we have the individual, moral, and psychological aspect of the general ethical problem of ends and means. And with admirable facility everybody avoids the personal question of his own conduct by politicizing it. The more the solution is in the future, the more *everything* is permissible today.

Jouvenel [1] properly reminds us that "the myth that there is a solution obscures our understanding of politics, and in all such matters only precarious settlements can be reached by political means." A problem is composed of precise and known facts and can therefore be solved: for any arithmetical problem there must be a solution. But a political situation is not of that order; what makes it political is "precisely the fact that the frame of reference in which it exists does not permit any solution in the exact sense of that term. A true political problem arises only when the given facts are contradictory, i.e., when it is insoluble." A political problem permits only an accommodation, never a solution. There can be compromise, evolution, conciliation, various methods of using authority, and so on. But these are not solutions. Yet modern man increasingly demands solutions. Increasingly, the technicians insist on formulating problems of society as though they were exact problems permitting exact solutions. The growing myth of "solutions" progressively removes from our conscience the sense of the relative, i.e., limited, nature of all true political effort.

There is one final aspect: the politization of a genuine, existing problem permits us to avoid its reality, its depth, its human aspects.[2] On the political level, what one says and does may be just, even though one pays no attention to individual or human values. But any attempt to consider the individual as a human value makes it impossible to think of the problem in political

---

[1] Bertrand de Jouvenel: *De la politique pure* (Paris: Calmann-Lévy; 1963), pp. 248 ff.
[2] How true in this connection is Rubel's formula: "The conquest of political power is a bait and a trap: it is the death of the labor movement." (*Arguments,* No. 25)

terms. The Third Reich had no doubt that the Jewish problem had to be "solved." In the eyes of the Nazi chiefs it was a political problem. Therefore they could give an abstract order for the massacre. But all historians of the Third Reich report that Himmler fainted when he saw a few dozen Jews shot. At that point, the matter had suddenly become brutally human again. But in the ordinary course of the political process, the human aspects are generally hidden. Celebrating the Don Canal helped it hide the fact that it cost 100,000 human lives to build. The war in Algeria clearly demonstrated this function of politization.

Actually, the political point of view allows people today to escape values, to obliterate the reality of human situations which, are individual situations and therefore no longer of interest. What is true and real is hidden under politics; people carry posters and in a leisurely way discuss future plans and revolutions. Political considerations permit us to think that we have the "general solution" because they permit us to do away at one stroke with all human reality and the search for truth.

2. Politics as Attainment of Values

Concerning the problem of justice,[3] it is an illusion to think that justice can be attained by a political organization of any kind. First of all, concepts of justice and its content vary greatly among civilizations and even individual points of view. Communists insist that bourgeois justice is only class justice. But it can be demonstrated that the same class aspects prevail in justice as conceived in the Soviet Union or China. Let us therefore leave aside the problem of juridical justice and even that of social justice, the ambiguities of which are well known. Let us deal only with two aspects of justice that fall within the purview of politics: justice of opinion and justice of decision. These ob-

---

[3] We could also take other values: freedom, for example. Among the innumerable treatises on freedom, I cannot resist referring to R. Ikor's, which is accurate but shows a remarkable ignorance as to the nature of the modern, or the more recent, state. Does Ikor believe that since 1789 freedom has ever been anything but a revokable favor? And can he imagine a modern, technological state structure in which freedom would not be exactly that? What innocence!

viously only delineate "periods" in political affairs, but if we give up the idea that someday, in unexpected fashion, the state will create a finished society including absolute justice (which is the vision of all utopians and most militants—proof that they have been propagandized), we must also admit that in political affairs justice is in reality expressed in fragmentary, and in some way prophetic, fashion, *here and now*, in *one* just decision, in *one* just opinion. That is the justice which, effectively and at best, politics might attain.

Let us begin by taking a perhaps extreme example of the justice of opinion. How can justice be administered to the Hitler regime? To be sure, all that was said against him was true and entirely deserved. But let us ask what would have happened if Hitler had won. We then would never have heard anything of Hitler's concentration camps, the massacres, or the experiments on human beings. Instead, Stalin's crimes of 1945 would have been discovered, and he would have been considered a war criminal. The Russians would have been charged with genocide because of their concentration camps, their massacres in the Baltic countries, the Ukraine, and Rumania. (Let us remember that of the 100,000 German soldiers captured at Stalingrad and deported from there, less than 5,000 returned—all the rest died in Russian camps!) In victory, Hitlerism would have softened progressively, after having liquidated all the elements to be liquidated—such as communism. And ten years later the moderation of the chiefs, who by then would have relaxed their hold, would have been admired. Historically, the struggle between races rather than the class struggle would have then taken first place. The Nazi doctrine would have been deepened and broadened, eminent philosophers such as Heidegger would have made their contribution to it, and Marxism would have ceased to preoccupy the intellectuals. Christians, after having been violently opposed to the Nazi doctrine, would have progressively doubted the need to oppose Hitlerism, in the same way they came to doubt the need to oppose Marxism, which surely no longer ruffles the Christian conscience. And, thanks to propaganda, because people would have known little of Communism except its crimes—nothing of its love of justice, nothing of economic progress in the Soviet Union—and because people would have been submersed perpetually in National Socialist ideology, the latter would have appeared perfectly just at the end of ten years, and the well-known Nazi crimes would have been forgotten.

This extreme example—and the changes in attitude toward Communism between 1939 and 1950 are probably sufficient to make such description reasonable—reminds us that the concept of justice in public opinion is subject to extreme fluctuation, indecision, and variation according to circumstances, even while giving itself the strongest doctrinal assurances. It was exactly this vacillation that was apparent during the distressing years of the Algerian war. The justice of one's cause, invoked by both camps, was nothing but a pretext to cover up political opinions.[4]

We are dealing here not only with the fluctuating character of public opinion, but also with the strange mixture of ideas, influences, prejudices, justifications, and irrational learnings which we call "our" opinions. The *same* people were opposed to the personalization of power in de Gaulle's case in 1962 and in favor of such personalization in Ben Bella's case. People will immediately exclaim: "That has nothing to do with it! Such personalization is reactionary in de Gaulle's case, and progressive in Ben Bella's case." These are just words. Was personalization of power reactionary in Stalin's case? It is being condemned by the same people who condemn it in de Gaulle's. And *objectively* speaking it was not reactionary, despite all the talk on the subject, because exactly that personalization of power permitted the Soviet Union to advance along the road toward socialism and attain a situation considered by Khrushchev as approaching communism. What justice of judgment is there in these opinions? As a corollary we can confirm that a just opinion in the political domain is necessarily partisan and therefore cannot be just by itself, whatever definition one might want to give to the word.

With regard to the second aspect of political justice, i.e., just political decisions, in political affairs, justice is not a matter of

---

[4] See the excellent issue of *Esprit* on the subject.

objectives or situations but a matter of moments. The possibility of a political solution or decision being in fact just or unjust depends on the moment when it is made, and not on the concept of justice of those making it or on their good will or political inclinations. Let us assume, for example, that a just solution for some delicate political problem can be found at the beginning, when the problem begins to emerge, and the matter is in the process of becoming twisted—before it has burst forth full-blown, before the contest has really begun, before the entire procedure is caught up in an inexorable mechanism. A decision must be made before irreparable acts have been committed or public opinion has come into play. In the former case, the matter would have moved into an area of force and of demands that will be either refused or unsatisfactory; in the latter case, public opinion's demand for justice will have made its appearance and political passion will have entered; from that very moment all just solution will have been rendered impossible. An example of the first: the Hitler regime could have been eliminated without much trouble in 1934–5, and a subsequent well-weathered crisis would have permitted a cleansing of Germany's political life and, probably, a reconstitution of the country.[5] But after 1936 no just solution was possible. An example for the second case is the relationship between the Western and Arab worlds. In 1918 it would have been possible to find a sensible situation and to establish true justice in the Near East. But after 1919 that was no longer possible. The same goes for the war in Algeria; in 1954–5 a just and generally satisfactory solution was definitely possible, but after 1956 no just solution could be found. From then on, either the F.L.N. had to be crushed and millions of Arabs murdered or the European population had to be sacrificed because of the *de facto* victory by the F.L.N. (which is what actually happened).[5] Partition would not have been any more just, as the Mohammedans would have been pushed back into economically inferior regions.

But if this diagnosis is correct, under what conditions can a just solution be applied from the beginning, as soon as a political

---

[5] After the ravages of war and political aberrations.—Trans.

problem makes its appearance? There seem to be three conditions. Firstly, the existence of the intellectual capacity to anticipate the problem long before it emerges, to predict what threatens to become a problem from a mass of often minor indications. Such foresight need be neither prophetic nor superhuman. A good and well-informed political scientist can predict certain developments accurately. But continually less attention appears to be being paid to such efforts.

Secondly, a just solution would require the capacity to engage in actions not required here and now. In effect, it would not be *necessary* to intervene in a developing situation; intervention would, in fact, seem gratuitous (whereas our attitude now dictates that a hundred urgent events press in on us and demand attention). But a just solution can be found only if there is a considerable range of solutions. If, as a result of some development, choices have been progressively eliminated and, eventually, only one solution remains, inexorably imposing itself, such a solution will always be an expression of the strongest power supporting it, and *never* can be just. A solution imposed by necessity in political affairs cannot be just.

A third condition for any just solution is generosity. He who feels master of a situation must act generously with regard to the weakest party. A just solution can only be found if the strongest will give full consideration to the true situation of the weaker party, not in order to dominate him, but to help him to his feet. The elimination of the Hitler regime in 1935 would have been just only if the rest of Europe had helped provide Germany with a better economic and political life. The solution at that point would probably have been a united Europe.

But these three conditions seem impossible to meet. The more the technicians' power grows, the more technological and, to a lesser degree, economic foresight grows with it—but always at the expense of political foresight. There seems to be a contradiction between the technological order and the proper methods of political prediction. For example, the sterility of all studies concerned with political statistics is striking. Nonmathematical prediction is held in low esteem nowadays: it is allegedly nonscientific and therefore chancy. This is considered a deadly criticism. It implies in turn that genuine political thought is no longer appreciated.

Because of the attention that must be paid to public opinion, the second condition is even less possible to fulfill than the other two. Could any just solution have been found in 1934 with respect to Hitler? Indeed, but the French Right would have cried injustice; the Left did not want to risk war at any price; and French public opinion as a whole wanted no excitement, only comfort and quiet. Under such conditions, why mix into something that did not concern us? Could a just solution have been found in Algeria in 1954? Indeed, but the European Algerians did not want to make any concessions and most Frenchmen in France did not see why "these people" should be taken seriously. Actually, because of the curious role played by public opinion in political affairs, public opinion's *inertia* impedes all possible just efforts at the *beginning* and *once public opinion is aroused,* it immediately turns partisan and insists on unjust solutions. On the whole, partly because people are deluged with information and current events, any matter that has not yet been blown up and become irreversible cannot be taken seriously. People cannot take seriously the indications revealing an emerging drama; they will not be interested in it, will not accept any sacrifices in order that justice prevail. They will not accept a sacrifice while they are free to do so. The people will make any sacrifice demanded of them, but only when the drama has descended upon them fully, when the monster is at their doorstep, when straight and simple necessity demands it, and when they are completely propagandized, i.e., after a just solution can no longer emerge.

The problem of whether certain values can be realized through politics may be approached in another way. A fundamental contradiction exists between politics and justice. Politics, as said before, can act only with material or psychological force—with spiritual, ideological, or police constraint. A well-conducted political move can never produce anything but power—the institutions created by it are only ends or instruments of such power. But, it might be objected, is the politically interested citizen not eager to see this power controlled, rather than see its growth further promoted? This is a great illusion. The more an individual has become politized, the more he will see and think about all problems as political problems, the more importance will he attach to political action, and consider it the only possible course and, by his attitude, endow that course with a maximum of power and effectiveness. At the same time, the more politized he is, the more will he be focused on and oriented toward that basic political force and form: the state. The more he takes recourse to the state, the more power he gives it. For him the *only* problem is: *who* will control the state? Will it be *his* party? All will then be perfect. Will it be another party? Then things will be bad. But he never thinks of reducing the state *itself*—on the contrary. All he thinks of is to replace the incumbents. No minority wants to reduce the state's power. The last fifty years have shown that each minority attaining power increases the state's power in order to prevent its defeated opponents from using the same means it used to gain power. At each step, state power is increased. The people under the spell of politics seek less and less to control the state; politizing everything, they consider it normal that the state should constantly expand its area of action and use ever more instruments of power. This is legitimate in their eyes, as they believe that all will be solved by political action.

All the phenomena already described can be seen here: the autonomy of political affairs with regard to moral values; the conflict between values and increasing state power; the connection between means and ends. This combination reveals the tragically illusory character of the belief that any justice, truth, or freedom can be attained by entrusting these values to the state.

It might be objected that my examples are partial, my approximations too rough, and that political activities are not everywhere or always of this kind, that they are more differentiated, that excesses should not be taken as examples, and that, in any event, American and British democracy is entirely different. That is true. But the *significant* facts all point in the same direction. It also is a sign of our present political development that a growing number of military governments that are neither dictatorships nor democracies are being established in a growing number of countries. We must evaluate the facts that bear upon the future; that is what counts, not the current precarious maintenance of parliamentary democracies and liberal traditions.

[VII]

DEPOLITIZATION
AND TENSIONS

─────────────────────────────────────

─────────────────────────────────────

1. Depolitize?

The reader, who has had the patience to arrive at this point, will say: "All this is just another plea for apolitical attitudes. But is that truly a solution? If the state really conducts its political affairs as described here even while the citizens and various organizations participate, or at least try to participate, in politics, would that state not do still much worse if nobody tried to control it, if nobody were to interfere in its exercise of power? Depolitization is no solution. On the contrary." Fauvet, summarizing the opinions of hundreds of political scientists, says correctly:

> There is no democracy without political parties. . . . By rejecting these parties one makes a double political choice: one embraces the Right, which is not structured into parties, and one fights against democracy. Personalized power is the general law in contemporary political societies. It does not exclude de-

mocracy where organized parties and decentralized institutions counteract the weight that necessarily accumulates in the executive branch. It becomes a danger where nothing stands between personalized power and depolitized masses . . . Gaullism, by aggravating the political void and institutionalizing it may be preparing the road for an authoritarian regime.[1]

It is true that depolitization is no remedy at all for the shortcomings of our political world,[2] or the increase in state power. I have never called apolitism a virtue. The apolitism of a great number—though surely not most—Frenchmen is not a good sign at all. Rather, it affords them a cheap feeling of relief to no longer consider themselves responsible for anything. People say:

---

[1] Le Monde, January 1962.

[2] Opinions on depolitization itself are extremely contradictory. First of all, there are analytical studies such as Merle's report (Inventaire des Apolitismes), which distinguishes between tactical apolitism (propaganda from the Right, efforts to weaken some adversary); organized depolitization (in which leaders try to "detach public opinion from the sterile games of politics" and to increase apathy and indifference); and, finally, a doctrinal apolitism characterized primarily by a Maurrasian inclination and technocratic conception. All this is not very encouraging.

Others detest depolitization, which proves to them that the regime is not legitimate in the eyes of public opinion; that the lower classes are held at bay; that the citizens are inept; and that in such cases democracy cannot function. They will then insist on the need for parties. According to André Philip (Pour un socialisme humaniste) and Georges Vedel: "Democracy can no more exist without parties than thought without language."

But some serious political scientists take apolitism as proof that a regime is satisfactory in the eyes of a majority of citizens, who do not want to change their government or constitution (Herbert Tingsten) or, are occupied with more useful tasks than political discussions (David Riesman); they also point out that the greatest political participation is found in authoritarian states.

Serious studies have shown that a rapidly increasing participation in elections is a danger for democracy because it is during elections that the least enlightened citizens are suddenly activated. As a result, apolitism is not automatically and in itself to be condemned (Seymour Martin Lipset: Political Man [Garden City, N.Y.: Doubleday; 1960]).

We find the same contradictions even in literary works. Hermann Broch's novel The Innocents is significant for its mixture of truth and fiction; Broch rightly stresses that political indifference is a solid basis for the establishment of a criminal dictatorship. But he is deliberately misstating the case when he tries to make every person responsible for everything on the ground that the total mass of all human beings is implicated in all that is being done—good or bad. As stated earlier, it is completely useless to insist that I am responsible for everything; I am actually incapable of doing something about everything. The problem is to determine what a man can effectively do in a political situation. This Broch avoids carefully, thanks to his philosophic generalities. On the other hand, Dostoevski in The Possessed, Heinrich Böll in The Two Sacraments, and Petru Dumitriu in Incognito approached this problem correctly. But when doing so, they left the realm of politics behind!

"After all, somebody else takes the trouble of making decisions, somebody else assumes responsibilities; I am therefore no longer concerned, no longer have to aggravate myself if something goes wrong; there is a pilot after all. I no longer have to find solutions—someone is in charge. I can devote myself peacefully to my personal affairs. Nothing collective concerns me any longer." This sort of apolitism is only a general retreat into private life, a flight or renunciation caused by cowardice or laziness in the face of difficulties. It must be condemned just like the refusal to admit that in our society everything is ultimately political. It is not true that a man can no longer be reached by politics because he has turned his back on it; it will still reach him. It is absurd to think that one could nowadays really retire into one's own corner and defend oneself against the inroads from the all-devouring state. The latter does not change its nature; and, whatever your intentions, it will find you easily. Besides, I agree with what a humorist said of the Fifth Republic's particular apolitism: "According to the government, an association or a group is apolitical when it actively pursues the government's politices."

My aim never was to lead the reader in the direction of apolitism. I am fully aware of the radical lie hidden there: to become apolitical is to make a political choice, and as a result apolitism hides some very definite political choices. The idea that one can escape politics by being nonpolitical is just as absurd as the political illusion itself. Therefore my aim is not to invite people to cease being interested in political affairs or to disregard them. Nor is my aim to demonstrate the uselessness of political affairs. They exist, after all; and the state, in one way or another, hews to politics. To be sure, it does so under conditions different today from what they were yesterday, but they still are political activities. In any event, the citizen is affected by them, and the state is of the opinion that it can do nothing without the support of the masses. Even when they are depolitized, the voting masses commit a political act that is indispensable for the state. The ideal situation would be for each citizen to be completely equal to the required political acts in this society. But it is a pure illusion to believe in such a possibility. Yet all this does not

mean that political activity is useless or that all attitudes toward
political affairs are the same, and seemingly illusory.

To ask man to depolitize himself does not necessarily mean
to lead him to a situation of apolitism or invite him to occupy
himself with other things. On the contrary, as the political problem is so essential, it means to lead man to look at the problem
from another perspective. The hope must be surrendered that
constitutional rules, good institutions, or socio-economic
changes will modify anything in decisive fashion. The hope must
also be abandoned that the citizen will be able to control the
state. Politics is a problem of life, and of life without respite.
The fundamental error in 1789 was to believe that controls over
the state could be found *in* the state, and that the latter could
be a self-regulating mechanism. Experience has shown that the
state will retreat only when it meets an unsurmountable obstacle. This obstacle can only be man, i.e., citizens organized
independently of the state. But once organized, the citizen
must possess a truly democratic attitude in order to depolitize
and repolitize; this attitude can only be the result of his being
freed of his illusions. The crucial change involved focuses not on
opinions and vocabulary but on behavior.

The actualization of this democratic behavior rests on two
major conditions. The first requires that political affairs be freed
of myths in an effort to put them into proper perspective. It is
strange and even incomprehensible that those who are so democratic in speech are the very ones who absolve themselves of
their political function, that the most liberal people are the most
intransigent.[3] Democratic behavior presupposes that a man
knows that opinions are unstable, that a pure system cannot be
attained, that justice cannot be had in politics, and that he
therefore admits the relatively limited scope of all political debate. To admit this relativity will prevent people from becom-

---

[3] I disagree with observers who believe the average citizen lacks political passion
and exhibits general skepticism and indolence. On the contrary, some latent
political passion appears to exist which erupts on any occasion and at every
event. What is lacking is truly reasoned personal opinions, certainly not passion.

ing agitated to the point of delirium as they become nowadays.[4] Any man writing on some wall: "To the gallows with such and such," is anti-democratic, no matter what the political crime committed. For a democrat, no political action, even if it can be called a crime or be seen as a threat to the structure of democracy, no political decision, deserves to be carried to that absolute point of life and death. In that domain everything is relative.

It is necessary to help the citizens' political feelings, reactions, and thoughts become less dramatic. But that means that one must free political thought of myths at the same time that our entire press does nothing but engage in myth-creation. The press can exist only if it attributes to any event it picks, an element of passion and myth that completely prevents individuals from knowing or understanding anything; the readers are thereby plunged into the arbitrary and illusory world of superficial political judgments and superficial emotional reactions. To be sure, that is the way newspapers are sold. But one must choose, and when I speak of myth I use it in the strict sense of the term, just as I have tried to show, it is characteristic for a myth to have different shadings, for example: "The construction of a set of events reduced to *one story,* beginning with a structure and ending with an absolute concept; it is a construct— like all political affairs or institutions—in which scaffolds are made of more or less synthesized events, so that by the way in which they are told, they end up as a story (which political affairs never are to begin with). Another shading is found in the explanation. Myths always *explain* a situation, a human condition, a construct; and political affairs, because of the way they are experienced and learned through the mass media. Politicians, are indeed always explanations—of the proletarian situation, of Germany's disintegration in 1918, of the science problem in the Soviet Union, and so on. A last shading is the character of the

---

[4] See Bertrand de Jouvenel's excellent analysis in *De la politique pure* ([Paris: Calmann-Lévy; 1963] pp. 244 *ff.*), according to which "if people want to keep the political game within the framework of fixed rules, the stakes must be moderate" (p. 265). This is the same as my notion of "relativization." But it must be remembered that the people and the technicians always carry the stakes to their limit.

colored, all-encompassing image in which political affairs are always dressed, pushing men into action. Politized man does not think rationally, but through images forming a set of constructed explanations, a total image of the world. This mythic dimension, which prevents all democratic behavior because it pushes man to radical actions and gives him peremptory fears and opinions, must be destroyed at all cost if men are to regain a personal conscience—which is much less facile or satisfying, but is the only thing that can save both democracy and what is real in political affairs.

A second major condition for true democratic behavior is a change in the citizen's personal development with a view to helping him know and understand things in such a fashion that he is no longer the plaything of orthodoxies. Nobody objects to that in principle; it is in fact a pure and simple banality. But the extraordinary difficulty is that *all* of the means thus far listed to make the citizen understand and know things exist nowadays in forms that conflict with this goal. Take education, for example: the more we orient ourselves toward practical and technical education adapted to the modern world, the more the child is being prepared to enter this modern world, but the more all true knowledge, all reflection, all opportunities of becoming conscious through anterior adaptation is kept from him. Jesuit education of 1930 seems much more suitable for the purpose than the most modern teaching provided by our audio-visual instruction, which is never anything but a pure and simple mechanism of adaptation to society, thus precluding from the beginning all true awareness, all reflection. the same is true of information. The problem no longer is to inform the citizen who is already overinformed. It is wrong to assume that the highly informed citizen is more capable. Rather, he is drowned in current events, thus becoming an easy prey for propaganda and the very symbol of the political illusion. This does not mean that instruction and information should be suppressed altogether, but only as they are at present (including the most advanced education and information), for as now constituted they can only prepare man to adapt to illusions. Knowledge and comprehension can come only to an individual, not to a social body. That is the crux of the basic misunderstanding.

Obviously "the subject of political affairs and the private person are identical," but the subject of practical politics can only be a private person existing as such and giving himself as such to the exercise of political efforts; it is necessary to be a self-aware person before assuming responsibilities in public life, and the task of education and information is to create self-awareness rather than political activity.

In *L'État et le citoyen*, the chapter devoted to private life is the best:

> The distinction between the political and the private is the fundamental presupposition of every analysis . . . private political interests are limited just as the interests of private life are limited interests. But there is no gradual transition from the one to the other, as political affairs presuppose a suspension of private interests, just as private life presupposes a suspension of political interests. Yet, while the political limitation is a suspension leading to logic rigidity with regard to problems, the typical limitation of the private interest is a suspension of the rigidity in the arrangement of the totality of preferences and choices.

That is a perfect statement of what ought to be, and the definition of the difference between public and private life seems absolutely essential. But it is compromised precisely by the present situation, in which politics claims to direct everything, including our private lives; the citizen has been politized or is told that he must be. The more he lives in the illusory world of political affairs, the more his private life changes, loses its sense, its savor, its justification, seems lack-luster and unworthy of the full capacities of the informed citizen consumed with the desire to serve, to bear witness, to commit himself. Even if a citizen takes refuge in private life in disgust, then his private life is no longer what it ought to be, but becomes a refuge, an absence, and an evasion; the problem is elsewhere. Private life itself must be re-established, but this cannot be done artificially, by technical and external processes. That would also mean an impermissible invasion by politics. Private life must be "re-invented."

It is necessary to "re-invent" a situation in which life's true problems are not posed in political terms.

2. Tension [5]

We all know the great slogan in our society: adjustment. The spreading of that term and the doctrines of social psychology that go with it are of American origin. But when the Soviet leaders speak of the Soviet citizen, his education, duties, and shortcomings, and when we are told of the identity of collective life and private life in the socialist world, the absence of the "screen" between men and socio-political reality, that is exactly the same thing as adjustment. The general idea is infinitely simple, in fact simplistic, even if the studies in quantitative psychology and sociology based on it are infinitely complex, meticulous, cogent, and irrefutable. But thousands of volumes written on the subject have not changed the general idea. At the individual level everybody learns from experience how distressing internal conflicts are, and that it is better to have an ordered, serene, and balanced life. But depth psychology has taught us a great deal that is new about these conflicts, and has revealed that they are much graver than they appeared to be. As psychoses and neuroses derive from uncontrolled internal tensions, the conclusion was drawn that these tensions had to be avoided to preclude their terrible results. All the known techniques of analysis (not practiced only for that purpose, of course) were then mobilized. Yet the point always was, more or less, to adjust the individual to himself and his own actual life, from which the majority of conflicts and tensions derived.

In groups the same problem exists; people have come to realize that a group in which conflicts, recriminations, and jealousies between individuals abound is not only a less happy group (as in the case of a family), but also a group much less efficient in

---

[5] Only very few admit this to be the key problem. Even fewer are trying to solve it. The essay in *Arguments* (1962) is rather tragic; it finally comes to grips with the problem, but presents it as hopeless. It remains in the realm of words, or regards as solution what is only the problem.

the performance of a task or the fulfillment of a function (such as that of a work team). It is therefore important to reduce these conflicts, first of all in order to enable the group to give its full measure in the accomplishment of its work. Human relations and human engineering experts occupy themselves primarily with this problem. A group is not an entity; it is a sum of individuals. The problem is to establish relaxed, happy, and conflictless interpersonal relationships among the individuals. That is not only in the group's interest, as all effort will become vitiated if two members are in conflict with each other, but also in everybody's interest; it is conducive to everybody's happiness. Each individual is a part of many groups and his happiness depends indeed on his place in these groups and his relations with others. If he has good and truly balanced relations in his family, in his office, in his sports club, or in his union, then this man *is* happy; he cannot fail to be: his happiness depends entirely on his network of social relations. Therefore all is a question of adjustment. If everyone is completely adjusted to his milieu, to his groups, to his work, to his companions in his groups, he is happy and efficient and helps to alleviate the group problem. If *everybody* is adjusted, there is no more group problem. Communism says the same thing in different terms.

But this is not just a solution offered by certain societies; it is also *the* solution for society as a whole. We all know the disastrous results for the individual when the cultural concepts and moral standards that he receives from his society are in conflict with the completely different behavioral patterns demanded by that society. Conflicts between idealism and technology, morality and competition, humanist teachings and professional activity—in short the conflict between ideologies deriving from the eighteenth and nineteenth centuries and contemporary realities. These conflicts must be resolved—in fact the ideologies must be adjusted to the realities and the individual must be adjusted to the new situation. Class conflicts must be resolved in the same fashion; this is a matter of both organization and psychology. The principal aim is the individual's complete adjustment to his diverse activities, his milieu, his functions, his habitat, and his entire mechanism. A maladjusted individual is not only unhappy but also troublesome and a cause of disorders and general imbalance. And his adjustment can be effected only by the reduction of all tensions, whether internal or external.

This doctrine is not merely a doctrine; it is inspired by thousands of books and is widely applied. But it must be realized that the doctrine makes sense only on the basis of certain value choices and presuppositions: it is primarily concerned with comfort and happiness. The gigantic effort at adjustment, the glorification of the extraverted individual, and the hatred of tensions and conflicts rest entirely on the idea that the only aim, the only sense, the only value in human life is happiness, and, further, on the conviction that the only means, the only road to this happiness is comfort—material comfort (high living standard, reduction of work, absence of physical pain) and moral comfort (security, easily applicable doctrines and explanations, idealism). These values are the same in the Western and Communist worlds. In this general orientation, politics plays an ambiguous role. On the one hand, it admittedly creates tensions and conflicts and, as a result, comes under criticism in a society like ours. This has led to all the psychological group studies undertaken to demonstrate that democratic behavior, which reduces conflicts, is both the most efficient and politically the most suitable, though only on condition that man be really and fully integrated in his group. On the other hand, political activity is the great agent for reducing tensions, not only because it presupposes a basic agreement on the state's primary value—to which all else must contribute and be subordinated—but also because in society's actual fluctuations it eventually establishes, as for example in the Soviet system, an effectively unitary society in which decisions by local groups inevitably coincide with certain common aims and end up by attaining an entirely non-controversial, collective objective. I do not say this is actually the case or has actually been attained in the Soviet Union, but it is the aim, which also happens to be admirable and convincing for all, even for non-Communist nations. Has the political ideal not always been to reduce the social body eventually to this type of unity? At present we are closer to it than ever.

But I think that all this is a terrifying error and that the course offered by all the doctrines coinciding with the political illusion are the worst course contemporary man can pursue. It is useful to remember the extrapolations made by Shannon to the theory of information from the theory of entropy in thermodynamics. Entropy increases with every spontaneous change inside an isolated system. It never decreases spontaneously. Similarly, information always decreases as a result of communication. Ultimately, when communication is total it remains constant. But information never increases as the result of communication. Entropy and information are given isomorphic factors, but of different types. Norbert Wiener has added that in every isolated system, entropy tends to increase spontaneously as information tends to decrease. That would make entropy a sort of "disorder" (but not in the sense of confusion or perturbation). Information, on the other hand, would be a measure of order. If someone who needs to be informed already knows the content of the information, the communication can be materially perfect and technically to the point, and yet have not object: there has been no process of information. In order to have information it is necessary that in a closed system (language, for example) an imbalance exist; the informant knows an item of information and transmits it to one who does not know it; in that case there is a process of information. When nothing happens, when nothing is communicated, there is entropy. Entropy, which is therefore a state of maximum disorder, is at the same time the state of greatest homogeneity; when all parties are homogeneous, there is no longer any exchange, and entropy will prevail. In a universe in the state of thermic equilibrium, no event could take place because of the absence of all imbalance. In a circle in the state of complete equilibrium of information, there can be no more information. In a group in the state of human equilibrium, of human homogeneity, there is entropy. But entropy is exactly the equilibrium of death. We must be cautious when accepting the generalizations made by others and understant that complete adjustment by all to all in a group in reality means that the group is no longer alive; it has been mechanized. Unity attained in a political movement means that life in a given system has disappeared. To be sure, everybody will exclaim: "This is not possible. There will always be the individual's singularity, and everything will always be troubled by his tastes and passions. There will always be competition, hatred, obstruction, laziness. All this prevents total adjustment or complete unification." True. The problem, however, is not the final result but the general orientation.

The fact is that the orientation toward a unitary conception of a nation under the state's organizing power, just like the orientation toward man's general adjustment to his environment, increases entropy and diminishes life. In this development, the political illusion plays a very definite role by representing a simulacrum, a false account of the living course of things, by directing human interests at false realities while the adjusting mechanisms are functioning, and by avoiding collisions and obstructions at the level of reality in the new society.

The only way to hold the state within its framework and functions, to return true reality to the conflict of "private life versus political life," to dissipate the political illusion, is to develop and multiply tensions. This is as true for the individual as for the political body. Only tension and conflict form personality, not only on the loftiest, most personal plane, but also on the collective plane. Of course, this is in conflict with the unanimous view of educators and psychologists. Yet I believe that as a result of methods now used, we are pursuing the wrong road, and that everything rests, ultimately, on anterior choices of a metaphysical character. It was the fashion in the nineteenth century to insist on counterposing the individual and society. A good many stupid things were then written on the subject. In the last fifty years, however, the problem has been solved by our insistence that individual and society coincide completely; and American psychological techniques, like Soviet political education, essentially aim at turning this presupposition into reality and making it effective. But, without any further discussion on the considerations of the nineteenth century, it can be stated most definitely that there is no society unless there are individuals; that these individuals do not fulfill themselves either in or through the state, the group, the society, or socialism; and that a too nearly perfect adjustment leads to group efficiency and individual degeneration. Personality is formed through tensions and conflicts. Rather than a complete analysis only a few examples can be presented here. With regard to the child, the contemporary orientation is that the child must learn without pain, that it must have agreeable, seductive work, that it must not even notice that it is working, and that in class the teacher must be really a sort of game leader, a permissive leader with whom there is no conflict, and so on. All this seems remarkably suited to prevent the child's personality from forming, though much is made of our respect for it. It is a perfectly hypocritical mixture that hides realities under artificial procedures, like sugar-coated pills.[6] What is really necessary is for the child to be confronted with work that is limited and much less time-consuming than is the custom nowadays, but requires true effort and conquest and is a genuine challenge. Only this struggle, geared to the full measure of the child's powers, can be useful and prepare the child to exercise his energies and face a society in which work certainly will not be a mere game for a long time to come. In the same way, his relationship with the teacher should be a relationship to authority, as with his father—an understanding, friendly authority, full of devotion and the desire to teach. To assert that there should be no conflict between teacher and pupil is an error that radically falsifies the child's participation in social life and keeps his personality from developing. In reality, the teacher can never be anything but the child's enemy—in the child's eyes—as the officer is to the soldier. What shapes personality is this very conflict, in which the subordinate "grows teeth," tests his strength, and learns the interplay of constraint and liberty. But in this conflict the teacher must know that his role is not to bully, crush, or train children like animals; just because he is superior, he must know how to limit his own force in relation to that of his adversary— that is what is at the core of true pedagogy.

It is exactly the same with regard to the famous democratic

---

[6] Jacques Ellul: *Propaganda* (New York: Alfred A. Knopf; 1964).

learning process so much sought after in group experiences. Apprenticeship in democracy cannot take place in an artificial group in which a so-called free discussion of the choices of group activities would lead to a sort of consensus. Apprenticeship for democracy presupposes a more severe, more extended, more virile education, without which democracy would turn into what its enemies accuse it of being—a regime of the soft, a vocabulary lacking sense. Democracy spreads itself through constant conquest; it is not a *normal*, natural, or spontaneous regime. If it exists, it is the most strained of all political acquisitions, the most jeopardized by reality, the most fragile and the most voluntary. How can it maintain itself without its citizens' voluntary compliance, which is the exact opposite of conformism and adjustment? How can it hold together if it is reduced to nothing but a collection of well-oiled wheels and institutions? If a citizen is prepared to become part of this machinery of wheels which he takes democracy to be, democracy can only be illusory, a memory of the past extolled by contemporary democracies at the very moment when they are dissolving. Washington and the Jacobins are the given names of dead democracies. The ancients were completely right in insisting that democracy presupposes civil virtue. And such virtue can be formed only by surmounting and being changed by the tension in conflict, not by adjustment.

Only in facing obstacles, constraints, rules, superiors, and imposed order can man feel his strength and live his liberty. But if liberty is conceived as a given fact of human nature, as a result of some social mechanism, or as a sort of available terrain offered to the individual by a benevolent society, with its variable limits determined by the state or the schoolmaster— as long as liberty is "inscribed" in laws and institutions, it can only be what B. Charbonneau has called the "lie of liberty." [7] There is no liberty except liberty achieved in the face of some constraint or rule. There must be a precise and rigorous order if man, placed in a conflict, is to conquer his liberty. The problem is similar to that of poetry: poetic liberty does not consist in the absence of rules in a free pseudo-poetry, which is only absence

---

[7] Bernard Charbonneau: *Le Mensonge de la liberté.*

of poetry, but in the poet's struggle with the sum total of all rules. And the stricter the rule, the more the poet's freedom affirms itself by surmounting it. Modern man has undergone this experience in his struggle against the necessities revealed by the exact sciences—by discovering to what extent he was determined in the physical and chemical order, man found a way of mastery that could be the road to his liberation: technology. But what he accomplished in that domain, he failed to equal in the social-political-economic area.[8] He failed for three reasons:

He considers himself an object to be treated like physical or chemical matter; in the social and political domain he wants to employ methods like those that succeeded in physics and chemistry; he avoids all confrontation with the social body, believing that the social body contains freedom, whereas he did accept hand-to-hand combat with inanimate matter. Put differently, he triumphed in the one case because he accepted the conflict, i.e., the tension between man and matter (or nature); he is in the process of failing in the other domain because he refuses to see the conflict, i.e., the tension between man and society, culture, and history, or insists on resolving it by adjustment.

Of course, a great deal can be said about the neurosis of people who cannot overcome tensions and conflicts, the trauma that authority inflicts on children, the risks of a rising dictatorship if the citizen has no civic virtues, and so on. But it is evident that if we take human life seriously, if we talk of "responsibility," we must mean at the same time "risk." Obviously I do not approve of tension for tension's sake, as a value in itself—tension has value only if it is a force to be surmounted and assimilated, which is not at all the same thing as adjustment. Also, tension must not be an artificial and theoretical test; it is a genuine struggle in which the child, and later the man, must engage all his forces.[9] Even more, tension must not become a

---

[8] I am partially in agreement with Barrère (*Semaines sociales* [1963]), when he says that "the great problem is where intermediary structures are situated vis-à-vis the public powers." But I think he is too optimistic in his conclusions.
[9] Tension must not be artificial or factitious. A good example of what it should

stabilized situation; it must be dissolved on one plane while at the same time it reproduces itself on another plane in another form. There is a risk, of course. But the risk of a failure or set-back is exactly the condition for a responsible human life.[1] To avoid risks by avoiding conflicts is to suppress responsibility and the capacity to lead a personal life: to reduce man to being a "fully insured consumer" in all fields is to negate man's creative capacity and, at the same time, to negate democracy. But the greatest danger of all is the mental sleight of hand—of which Teilhard de Chardin is an advocate—which consists in pretend-ing that tensions one meets will dissolve by themselves. That is a false appearance that diverts our attention, our will, and our intelligence from real confrontations by shrouding them in idealism—as we have seen in our confrontation with technology —or by adjusting man to the objective situation. If that is done, man has no longer any chance to realize his true condition.

Regarding man and his personal development, we have pri-marily considered the problem of tension from the viewpoint of conflict with some rule or constraint. But tension is deeper and more complex still when it is the result of two existences in conflict and being formed through their mutual encounter. This is one of the possible meanings of Christ's demand: "Love your enemies"—not your comrades or your equals.

Tension, then, presupposes two poles: a profound difference, without which nothing would happen (this is the dimension that adjustment avoids or rejects) and a common measure, without which human relationships would not exist. At the in-dividual level there is the relationship between man and woman based on tension, which is the most characteristic in the uni-verse, (our obsession with adjustment is seen here in the tend-

---

not be is represented by the Soviet poet Yevgeny Yevtushenko. He is described as an opponent and innovator, whereas in reality he really represents exactly the party line. He is actually an official poet who limits himself to trying to improve his country's system; and when he is "enraged," he is so—as he himself states—on "party orders" (*Le Monde*, February 11, 1963).
[1] Obviously, by "intermediary bodies" I do not mean the same thing as L. Armand, who believes that these bodies are merely diversified, yet collaborating, elements.

ency to reject love as a conflict or to insist that the woman should ultimately be the same as the man). To a lesser degree, this tension exists in all people belonging to a group, if the participants have attained an appreciation of their worth as individuals. Man shapes and proves himself through just such a network of human relations. It is distressing that some people consider this type of human interaction injurious because it reduces efficiency and disturbs tranquillity. Others insist that it be transformed into a network of "social" relations with an economic infrastructure but without any definite personal significance. This amounts to saying that man must be an element of a collective system, and that he exists only as part of that collective system. People holding such views should also have the courage to face all the consequences, particularly to stop talking of humanism or values and even individualized language under such conditions. For example, language reminds us of the necessity of tension at two levels: tension or contradiction is based on a similarity between the signifier and the thing signified (when that tension disappears, there is no more language—that is why, whatever one may think, imagined reproduction of reality is not language); the other aspect is the tension between two interlocutors: if a difference does not exist, if they are identical, there would be no language because it would have no content; if a common measure did not exist, there would be no language because it would have no form. The aim of these examples is to show that in my concept of tension conflict can have positive value only if we are not trying to eliminate or absorb one factor by means of the other: tension makes sense only between two elements that are part of the same system, of a whole that does not destroy itself, that does not disintegrate because its elements are in opposition (and we are not describing here a static whole in the state of equilibrium); tension presupposes a progression of both factors by a suppression of the conflict which entails the creation of a new tension, situated normally at a higher, more enriched level, but also one that is more demanding for both partners.

If we now look at the social body, the "entire society," we see that it lives and progresses precisely to the degree to which such tensions exist. We will find in society the two types of tension that we have discerned in the individual. On the one hand there are obstacles, rules, and limits, whether geographic conditions, political competitions with neighboring groups, or demographic factors. For an entire society, such conflicts have a certain importance because its vitality is affirmed there. And, without creating a general philosophy from it or claiming to find an explanation for cultures or a key to history there, we can accept Toynbee's theory of challenge on this modest level. It is true that a society can exist only if it has the vitality, malleability, or inventive capacity to resolve problems facing it as a result of population growth or decline, the exhaustion of its resources, cultural or military competition, and so on. What we can call constraints and limitations for the individual on the social level is in reality a system of tensions and conflicts in which the society is obliged to assert itself or perish. A society not experiencing tensions, like an individual in the same situation, would become progressively weaker and would progressively lose its inventive facilities.

But the other aspect of tension is more important. In order that a society be able to live and evolve, there must be centers of conflict and poles of tension in all domains, cultural as well as economic. It is a monumental error to organize and conceive a unitary society in which all elements, well integrated and adjusted, are the wheels of a machine. From that moment on, whatever the structure of the machine, the result will be the same. Most often conceived on a pyramidal and hierarchical plan, with all elements well coordinated and meshing at the summit from which all social impulses derive, such a society appears to be a harmonious whole. Obviously such harmony is seductive; be it at one moment the fruit of the philosophic spirit, with its thrist for unity; be it the fruit of the conviction of some universal reason imposing a rational pattern on the world; be it the fruit of contemplating the machines, so perfect in their limited function, focusing our attention on the imperfections of the social body; be if for other reasons—man was always tempted by this unitary view of society, for which all utopias since Plato offer terrible examples. But the contemplation of history and evidence that society is ultimately made by men for men, teach us another lesson. Unitary societies—though in reality social bodies have never attained such complete unity, neither the Egyptians nor the Incas—are ultimately societies without progress, sterile societies. Only societies in which tensions are very strong between groups, as in India, Greece, the European Middle Ages, France and England of the eighteenth and nineteenth centuries with their class struggles, can be inventive, evolutionary, and capable of assimilating new cultures and dealing with man's "problem" in all its dimensions. Let us not fool ourselves: if our society is still haunted by the problem of man, it is not some fleeting remnant of philosophy or Christianity, but the fruit of the nineteenth century's class struggle. Tension between groups composing the entire society is a condition for life itself, or life susceptible to creation and adaptation in that society. It is the point of departure for all culture. There can be no culture in a unitary society; there can be only diffusion of knowledge developed and applied for the greatest good of the social body. To say this is no more than to affirm the reality of a certain dialectic movement in history. There, too, no key or universal system can be provided. There is no *necessary* dialectic. The possibility of this dialectic movement is the condition for life in societies. But this possibility is not always attained. One must not blindly believe that contradictions—still less the same contradictions—will arise under all circumstances. Man's dream—including the socialist dream—is to suppress these contradictions, i.e., to arrive at entropy, at the equilibrium of death. This dialectic movement is no more mechanical when it relates not to abstract forces, but to the relation between social groups that can be of completely diverse natures, depending on periods in history—for example, church vs. state, or state vs. nobles, or tension between social classes—and cannot always be reduced to the class conflict, of which all the rest would be only a reflection.

We have never really arrived at a unitary society, but we have seen certain patterns in the course of history that serve to illustrate its elimination of internal tensions when the dialectic movement is no longer prevalent. "But," it will be said, "it is impossible to suppress tensions in entire societies—they are inevitable because there are always opposed groups. It is an impossible simplification to speak of a unitary society." That is very true; man will never create a perfectly mechanized society any more than a constant and complete adjustment of the individual to his group will be achieved. But it seems certain that there is a threshold: on this side of it, tensions are true and fertile, and groups are genuine poles around which societies can structure themselves; beyond it, tensions are only appearances that make no demands, have no rigor or force. They no longer menace anything, and society is no longer structured with relation to them. It no longer even needs to pay attention to them. Tension between church and state was a reality in the Middle Ages, but no longer is today; to be sure, the church is not the state, as it keeps protesting a great deal, but that difference has no great value. Similarly, the relationship between bourgeois and labor classes from the nineteenth century until around 1930 exhibited true tension but that has now greatly declined and will soon disappear. Certainly the labor class will not have entirely become the bourgeois class, but the contrast will be mainly in the realm of words. Similarly, studies trying to show that a new social class has been created in socialist countries—which is certainly true— do not permit us to conclude that, as there are now two classes, there is genuine tension and struggle. Soviet society seems remarkably unitary, and the emergence of one, two, or three social classes will change nothing whatever in that respect; tensions between them will have no more significance than those between an engineer and the general manager of a project in a small, otherwise well-organized factory. It will be a question that can always be resolved without great damage. But the threshold in question is that of risk: for tension between social bodies to be fertile and serious, it must constitute a true risk for the entire society. If we deal only with some small problems of co-existence between groups with slight contradictions—having, aside from that, little vitality—such as those among our unions, our political parties, our communities, our churches, our agricultural movements, our universities, our families, our free masons, our pressure groups, or our trusts, with everybody living under a peaceful gentlemen's agreement counterpointed only by the violence of their declarations, protests, proclamations, and petitions that have neither content nor effect, then we cannot talk of tension. Furthermore, there can be a genuine federalism—a good example of tension—and an illusory federalism. True federalism fundamentally challenges a central state, and finally destroys it. For three quarters of a century there was in United States a system of tension between the federal government and the elements of the federation. But nowadays we are being offered illusory federalism by everybody: the central state is no longer challenged in any way, but some vague and timid decentralization is sought; no source of tension of any kind exists there. The social body is unitary, and all possibilities of its making progress are excluded.

We are dealing here only with the internal problem, the internal structure of an entire society (such as the French nation), and not with external challenges. It is quite true that a serious tension exists between the Western bloc and the Soviet bloc. But here we are faced with a profound choice: it would be catastrophic to take the tension between the two as our only reason to act, i.e., to supress all search for internal life in our own society only to sacrifice them for the sake of parading them to defy the Soviets; to accept having a unitary society in France in order to be more efficient in economic competition, technological progress, and military defense is to agree to having all possibilities of human life and all evolution in our society greatly reduced. The true response to external challenge is not forceful supremacy of one group over another, but invention of a new form, of new activities provoked by that tension. Engaged in competition, we are not experiencing authentic tension, as the aim is the exclusion or the elimination of one of the poles. In that case, development is unilateral. In this fashion states engaged in war against Hitler came to imitate Hitler's methods, and the losers were remarkably able to corrupt the winners, who in turn began to practice propaganda, torture, internment in concentration camps, racism, destruction of rights, and so on, because we placed ourselves on the platform of power. Similarly, in peaceful co-existence the reduction and elimination of tension run the danger of coming about by a progressive and reciprocal imitation on the part of the two adversaries, both engaged, besides, on the one-way street of technological growth, so that tension is eliminated without any fruitful effect—without dialectical progress. Yet for the benefit of this single effort all internal possibilities of human development are sacrificed (and efforts are made to persuade us that the only human development is technological development).

Our French society has become a unitarian society from which tensions are practically excluded,[2] or, more precisely, only one form of tension exists—political tension. When speaking of politization, I pointed out that political conflicts are being carried to a state of paroxysm, passion, and violence. I know the reader will retort: "What more internal tensions do you want in a country than those we have already experienced! Tension between collaborators and the Resistance from 1940 to 1945 (with all its sequels), tension between French and Independent Algeria, between army and nation, between the OAS and the anti-fascist Left . . . we live in terrible and permanent tension, and cannot see that it is fruitful." The problem is that the conflicts we know today are exclusively of a *political* order. In France there are no longer any other tensions because all the rest has been reduced to and assimilated into a monolithic whole.

But have I not tried, precisely, to demonstrate throughout that politics in our society, structured as it is and undergoing its current transformations, has become illusory; that the real problems cannot be resolved by political means; that political debates are revealing around illusory problems? Therefore, these tensions, of which so much is being said, and which are tragic for us because every twenty years they must be paid for with human lives, are the more tragic because they are absurd

---

[2] The new feudalist elements are not elements of tension, nor do they set limits to state power. These pressure groups, unions, parties, and so on are completely integrated into the state's monistic political structure. They are "feudal" only with regard to their adherents, who lack all real power because of them, and must seek refuge in them for their own protection.

and illusory. The only tensions that still exist are political tensions, but despite their hard and violent character, despite
widespread commitment to them, despite some people's seriousness in the debate, they are false tensions, emptying into a void,
dealing with nothing serious in the structure of our society, and
incapable of producing any solution or basic innovation. All
"innovations" being proposed either are on the level of the ever
necessary technician or burst like soap bubbles—this is depolitization. Ultimately, politics obsesses us and gives us hallucina-
tions, fixing our eyes on false problems, false means and false
solutions; we must therefore leave politics behind, *not* in order
to abandon all interest in the *res publica,* i.e., collective and
social life, but, on the contrary, in order to achieve it by another
route, to come to grips with it again in a different way, on a
more real level, and in a decisive contest. The point is not to
give free rein to a state that would then no longer encounter
even the obstacle of an illusory public opinion, but on the contrary, to erect in the face of the state a rigorous arbiter whose
several poles of attraction would force the state to adjust itself
to them. The point is no longer to orient all channels of public
action in the sense and direction of the state, in the way our
railroad network is oriented toward Paris. This does not mean
at all that we must rediscover local autonomies. It would be
illusory to go against the trend of the times. When labor unions
increasingly enter into the state's unitary structure there cannot
even be any question of asking them to rediscover the seriousness of their mission. Unions were, in their time, definitely poles
of tension—in France, for example, between 1880 and 1906. But
today their opposition to the regime and their methods of action
have become fictitious. They engage in routine demands, false
defenses of the labor class, and symbolic strikes to show the
persistence of class struggle—that is all. And, what has lost its
sense in the course of time cannot be recovered artificially. An
obsolete institution *is* obsolete: it cannot be reinvigorated—that
is the historic lesson of all institutions.

We are therefore in the presence of the following dilemma:
either we must continue to believe that the road to solving our
problems is the traditional road of politics, with all sorts of

constitutional reforms and "revolutions" of the Right and the Left—and I have already tried to demonstrate that all that no longer has any significance, but merely represents shadow-boxing—or we turn away from the illusory debate, and admit, for example, that "public liberties" are but "resistances," admit that for man "to exist is to resist," and that, far from committing oneself to calculating the course of history, it is important above all never to permit oneself to ask the state to help us. This means that we must try to create positions in which we reject and struggle with the state, *not* in order to modify some element of the regime or force it to make some decision, but, much more fundamentally, in order to permit the emergence of social, political, intellectual, or artistic bodies, associations, interest groups, or economic or Christian groups totally independent of the state, yet capable of opposing it, able to reject its pressures as well as its controls, and even its gifts. These organizations must be completely independent, not only materially but also intellectually and morally, i.e., able to deny that the nation is the supreme value and that the state is the incarnation of the nation. The idea should be opposed that because a group is *inside* a nation, it is therefore, above all, national, and that the state, representing the nation, can therefore control it and dictate to it. What is needed is groups capable of denying the state's right—today accepted by everybody—to mobilize all forces and all energies of the nation for a single aim, such as the grandeur or efficiency of that nation; we must not give in to blackmail such as: If all intellectuals were not used by the state, and if all resources were not concentrated in the hands of the state, and if all private interests did not subordinate themselves to the state, we would never have the Pierrelatte establishment. All right—so much the better. What is needed is groups capable of extreme diversification of the entire society's fundamental tendencies, capable of escaping our unitary structure and of presenting themselves not as negations of the state—which would be absurd—but as *something else*, not under the state's tutelage but equally important, as solid and valuable as the state.

They must, that is, be poles of tension confronting the state, forcing the latter to "think again" and limit itself to considering real political problems without being in a position of omnipotence.[3]

It would obviously be dangerous if groups of that kind were to emerge, and would in a certain sense perhaps reduce the power of the nation, the growth of technology, the economic and military competition with other nations. But this is the condition for life itself. Tension presupposes risk, but it is a game that must be played; the stake ultimately is the authenticity of human life and social development. Confronted with such terms, people will shrug their shoulders and the more strictly scientific minds will say: "What is all that?" It is, *for example,* not to bandy words about, not to feed on illusions—of which my example has been the political illusion—as many strictly scientific minds do in our day! Creating such poles confronting the state, one must not forget that opposition factors would be part of the system; to put it differently, they would not aim at disregarding the state or tend to destroy it, but, by returning an autonomous vitality to certain parts of society, would make possible a political life that would be something else than mere illusion. This would provide the state with the possibility of true life. Here the objection will be: "All this is entirely utopian, and in fact it is an illusion to believe that the establishment of such organisms would be possible." I have never said that it *is* possible. I have only indicated what I consider to be the basic condition for social and political life and the *only* way to escape the political illusion. If one does not want to follow it, so be it. The future is clear enough under such conditions. More or less quickly, the political illusion, which is transitory in nature, will dissolve into ashes, and what will be left will be an organization of objects run by objects.

---

[3] An authentic new tension between the intellectual and political realms should also arise again.

CHAPTER

[VIII]

MAN AND
DEMOCRACY

These timid propositions are not imaginable, much less realizable, unless political man is above all else a man.[1] Whether we like it or not, all depends entirely on the individual. Man? I will not venture into the thicket of present-day debates on that subject. Let us simply say: man is an autonomous center of decision, not merely a product of sociological currents which, in confluence, produce a semblance of man. Nor is he a planned product, the result of systematic influences precisely calculated to make him such as to be of the greatest good for society and

---

[1] Very significant in this connection is Pierre Mendès-France's position. Following the best tradition, it completely eludes the problem of the citizen's reality, and proceeds in all respects on the basis of the purely abstract notion that the average citizen is reasonable and competent.

Jean Barets, on the other hand, innocently admits that his system cannot work unless men undergo a sort of spiritual conversion. In his view, a moral revolution is needed. But, while decrying the views and means of technological dictatorship, he, like everybody else, stops short of such a needed moral revolution; still, the fact that he poses the problem at all makes him more serious than if he ignored it altogether.

for his own greatest happiness. Nor is he, finally, an undiscern-
ible fragment—even though potentialy full of promise and a
future—of the Teilhardian social magma, converging toward
some hypothetical mutation.

When I insist on man's indispensable, irreplaceable character,
the reader will have the feeling, both deceptive and reassuring,
that he is returning to a well-known political problem. He will
say: "The republic is worth only what its citizens are worth."
And he will call Aristotle, Octavius Augustus, and Saint-Just
to the rescue. But I think that there is a great misunderstanding
here. Our situation is no longer the same, and we can no longer
appeal to civic virtue. The classical position, called reactionary
in our day, was an ethical proposition; everybody was faced with
the choice of civic virtues in his private and public life. But
because of its chancy and illusive character, sensible men have
tried to elude this ultimate decision and inevitable standard.
The civic virtue of *a* citizen and of *the* citizens was never assured. It was necessary that the republic function even without
it. The great task was to invent institutions permitting the reduction of appeals to the individual; democracy, though based
on popular adherence, was designed to function even if the
people were corrupt, senseless, cowardly, spoiled, egotistical,
and flabby. Institutions, rules, organizations, and constitutions
were formally constructed and combined often neglecting
human "presence" and variability. This eventually led us to the
impasses we have noted. Another element was soon added: the
inevitability of history's course; whether in the Marxian or Teilhardian sense, the important thing was that people be assured
that "things take care of themselves" and that there is a happy
ending to all experience; that secret mechanisms will produce
solutions, without effort, energy, morality, or civic virtue. The
model is not: "I do." It is: "Things develop." This means that
something outside of man is relied on to make the social and
political machinery function, regardless of the particular nature
of man. To be sure, this provides much greater security—if
people truly "believe" in these mechanisms—and allows us to
"reason" without taking account of the uncertain human factor.
The acceptance of a kind of inexorability in societal behavior

can be seen in the "social sciences," though in more modern and subtle fashion. It is quite as remarkable that many lucid people fall for this and think of the methods of statistical sociology and social psychology as a way of providing answers to actual political questions. This means really that they look to such methods for the manipulation and adaptation of man to his political role.

1. The Unprecedented Nature of the Problem

It is my view, however, that both the old and the new direction are wrong, that today's situation is unprecedented to a much greater degree than is generally imagined, and that the ties between individual and democracy are much stronger and more profound.[2] The great new facts, such as our increasing technology, our propaganda and psychological techniques, and the systematization of all institutions attack man and democracy simultaneously: they attack man to make him conform and to reduce him to a mere piece in the system; they attack democracy, by substituting a mythical system for one based on reality. We now apply the term "democracy" to to reify existing situations, and search for subtle definitions provided by political science or sociology, in order to avoid the simple evidence provided by this word, which has absolutely no content except when based on complete individual liberty. I feel particularly entitled to say that without such liberty the word has no content when I see the complicated analyses explaining that the Yugoslavian or Czechoslovakian dictatorships are also democracies, or analyses describing the democratic process as a form of group dynamism. All that is only a hypocritical cover-up to keep us from giving up the magic word and admitting that the demands of technology and all the psychological seductions have eliminated the substance of democracy.

---

[2] Obviously, I am not repeating in these pages what is commendable in the many recent articles treating democracy, for example: "Colloque France-Forum," *La Démocratie à refaire* (1963), and "Action populaire," *Démocratie aujourd'hui* (1963).

What seems most remarkable nowadays is that the attack against man is a political attack. Our political world, summarily described here, is not a formal dictatorship coercing or crushing man by violence, police, or concentration camps. It is a world that seduces, absorbs, appeals to reason, neutralizes and forces man to conform, i.e., it is no longer a threat to man's overt behavior, but to this heart and thoughts. That is the reason why the problem of civic virtue is no longer the same. The problem used to be: "For democracy to live, the citizen must have civic virtues." That was a personal problem. Today the problem is: "The growth of political affairs destroys man in his innermost being. And yet nothing can be done without man." But which man? The type of man needed today for politics—for we know well that man cannot declare himself an absentee in that area— is the type that must give his heart if political affairs are to work. The attack against him is thus political. Conversely, if one hopes for a return to democracy, such a return could take place only as a result of a restitution of man, who would then cease to be integrated in the present mechanism whose results are actually authoritarian.

To want man to be, means to want him to exist despite propaganda and psychological techniques of influence, and surely despite the hypocritical "sciences of man," which claim to act on him in order to lift him to the level of his destiny in society, to the level on which he can exercise his responsibilities, but which, in reality, dispossess him of himself in order to possess him more thoroughly. Himself? Yes, a mediocre, maladjusted, uncertain, fragile "himself." Still, himself. Undoubtedly with our psychological therapy, we will do much better, and create a nice, extraverted, responsible, adjusted, efficient man. I always hear that famous objection: "You think you should defend this man? Go on, he is just a product of chance, family influences, his milieu, profession, tradition, climate . . . why should that 'himself' be respected?" The answer is simple. To be sure, all these determining factors exist. And because they are quite heavy, constraining, and numerous, one should not add, on top of them, complementary determinants stemming from "scientific" inroads made by other people. All the less because it is possible to struggle to some extent against the first-named orientations, which are the fruit of chance and circumstance. But, gripped by such proved, rational, and profound techniques, how can man escape? And if he tried, would he not immediately be regarded as abnormal or as a dangerous anarchist? What is more, in the name of what authority, what virtue, what certainty, are we interfering with his life? We have the means to make this man conform, but are we sure we know all the consequences such action entails? Are the psychologists and sociologists supermen, and therefore entitled to "treat" the vulgar herd? Is this new aristocracy quite certain what its wisdom will turn them into? The "head" men also have certain centers of equilibrium and certain orientations, but these, too, are subject to serious questioning nowadays. Are we certain that our inroads will not be even more traumatic and destructive of that equilibrium? If we consider the terrible errors committed against the natural equilibrium in biology or chemistry by technicians of various kinds from 1850 to our day (of which scientists see the consequences now when it is too late to do anything about them), we cannot remain quiet when we are told of these psychological and social inroads. Errors in that domain can be even graver and more decisive.

But to demand that the soul of this clumsy, badly adjusted, mediocre man should not be lanced, to demand that he should be respected and permitted to evolve spontaneously, also means to favor a political type that is the opposite of what the combined mechanisms of technology, organization, and propaganda tend to produce automatically. One can no longer opt in favor of man without making this choice; it is evident that regimes created by these techniques will lay their hands on man in order to adjust and conform him. But making such a choice would then mean going against the current of history, which tends toward such combination of forces and runs in the direction I have described.

To want this particular political type is to want democracy. Is that somthing new? People should realize to what point it has now finally become new. For, first, it implies the radical rejection of empty formulas on "massive" or "popular" or "organized" or "planned" democracy. But at the same time there is no question of turning back to a democracy patterned on that of the nineteenth century.

Second, we must understand that it implies a democracy of choice, decision, and will. Put differently, we must abandon all our customary assumption that democracy conforms to nature. This idealist view current at the end of the eighteenth century is still very widespread; innumerable works by American sociologists on small groups try to demonstrate that in democratically organized groups there is the most equilibrium, the least tension, and the most adjustment.

Thence also stems the customary conviction on the part of the Leftists that democracy is a natural regime, ultimately desired by man in expressing his nature. A non-democratic regime seems opposed to nature. Many other tendencies of the same kind can be adduced. People say: "Let things take their course, and you will have democracy." Today, in the present politico-technological setting, this proposition must be reversed to read: "Let things take their course, and you will have dictatorship."

For others, democracy is also history's necessary product, its inevitable fruit. The "course" of history empties into democracy. It emerges—spontaneously. That same resignation to spontaneously emerging events may be seen on the part of man, based on his expectation that history will do something. But proceeding from that first resignation resting on a belief, there can be no democracy, for man will not resume his responsibility again at a given moment, and, moreover, will think he knows beforehand that whatever actual regime will eventually materialize can only be a democracy. But such resignation and passivity are not grounded in any reasoning, philosophy, or belief; they merely correspond to the current willingness to settle down in a ready-made situation, to sit back peacefully in democracy. The latter is unconsciously considered a natural gift, an irreversible acquisition; and everything else then seems abnormal and strange. People rest themselves cozily on all the clichés of people's sovereignty, equality, liberty, our Jacobin ancestry, and education for all. Occasionally people organize meetings to "defend democracy." How stupid to believe that one is defending something that disappeared long ago! Democracy cannot be defended: it is not a capital city, a fortress, or a magic formula (as a constitution is). Democracy becomes possible only through *every* citizen's will; it remakes itself every day, through every citizen. If we accept the view that democracy is now a given fact, everything is lost. On the contrary, it must be understood that democracy can no longer be anything except will, conquest, creation. It must be admitted that democracy is the exact opposite of our natural and historical inclinations, our laziness, our blindness, our taste for comfort and tranquillity; contrary to the automatic features of techniques and organizations, to the ever more rigorous demands of sociological structuration and the economy's growing complexity. We must understand that democracy is always infinitely precarious and is mortally endangered by every new progress. It must be forever started again, rethought, reconstructed, begun again. More than that, today as yesterday—though perhaps for other reasons —de Tocqueville's proof that democracy dooms itself by its own internal evolution remains true. Therefore it is more than ever the fruit of decision, vigilance, self control, and the public will.

But every citizen, not just some group leaders or some organized marching and shouting mass, must want it. That already shows us how little chance democracy has. But if each citizen does not want it, then the established regime will inevitably be of the aristocratic type, produced by technological progress in the authoritarian manner; and if the citizen is made to enter into democracy, it is only pseudo-democracy, a game with juridical formulas and rules, not man's expression.

The situation seems even more desperate when we consider the object of choice and will. Man must want democracy? But where is that democracy? For a century and a half, a general development has been modifying the possibilities of democracy and necessitating a deepening of the democratic view. Man started from the most superficial levels, and has now attained the deepest levels. In the beginning, democracy was purely "political" in the superficial sense of the word. It was a question then of constitutions, of organizing the central powers, or setting up rules and courts, laws and principles, of defining the "rights of man" and providing for the separation of powers. Today, that trend can be seen in the search for the most adequate electoral system, the structure of parties, and so on. But all that was very superficial, and did not at all guarantee democracy, for institutions must be the expression of a certain socio-economic structure. If society itself is not democratic, institutions serve no purpose, and eventually democracy no longer exists and democratic talk is only a snare and an illusion. In this connection, Marx's critique is decisive and completely adequate. But, at the same time, Marx's disillusionment could not lead to purely negative judgments. It soon became clear that juridical democracy was not just a simple lie, but a point of departure; it was necessary to push on farther and dig deeper. Democracy tried to establish itself on a different level. As a result, the quest for social and economic democracy began. In the beginning there was confusion between the two, or rather a misunderstanding. Most of those who spoke of economic democracy meant social democracy—except for Karl Marx. People therefore aimed at equalizing conditions, spreading comfort to more people, raising lower salaries and reducing the range of salaries; they aimed at institutionalized security of various kinds, at broadening and democratizing education, mass culture, and constructive leisure and at obtaining decent dwellings for all. But it was realized very quickly that social democracy was extremely fragile if it did not rest on a deeper and more solid foundation. Just as juridical democracy is nothing without social democracy—but demands it and leads to it—so social democracy is nothing without economic democracy, and demands it and leads to it. It leads to it. To be sure! For the acquisitions listed above lead any man to desire a greater share in the economy and to increase his powers in society. But all these acquisitions are easily endangered if economic democracy has not been established. Popular participation in the great economic decisions, development of enterprises, plan fulfillments, the direction to be taken by production, the level of employment, the redistribution of national revenues: these are the problems that concern most democrats today; they are now at that level, that is the topic of their discussions—which places then a century behind Marx.

It is true that at this level people run the risk of reaching a more solid level of democracy. But the problem is already obsolete. Efforts made in that direction end up in empty phrases. Just as generals are constantly behind with respect to war, politicians and economists are constantly behind with regard to evolution. When battles were fought for the establishment of political democracy, the question already had been rendered obsolete by the facts, and what arose in reality as the problem at that moment was economic democracy. Now, today, the point of contention is economic democracy. But democracy already is no longer possible on this level; the problem is already facing us on a much deeper level. The growth of technology, the interference in all domains by the new "class" of technicians, the processes of propaganda, the attempts to establish a systematic sociological structure, the desire to create democratic processes by "conditioning"—all this has now turned the debate toward the heart and mind of individual man, his *personal* relationship with the groups to which he belongs. There, and there only, can the issue be faced. If man were left to himself—his inclinations, his responsibilities, his personal choices, on his own level, without systematic influence, propaganda, "human relations," group dynamics, obligatory information, directed leisure, then, slowly, humbly, modestly, democracy might perhaps be born. But how newborn, weak and fragile it would be!

This presupposes a radical question with regard to everything we call progress, just as economic democracy led to radically new questions concerning bourgeois politics. If these questions are not posed, if efforts at adjusting and conforming man are continued, as well as the efforts at structuring him "to make him capable of playing the role demanded by progress," then man will no longer be anything but a cog in the social machine —as essential cog; economic democracy will be a joke; and social democracy will consist of the distribution of objects to satisfy needs of other objects. But it must be realized that we are really in the presence of a choice. In the course of a century of trial, we have learned with great difficulty to understand that democratic political institutions did not automatically lead to liberty or equality, did not by their very nature produce economic democracy. Today we must accept the equally hard and distressing discovery that economic democracy does not automatically lead to human democracy, does not *ipso facto* produce democratic man. In that respect, Marxism is obsolete. As long as the true problem was that of economic alienation, one could legitimately conclude, as Marx did, that if this alienation came to an end, men would really beome Man.

But a new attack on man emerged, a new alienation to endanger his progress; or rather, political alienation, which at the time of Marx was incompletely envisioned superficial, has now become definitely established, is now the result of the use of new means at the state's disposal. Now the problem is for the powers that be—political or technological—to possess man internally, to organize fake appearances of liberty resting on fundamental alienation, to organize false appearances of responsibility resting on systematic collective resignation, to fabricate false appearances of personality resting on integration and radical massification.[3] Under such conditions Marxism is an asset, but no larger a solution or a remedy. But the more the debate deepens, the more difficult it becomes. It was more difficult to invent economic democracy than juridical and constitutional democracy. So today it is more difficult still to invent human democracy, to want the kind of man who would be consonant with it, and to select him. For we are now at a level where everything becomes more risky. We are faced with a set of problems much graver than those confronting the bourgeoisie or property-owners of another day. We are faced with a choice that cannot be taken by one man, a group or a party *for* the others or *in the*

---

[3] Michel Crozier (in *Le Phénomène bureaucratique* [Paris: Éditions du Seuil; 1964], p. 370) shares the common error that an improvement in prediction techniques and a clearer view on the part of individuals of their culture would contribute to making the organizational system less rigid. This is true with regard to its formal rigidity, but that rigidity diminishes only to the extent that a greater integration of the individual into the system is attained. Once the manipulated individual has come to do precisely and spontaneously what is expected of him, the mechanism's external pressures and bureaucratic organizations can of course be made more gentle. This is happening in the U.S.S.R., where liberalization coincides with a more complete integration of individuals. The Soviet state is no longer endangered; therefore it can liberalize itself. But no elements of internal opposition will appear.

place of others. It is all or nothing. We are faced with a choice that must be made on the personal level, but *at the same time* implies political and economic transformations. Only in this connection does the immense task become clear: for the first time, human personality and political institutions must be examined jointly and decided on together, for if man is truly man, that fact should reflect itself (and I will say today cannot help revealing itself) in a certain political behavior, in certain new ideas coming from the grass roots, oriented perhaps in the direction I indicated in the preceding chapter.

All this presupposes a profound change in the citizen. As long as he is preoccupied only with his security, the stability of his life, his material well-being, we should have no illusions; he will certainly not find the civic virtue necessary to make democracy live. In a society of consumers, the citizen will react as a consumer. Comfort will weigh more and more heavily on all possibilities of truly serious political life, and will progressively restrict them. Certain writers have stated with satisfaction that increased material well-being leads to the liberalization of regimes. In reality, it leads to the citizen's political indifference, and in fact the regime can then afford to be less of a police state. Similarly, it is on the basis of the individual citizen, particularly on his obsession with efficiency, that we must judge the evolution of regimes. Democracy is not an efficient regime. If the citizen judges everything from the perspective of efficiency, he will inevitably be lead toward regulatory and authoritarian systems. What is needed is a conversion of the citizen, not to a certain political ideology, but at the much deeper level of his conception of life itself, his presuppositions, his myths. If this conversion fails to take place, all the constitutional devices, all studies on economic democracy, and all reassuring sociological inquiries on man and society are vain efforts at justification.

2. *Democratic Man*

Is man really Man? That question has been asked since time immemorial. Who can define it? Here I can only trace certain choices and say what I consider indispensable for democracy, reminding the reader once more that the problem is not one of "fabricating" this man from the outside by means of propaganda.[4]

The problem is, first of all, rational man, which, to be sure, does not mean rationalistic man. There can be human democracy only if man is determined to deal with everything by the use of proper reason and some cool lucidity based on great intellectual humility at the level of reason. Man learns to try to judge for himself by the use of reason; he then begins to see the limits and uncertainties of all the information in his possession, the relative aspects of his ideas and opinions, the restricted utility of institutions that must never be exalted, but must not be despised either. This man is then called upon to pass everything through the sieve of his reason, marshaling in his conscious mind all of it that he can—everything, i.e., his own passions, his own prejudices, his own doctrines, and also the groups and the society to which he belongs. And when he sides with what is reasonable, he must reject all exhortations, all appeals to the irrational addressed to him under the guise of man's highest expression, all calls to political action. He must reject the notion that socio-political matters are sacred, and he must reject at the personal level, as well as the collective, the obscure forces some have now tried to unleash for half a century. He must reject political or economical myths, in fact all myths—of democracy, socialism, progress, productivity, history, Western civilization, Christianity, the individual. He must reject all forms of idealism and all explanatory doctrines of the world, of science, of society, and the kind of man propounded by Teilhard de Chardin; he must reject them as the principal ways by which man is being reached by propaganda and psycho-sociological manipulation. I do not bring to bear here a value judgment or a metaphysical judgment on the sacred, irrational, and profound; this is only a relative judgment on man's vulnerability when he trades for such forces all that is reasonable. Today he is no longer vulner-

---

[4] I will give only a very brief indication of lines of inquiry I shall develop in a later work.

able with regard to God, but with regard to other men possessing the means to exploit the "easy mark."

This reasonable man, without whom human democracy cannot exist, is the one who at the same time can restore to language its true reason and its communicative substance and who will seek neither a metalanguage, nor a "point zero" in language, nor an expression of the inexpressible, nor an original language opposed to artificial rhetoric. To be sure, we know that this reasonable language is artificial. And so? That only means that it must be maintained as a modest utensil, irreplaceable and reliable. You want absolute language? The word in itself? Here too, I repeat: I do not apply value judgments, but judgments of fact. To lay oneself open to mystical and hypnotic language is to provide a total opening to propaganda action upon oneself. The more that language loses its content and reasonable structure, the more man is delivered to propaganda's delirium. Such propaganda is made to lead man into the world of technology; those who want to recover an absolute language, a natural language beyond all artifice, by a strange though not surprising turnabout—considering the world we live in—are delivered, defenseless, to complete immersion in and total adaptation to the most artificial world that ever existed. We must be aware of this general situation in our present society, in which mechanisms mounted by multiple technology have the power to turn man's best intentions against himself. Ultimately, reasonable man will have to face the hardest and most honest, the most realistic and humiliating realizations of his *condition* as man in *that society*. This hard labor cannot be done except by the use of reason.

Another dimension (upon which I also only want to touch) of truly democratic man that we must choose, and decide to have as ours, is respect. Absolute respect for adversary, fellow man, minorities: respect that has nothing to do with liberalism (which is indifferent to truth or grants equal footing to all opinions), respect that has nothing to do with tolerance (which means that one admits wide divergences while restraining them). With regard to what I said earlier about tension, such respect would imply two orientations: first, is the full apprecia-

tion of minority opinions, which must receive the more attention
the feebler they are. As a result, there would be no more question
of a massive democracy or of tendencies to eliminate minorities
by whatever means. The second needed orientation is dialogue:
dialogue is the opposite of identification. It is coherent affirmation of differences and common measures. In it, two elements
are closely interrelated.

For democracy and man to exist, it is necessary to maintain
at all costs the differentiations that spark communication and
relationships. All assimilation (such as of an inferior or minority
group to a superior or majority group), all adaptation (of the
individual to society), and all integration on the Teilhardian
pattern must be avoided. They must be rejected even though
they are exactly what modern man demands for reasons of ease,
laziness, or economy, and are rejected by society as desirable
because of its concern with efficiency and self-determination.
It must be understood that if adaptation takes place, there will
be no more dialogue, as there will be no more differences, i.e., no
more reason for communication. The only thing that will remain
will be a tremendous dissemination of collective and anonymous
news items without real information content. Such desire to preserve opposition cannot lead to the desire to eliminate those
who provoke tension; on the contrary, it would stimulate the
quest for meaningful communication and satisfy the desperate
desire not to be "strangers." This would mean to live on the
presupposition that a common measure is possible; that even
in our differences there are possibilities of agreement.

But this common measure is not a fact of nature or a simple
given fact. It is always possible for us to suppress or break it.
It is always possible for us to become strangers again; or, what
is worse, it is always possible for us to treat our fellow men as
strangers. The militant Nazi or Communist, on the one hand,
establishes an identity with those in his group (with whom no
true communication is possible) and, on the other, breaks off
all common measure with his adversary, who must then simply
be eliminated. The common measure of what we have to say to
one another and of what makes communication possible, of what
we jointly have to live for (which makes it possible for us to

work together despite differences), must be constantly rediscovered and recreated—for it is quickly lost, either in generalizations like "humanity" or "science," or in banalization.
This exhausting quest for a common measure within differences
is man's true mark.

But our vigilance must also be turned to another area. It must
always be stressed that our civilization is one of means and
therefore the true problem is not on the order of a discussion
about man's ends—which is an evasion—or on social philosophy,
or on the obvious subordination of means to ends. We must give
up big, general ideas, vast judgments, grand syntheses. We must
give up the idea that the means are something special, concrete,
immediate, and therefore of subordinate importance and easily
controlled. On the contrary. We must learn that three facts determine the world we live in:

The prodigious increase in our means of action makes it impossible for us to claim any control whatever over those means.
Rather, they control us.

The intensity of these means of action and their immediate
and constant presence in our lives provoke, without our wanting
it or even being conscious of it, a definitive primacy of action
over thought, mediation, choice, judgment.

The means determine the ends, by assigning us ends that can
be attained and eliminating those considered unrealistic because our means do not correspond to them. At the same time,
the means corrupt the ends. We live at opposite ends of the
formula that "the ends justify the means." We should understand that our enormous present means shape the ends we pursue. The means of national or class war have become such that,
just because they exist, we can no longer hope to establish peace;
the means of coercion are such that they no longer permit us to
claim that thanks to them we will arrive at liberty.

The difference between democracy and totalitarianism is precisely in the area of means. If a government increases technology
in society, steps up propaganda and public relations, mobilizes
all resources for the purpose of productivity, resorts to a planned
economy and social life, bureaucratizes all activities, reduces the

law to a technique of social control, and socializes daily life, then it is a totalitarian government. At that level, concentration camps, arbitrary police methods, and torture are only secondary differences between dictatorship and democracy, depending on the degree of both the government's cleverness and the acceleration of the movement. We should forever be concerned with the means used by the state, the politicians, our group, ourselves. They should be the principal content of our political reflections.

Finally, any quest for true democracy demands that we question all our clichés, all social evidence at present admitted without discussion, all collective sociological presuppositions that permit us to be in agreement at the most superficial level with our fellow citizens. These clichés are the basic ideological drug insidiously slipped into our consciousness by our society's actual development, designed to justify that society, and by which we adjust to it without too much suffering. These stereotypes provide the unconscious basis on which we build our glorious ideologies and even our doctrines. They must be tracked down and exposed, so that we can see in them our true social image: man is made for happiness; man is good; everything is matter; history has a certain direction and follows it inexorably; technology is neutral and under man's control; moral progress inevitably follows material progress; nation is value; no more words, but deeds; work is a virtue; the raising of the living standard is a good in itself. And so on through all the thousands of aspects of our judgment and consciousness. To attack the problem on this level is not just an intellectual game, or a morose critique, or a perverse investigation with a view to examining our conscience. Rather, we must come to see that precisely these beliefs open the way for propaganda to take hold of us, convince us, and drive us to action. The existence of these stereotypes in us is the social weakness of our existence, the central point at which we are vulnerable. If it weren't for that, we might be remarkably intelligent, informed, concerned with democracy, impervious to outside influences, openminded and liberal, humanist or Christian—but all that matters very little. In our relationship with the political world, the fundamental law

is that of the chain and its weakest link. This goes for us: our
weakest point, through which all bankrupt political matters enter, is our basic adherence to these stereotypes. Where they exist
no freedom or democratic creativity is possible.

Why draw this out further? I am well aware of the reader's—
and also my own—reaction: in all this there is nothing new.
All these views have been expressed and heard a hundred times.
True. But the point is this: while my response is not new, the
situation in which we find ourselves is. The question is new. It
just could be, and I think it is, that the old response is still valid
—and the only one that is valid. Only, in this new situation, the
old response also becomes new.

Let us consider what I have said in this book neither *sub
specie aeternitatis* nor from the over-all historical perspective,
but with respect to our present-day political world. We will
then be surprised by the striking strangeness of that ancient
response. But this response cannot be a solution; that is the key.
For if the response is already known, has it been experienced?
And if it has not been experienced, it amounts to nothing. In
the present political evolution, we find ourselves at the foot of
the wall; either we stay there, or. . . The dilemma is upon us
these days as it never has been before. Escape is no longer
possible. But one thing must be made clear. I have never claimed
that man is *by nature* as I have tried to describe him here, or
even that man ever was that way in another day, and has only
sunk to his present level. I merely claim that man as I have described him is *possible,* and that we must want him to be. If he is
not possible, if we do not want him to be, if we do not fulfill
ourselves, we should stop talking about democracy, even about
political affairs. We should stop pretending and attributing to
ourselves values and virtues (freedom, for example) that do not
exist even in appearance. We should then follow the course of
history—not like men, but like things—and cease pretending
that we reflect on and engage in political action. Then the die is
cast. This brings us back to the beginning: in our day man and
politics are closely tied together, and that type of politization no
longer resembles the kind outlined in my preface. It is the reflection of man's greatest risk and most important choice.

THE DEMOCRATIZATION OF ECONOMIC PLANNING

In this section I shall review the reasons that have led me to adopt in the text an opinion that may appear too dogmatic. I shall not try to describe the French system of planning—everyone agrees that it is highly technocratic, and certain critics have denounced it as a mere means of capitalistic survival or adaptation.* I shall rather address myself to the problem of discovering whether the democratization of planning is possible or whether, in the last analysis, planning must remain technocratic in spite of all proposed palliatives. As far as the facts are concerned, I shall confine myself to the reminder that *no* democratic system of planning is in existence today. Soviet planning is just as technical despite the appearance of popular participation. As for the Yugoslav planning so often cited as a model, it is perfectly true that popular participation is relatively more of a reality (although it is very tightly confined to choices narrowly set out by the technicians), but it is generally agreed that the Yugoslav plans are rather inefficient and for the most part unexecuted, owing no doubt to the very method by which they are laid down.[1]

On the other hand, in putting the question I am not considering it on an abstract or doctrinal plane, where there appears to be a solution for everything, but keeping in mind the reality of Western man and of existing groups. If we are thinking of a man who is intelligent, reasonable, in control of his emotions, informed, and interested in economic problems; if we are thinking of political parties and trade unions that are liberal and democratic in conducting their affairs, free from petty partisan influence, devoted to the common good—then practically no problem is involved in the democratization of planning. The reality is quite different, however, and will be for a long time, if not forever. This may be inferred from the fact that there is not a trace of change in that direction.

What is meant in speaking of the democratization of planning?[2] Writers on the subject give very different answers. For some, it is the choice of broad options for planning on the part of the interested parties, the citizens themselves. For others, it is parliament that must make the decision. And often the same writer wavers in the course of his work and, as if the problem were one and the same, confuses the citizen with his elected rep-

---

[1] As far as the Soviet Union is concerned, the instances of authoritarian intervention in planning since 1956 are well known. As for Yugoslavia, the Congress of Yugoslav Trade Unions (April 1964) shows, on the one hand, the technicians' reaction to political intervention and, on the other, the imbalance between production and consumption, and the unevenness of growth.

[2] Pierre Mendès-France: *La République moderne* (Paris: Gallimard; 1964), pp. 109 *ff.*; *Économie et Humanisme* No. 136 (1961); "Colloque de Paris pour une planification démocratique" (July 1962); "Travaux du Conseil économique et social pour la préparation du Ve Plan" (October 1963); "Colloque de Grenoble (fondation nationale de sciences politiques) sur la planification démocratique" (May 1963); Jean Meynaud: *Planification et politique* (Lausanne, 1963) and *La Technocratie: Mythe ou réalité* (Paris: Payot; 1964).

I shall try to describe the facts and show the illusory character of the ideas on the democratization of planning. Hence I shall not study the tendency, which elsewhere seems to be in favor, according to which absolute autonomy would have to be given to the creators of a plan, with regard to political power as well as private groups.

resentatives, a decision by the interestd parties with one by
parliament. Some are much stricter [3] and not only consider that
the general choice must be left to the politician—only then con-
signing formation of the plan to the technicians—but also wish
to associate parliament with the entire undertaking, with all
stages in the formation of the plan. This is indeed the only serious position: the politician called in to intervene on the level
of preparatory studies, on the estimate level, that of determining objectives, of the choice of methods of execution, and finally
continuing to a position of control. Later I shall examine the
difficulties and flaws in these proposals.

Another aspect of democratization is the participation of the
trade unions in the preparation of a plan. But here I find a wide
range of opinions. At the least, this is a degree of participation,
generally considered unsatisfactory as it is now actually practiced in French planning; however, at the most, practically all
the power would devolve upon the trade unions in the matter of
planning, the technicians simply executing their orders. [4]

A fourth view—and one that is growing in favor—recognizes
the importance of regional councils. The regionalizing of the
plan seems to be a way of democratizing it because on the
regional level local needs and possibilities can best be discovered
and because on this level the ordering and execution of plans
can take on a human aspect, a flexibility that the technician
alone is incapable of giving. One last aspect of democratization
must not be overlooked: the flexibility of administrative structures, their adaptability to the necessities of planning, their
receptiveness to this problem; for an administration can, to a
certain degree, represent both the democratic state and the interested parties.

Everyone, of course, emphasizes the conditions necessary for
democratization: technicians whose loyalties are not bound up
with special interests, or the ruling economic class [5]; enlightened

---

[3] Bernard Gournay: "Technocratie et Politique," *Économie et Humanisme*, pp.
27 *ff*.
[4] Congrès C.F.T.C., 1963: Report of R. Jacques Declercq, "Les Syndicats et le
Plan," *Esprit* (1961).
[5] Guiducci: *Arguments*, No. 25, p. 90; J. Meynaud: *La Technocratie*.

citizens or deputies who are informed, trained to make decisions, guided by a vision of the general good, ready to cooperate with the technical staff, and capable of checking on the development of the planning system. I shall not insist on the near-impossibility of realizing these two conditions. Even that which everyone insists on—knowledge of economic problems and of the choices to be made,[6] seems to me almost unrealizable for reasons I have gone into elsewhere.[7] But I shall stress neither this point nor the traditional theme of the imcompetence of politicians.

A body of facts which never ceases to impress me is made up of the contradictions one encounters in writers who extol the democratization of planning. Thus, in L'État et le citoyen, we find that the plan can be "a way of rendering the participation of citizens effective in the exercise of economic power." The man who wrote that sentence then curiously enough proceeded to an elaboration under this heading to prove his point: 1. that the plan is the expression of social constraint; 2. that it is undemocratic in essence; 3. that its positive value is to stabilize the economy, to justify the sacrifices demanded of the worker, to make the world of the organization tolerable. I see in this not the introduction of liberty, but merely a way of making necessity acceptable.

Likewise with Mendès-France, in whom we find an assignment of the function of planning outside any political choice; planning must be directed toward the following objectives: "Elimination of the see-saw curves, combatting depressions and recessions in order to have as regular and rapid an expansion and increase as possible." But how is it possible not to see that these "preconditions" of the plan, this assignment of objectives not to be discussed, represent an extreme limitation in the possibilities of political decision? That is a part of the "upper limits" I mentioned in the text. Turin likewise speaks of the necessity

---

[6] Turin: "Le Plan, acte politique," Économie et Humanisme; François Perroux: Le IVᵉ Plan, pp. 15, 120. Mendès-France: La République moderne, pp. 117 ff.
[7] Jacques Ellul: "Information et Propagande," Diogène (1957).

of realizing "unfelt needs, the meeting of which can appear to be of primary importance in a certain conception of man." How is it possible not to see that if there is a question of unfelt needs, it is not just any citizen who will win acceptance for this orientation, that it is not even the politician, strictly bound to his constituents and their interests? It will be the technician (not necessarily the one in charge of planning, but the one occupied with urbanism, hygiene, social psychology, etc.) and, more generally, the enlightened élite who will win acceptance for this orientation of planning toward meeting unfelt needs. If, in the same way, planning must be destined to "*create* new needs, form habits, orient life itself," [8] then it is certainly neither the people nor the politicians who will make decisions in this direction. In addition, the same text (like Massé pointing out that one must "stir up the mentality of the people") speaks of the utilization of means of pressure on public opinion "to oblige it to head in the right direction and accept the plan," which is nothing less than democratic.

This article is at least honest. But apparently no one sees in it the contradiction between democratization, described as possible, and the use of means of pressure on public opinion. Finally, the most striking example of these contradictions: "Planning cannot fix as its goal the creation of a human being undisturbed in his ease." [9] What then follows is a description of the kind of man planning must not create, but that type is exactly the ideal that Western man and the politicians, too, desire. From that point on, whenever democratization is mentioned, the type of man that democracy would have to require (not because it is democratic, but because it corresponds to popular feeling) is rejected. A noble objective is then assigned to planning, but one that springs from the élite's vision of what men should be. We find the same tendency in Lebret,[1] the same preconceptions about planning, outside the reality of democratic participation,

---

[8] Turin: "Le Plan, acte politique," *Économie et Humanisme*, p. 19.
[9] Ibid., p. 17.
[1] Lebret: "Le problème de valeurs et des relations dans la planification," *Développement civilisation* (1963), p. 22.

when we read that cultural and spiritual life must be safe-
guarded in the perspective and options of decision. I am in absolute agreement, but I doubt that this result can be obtained by
a popular vote on the orientation of planning or by involving
politicians in the working out of a plan.

These contradictions seem to me highly indicative of the ultimate impossibility of maintaining a demand for real democratization.

Several possible types of choice would have to be proposed
to the people or to parliament—either, before planning could
begin, a choice must be made of its general direction, or else
the technicians could be asked to make several proposals from
which to choose. In the second case, obviously only parliament
would be fit to choose. But as far as preliminary general decisions go, I can already see the outlines of an opposition rising
even in the formulation stage. In political speeches, simplified
choices are presented, for example: the choice between the
atomic bomb and housing, between the capitalist formula and
the socialist conception of the relationship of property and labor
(these are *real* examples). Here one is confronted with simple
propaganda proposals that have nothing to do with possible
choices in planning. Mendès-France puts the matter in terms of
sterner choices to be made: the rate of economic growth, the
mutual importance of labor and leisure, of consumption and investment; a decision must be made as to the priority of individual or collective consumer goods, the apportionment of
investment among the diverse branches of production and the
distribution, by sector or by region, of these investments, etc.
Here one is confronted by real decisions to be made, ones that
really involve planning. But then can one be serious when one
insists that the citizen must make the decisions these problems
require?

I have already observed that almost all the writers presuppose that the consumer is a rational and competent man capable of making a political choice unaided, endowed with a
clear conception of the future. But can this idea really hold up?
Without stressing the problem of competence, I am forced to

agree with Frisch [2] that "the dimensions of current problems lie beyond the understanding of the average man. . . . Despite the enormous expansion of means of communication and instruction, his knowledge has declined in proportion to the knowledge required. Technicality has reached such a point that important details of the agricultural policy of the European Economic Community, to cite an example, cannot be given real and decisive attention by governments. They are part of the domain of technicians, whom the majority of the ministers must trust. Under such conditions, how can the citizen participate in politics?" I shall not lay stress on this theme.

I mentioned earlier that the citizen must be asked to make choices as to general orientation.

The preliminary question is obviously that of who will determine the choices available and the particulars of these choices. After all, one can choose among a thousand objectives or directions. Then there is a preliminary decision to be made as to the objective of each choice. If the making of this choice is left to politicians, it will necessarily be of the "atomic bomb or housing" type, or even that of "France's greatness or stagnation." To make real economic choices, recourse must be had to technicians to determine the ramifications of the choice, which rests not on a flight of sentiment or an ideology, but on the concrete possibilities of realization that only technicians can know. A current popular dictum has it that the electors must be correctly informed of these particulars and the technicians' first task will be to explain the elements of the problem fully and simply. Thus a preliminary technical intervention already determines the limits of the draft plan according to the possibilities. But, even given a simple explanation, can one believe that the citizen is fit to choose?

A little example (which I have cited before, but refer to again because I think it significant) will shed some light on this illusion of the possibility of citizens themselves deciding on the "grand designs," leaving merely the choice of ways and means to the

---

[2] Max Frisch: "Evolution de la Démocratie en Europe," in *Bulletin* s.e.d.e.i.s. (1962).

technician: the problem of the fourth week of vacation. Alfred Sauvy (whose belief in democracy is above suspicion and all of whose works are written along the lines indicated above) wrote two articles on this subject in *Sud-Ouest* (January 17 and 18, 1963) in order to show the average reader just what the problem was, and that choices had to be made, that is, that the decision could not be either "political" or a subject for passion and demagogy: the question was of an exact economic matter. These articles were excellent. But after making a little investigation among certain readers of *Sud Ouest*, I was able to ascertain that of the average readership (not, that is, among students and professors who already had some familiarity with the problem), 3 per cent had read the two articles. In addition, the articles themselves had already made a confession of futility. Sauvy makes the point that if the fourth week is to be granted, it will mean certain restrictions, for instance, fewer dwellings or schools built and, conversely, more probable expenditures. Sauvy gives some examples, then states: "This is not the place for us to describe the background of the decision." In other words, the "country" itself must choose. "The country must be placed before clear and unequivocal choices" (splendid!). But . . . these choices cannot be formulated here, that is, in two newspaper articles. But then we must ask: "Then where would the background of the decision be described?" In long, dense studies laying down all the correlations and all the implications, that is, in studies that would be quite unreadable for the nonspecialist, who is completely outdistanced even by clear, simple articles. Without even taking into consideration the fact that even if there is correct information, the greater the number of choices the more difficult it will be for the citizen to choose, as in most cases he will find himself confronted by elements he is equally attached to.

In addition, what one comes up against is not only an intellectual incapacity, but initially a spontaneous impulse. Simply suggest to some citizen that a fourth week of paid vacation be granted, and nothing will hinder his making a decision in its favor. If you offer the choice of "an automobile for everyone or else a more developed social structure," the decision is made in advance, and if the problem is more complicated how will it be possible to "get it across"? Pierre Bauchet is right in saying that the "French consumer of energy runs the risk of making a rather irrational choice between coal that is taxed at an average rate, electricity at a marginal rate, and oil products whose rates depend on multiple factors, including the tax structure." [3] If spontaneous choice is irrational, what would happen if the consumer was consulted for the purpose of making a theoretical choice among data that are so complex? In reality, a reasonable planning system ought to meet spontaneous choices half way, ought to act as a brake on "obvious" claims, and ought to dissociate itself from ideological decisions. It may be true, for instance, as Devaud says, that, in planning, housing should be put ahead of the automobile, but in a society that is getting richer, housing also should be paid for *at its* real cost by a growing number of families,[4] which would not be easily accepted by the mass of consumers. Likewise, François Perroux says, with evidence, that support for the plan would be improbable if one were to announce an increase of investments at the expense of an increase in consumption,[5] etc. One should, of course, always reject the rational and technical character of planning, and prefer the large-scale ideological decisions, prefer adventures—but in that case let us stop talking about planning! Yet we must talk about it, for it is precisely toward this method of organization that all societies are now turning.

Finally, it is a complete illusion—despite Massé's study of the Fifth Plan—to believe that the citizenry has been familiarized with the decisions that are to be made. Only a few circles of varied specialists will be able to play a role and influence decisions within narrow limits.

Moreover, almost everything I have just said about the average citizen also holds true for the deputy representing his electors, a man whose competence is generally scarcely superior to

---

[3] Pierre Bauchet: *Propriété publique et Planification* (1963).
[4] Devaud: "Faut-il réduire la consommation?" *Le Monde,* August 20, 1963.
[5] François Perroux: *Le IVe Plan,* p. 112. See also the excellent article by André Philip in *Le Monde,* October 1964, which shows that, to have a discussion of any value, parties and trade unions must make use of technicians, and will have the greatest difficulty in proposing a "counterplan."

the "upper-middle class." But here we run into other problems: how can politicians really be associated with a planning system? We are told, rightly, that this would occur not only on the level of the large-scale decisions, but also at each stage in the working out of the plan. For the preparatory studies, the politician would check the value of documents and statistics and see to it that they were objective. As far as forecasting is concerned, the politician's role would come about because of the ignorance and uncertainty of the technicians themselves, of the extremely rudimentary and conjectural character of the projection: because presuppositions and decisions serve as starting point for the technicians, those assumed by the politicians are, after all, no worse, and so they must be associated with planning.[6] As a matter of fact, this does not seem very convincing to me; the conclusion does not seem to me to be a necessary consequence of the premises. These latter may be accurate, but they do not justify the intervention of the politicians: in order to make that decision, and that critique of the presuppositions (it being impossible to enter into the substance of economic projection, which is very difficult), what would be required would be intellectuals and philosophers far more than politicians. It is not a question of competence, but of a general intellectual attitude. At the third stage, that of the actual planning, of quantification, of figures and adjustments, it is the parliament, and the "nation" (trade unions, consumers, parties, etc.) that can best decide here. Some people have proposed that these intervene in the parliamentary debates [7]; these debates must be made as broad and deep as possible. But here we come across all the difficulties that we have referred to with respect to the general consulting of public opinion. For that matter, Cazes admits that a real training of the political personnel would have to be achieved in order to make it psychologically fitted (he is speaking of intellectual retraining) to enter into such work. Concretely, only two possibilities can be conceived: either really very broad debates, large-scale consultations, in

---

[6] B. Gournay: "Technocratie et Politique," *Économie et Humanisme;* Meynaud: *La Technocratie.*
[7] Cazes: "Élaboration du Plan et Démocratie," *Économie et Humanisme,* pp. 44 ff.

which case they could no longer be confined to parliament: and
why ask only the trade unions and the parties what they think?
If it is a question of the fundamental decisions concerning
human life, the universities, the churches, the family associations, the philosophy societies, the numerous groups of artists
and writers seem to me far more qualified; but in that case the
consultations would produce an extraordinary cacophony, and
who will decide? And for what motives? Granted that most of
the arguments in all directions would be substantial, the politicians would have to go back to their partisan political presuppositions, which do not seem to be very certain criteria, or else
base themselves on what the technicians themselves finally consider to be possible amid all this. I should imagine that very
large-scale consultations of this kind would finally go back to
be refereed by the technicians, "enlightened" at best by hundreds of opinions.

Or else one may think of an association of deputies working
on the formation of the plan. But what will happen then will be
what always happens in all technical commissions: at the beginning the politician or the intellectual is not up to the discussion, and does not dare express himself because the technician
has (seemingly) irrefutable arguments; as time goes on, the
politician who has been at his post for a long time becomes
specialized and acquires a genuine competence. But at the same
time he acquires a point of a new view and a cast of mind similar
to that of the technicians. That is, it is not the technician who is
won over to the general conception, the ideas of the politician,
but the politician who takes on the technician's global outlook
and motivations. At that moment the decisions no longer are
really those of the politician. For that matter, if we look closely,
those who recommend this transfer of decisions to the parliament have very little *concrete* to propose, the moment the pro-
nouncement of general formulae is abandoned in order to see
how they could be turned into facts from an institutional point
of view; [8] it is always a source of surprise to see the gap between the breadth and apparent rightness of the formulae of

---

[8] The concrete proposals of Mendès-France, Gournay, Cazes, and Halff (Report
of the Economic and Social Council, October 1963) are very slight, and do not
appear to lead to real power of decision on the part of parliament.

democratization and the possibilities of practical action suggested. The following paragraph will deal with the technical difficulties arising out of the very nature of the plan.

We come to another aspect of parliamentary intervention, the vote on the plan after its technical elaboration. Everyone agrees that a plan, once it is laid down, is a whole whose parts all hang together. Every element has its place and, having been laid down as a function of everything else cannot be modified. If some of the data is changed, the rest must also be modified. Hence the vote on the plan must be global, not piecemeal. What is perforce at issue is thus a vote of acceptance or of rejection, but with no modifications. Hence there is a feeling that parliament is being frustrated in its function.

To avoid this, it is proposed that the planning commission set up several plans for parliament to choose between. As a matter of fact, Halff proposes the presentation of five or six models of development, with an analysis for each one of the general goals, the broad constituent elements, and the directives for regional expansion. This system would seem to be the most serious, and would allow parliament a real choice. But here another difficulty is met with: when five drafts of a plan are proposed to us, we see only a very restricted number of variables. If, for instance, one retained only the five basic points indicated by the law of August 4, 1962, and that would have to be decided on, and if for every one of these five points only two hypotheses were presented, this would, in reality, lead to the presentation of drafts for a plan. How could parliament get around to a real discussion of these twenty-five drafts and, if that did not take place, if they were reduced to five, who would make the preliminary selection? Very obviously, the planning commission, which once again would thus remain the master of decisions and directions. All this shows the degree to which the genuine participation of the political people in parliament and, even more their capacity to decide, are slippery and hard to apply.

We must say the same with respect to the trade unions. All the difficulties analyzed above may be brought up concerning them, too. In particular, it very quickly becomes vital for the trade union to detail specialists for any real discussion of planning problems with the technicians. And then we find the same development we indicated with respect to the politicians.

There is, moreover, still another difficulty with respect to the trade unions.

In a general way, the position of the trade unionists is clear: they wish to participate in the working-out of the plan, and even to play a preponderant role in it. But from another point of view, if—when the work of the technicians is finished and parliament has voted—the result does not suit them completely, they wish to be released from the obligation of carrying it out. They no longer wish to feel themselves bound by the plan. Now, this is far more than a mere question of form. The ambiguity here has been very well illuminated by an article in *Économie et Humanisme*,[9] in which it is shown that the trade unions are not fit to "define new needs" and "penetrate deeply into the nature of complex needs" because they are basically rooted in a false position with respect to the economy. They believe that the sole problem still remains that of surplus value and, on the other hand, that the satisfaction of needs is bound to take place via the raising of wages—both of which economic concepts now have been outmoded. Now planning, even if it is not "capitalist" from a simple technical point of view, cannot be based on ideas as out-of-date as those maintained by the trade unions. In addition, it is easy to understand the position of the politicians, who maintain that if the trade unions take part in the working out of the plan, they are committed to its execution; that there is a "quasi-contract," that they cannot simply wash their hands of the matter and start going into the opposition again.[1] But if they support it, that means that the trade unions will abandon their policy of agitation and demands for the duration of the plan: in which case they will lose their importance and value within the working class. Conversely, if they are determined to maintain at all costs their oppositionist and exigent attitude, then their substantial collaboration in the establishment of the plan can hardly be accepted: it would not be serious. It can be seen

---

[9] *Économie et Humanisme*, No. 136 (1961), pp. 25 *ff*. F. Perroux: *Le IVe Plan*, p. 125.
[1] Among others, Mendès-France: *La République moderne*, p. 181.

that the problem is far from being as clear and obvious as some are pleased to maintain. Finally, still with respect to the trade unions, in order for any democratization to take place with their participation, they would have to be democratic themselves; for this, see Chapter IV.

Summing up: the methods of democratization, of the participation of politicians in planning, of deciding on choices on the political plane seem, the moment they are closely examined, to be highly illusory and ultimately of no consequence.

But a final category of questions must be studied: the obstacle that the exercise of any real influence on planning by the politician has to do with the technical reality of the plan. The first thought that comes to mind is the middle-range plans. Now, it seems more and more that what must be envisaged is two types of planning, one middle-range, the other long-range: for instance, along side the problems of the rationalization of investments is the problem of the "human material" that must be trained. Now, the latter cannot be trained in one or two years. It is being conceded more and more that what must be forecast is ten or fifteen years in order to train the personnel that will be needed in a given sector. There is an obvious correlation between human arrangements and the evolution of production,[2] the latter becoming more and more dependent on the former. For a projection of this kind, no political decision is possible: we are in the presence of precise facts and of a very objective tendency with no room for nuances of opinion. Confronted by the detail and the rigorousness of the studies that have been made along these lines,[3] one cannot see how any discussions of value by nonspecialists can be inserted anywhere. It is very plain that this long-range plan in its turn conditions all the middle-range plans, which cannot be thrown over en route, for instance in the case of the training of people. The plan for investment must accept a period of waiting. Here I found another example of

---

[2] Grimanelli, in *Bulletin* s.e.d.e.i.s. (1963).
[3] E.g., Gauchy Vermot's admirable "La Planification à long terme," three studies in *Bulletin* s.e.d.e.i.s. (1963).

what I referred to above as the lower limits of choice. Another one of these lower limits, which reduces the dimensions of the choice—as well as the number of choices—still further is the existence of the preceding plan. A plan does not make its appearance in a virgin situation; it has been preceded by some other plan (unless a revolution occurs, which is always possible, in which case the politician in fact gets the upper hand once again—but here we leave the field of planning). Whether one likes it or not, there is bound to be a continuity between the two: the second is bound to be conditioned by the results achieved thanks to the first. This continuity is even felt to be so necessary that Mendès-France based himself on it in order to set up his procedure in parliament [4] (the documentation was to be provided a year before the end of the legislature and two years before the end of the plan, to allow for the results to be examined and new choices to be envisaged). Here, too, brusque switches are impossible, that is, it is really impossible to hold up to the electorate every four years the "grand decisions," the "basic directions," the "decisive choices"; whatever changes of opinion may occur, the facts themselves are molded within a non-elastic period of time; the grand decisions are most often decided on in advance by the continuity of events and of planning.

A third limitation of these possibilities, which I shall not enlarge on, is the combination of technicians and administrators for the observation and application of the plan. On this level, the political authority is in the presence of a singularly redoutable power, constituted by the mutual support given each other by these two elements—often separate, sometimes opposed, but here united. The activity of the administrators of the plan, far from being a factor of democratization, gives them a power that can more easily bypass the influence of the politician.[5] The two elements combined create a streamlined efficiency against which there is very little that can prevail. A fourth difficulty

---

[4] Mendès-France: *La République moderne*, pp. 128–9.
[5] Lebreton: "Plan démocrate et Réformes administratives," *Économie et Humanisme* (1961), p. 98.

arises from the fact, often mentioned, that in planning it is very difficult to distinguish clearly between the means and the ends, between the grand political decisions and their technical implementation (the plans themselves). Only the technician can tell, on the basis of the means in existence, what is possible with respect to the realization of such and such an end, and similarly the simple technical formulation of such and such an intention is bound to transform it by eliminating the imponderable, the contingent, the emotional, the "human" element contained in a speech. The simple citizen who gives his opinion will no longer recognize it once the rigorous method of economic calculation has passed over it and implemented it. In other words, in formulating a choice on the level of a speech, of opinion, or of sentiment, one does not know with precision what the end-result will be in terms of work schedules, the possibilities of consumption, investments, or the general equilibrium of the economy. In going on to such calculations, the technician is compelled to undertake rectification, to take his bearings once again in order to avoid any incoherences or disasters.

This leads us to a final difficulty: it is well known that it is often necessary to bring about modifications and rectifications of the plan while it is being put into effect, not necessarily because of errors in the plan, but because of circumstances. What is then sometimes spoken of is "active" planning.[6] For instance, how can our plan be adapted to the bad harvest of 1963, to the inflow of refugees from Algeria, to the fourth week of paid vacation, etc.? Here we are in the presence of modifications that can be decided only by technicians. It is quite certain that, while the plan is being put into effect, it is impossible to start the consultations and political discussions all over again, these problems being generally purely technical and supposing a great number of changes in the plan, for which a political discussion would merely obscure the situation without leading to any solution. But here once again we see the degree to which the intervention of political authority and the choices to be made are limited; once again, we find another *"infra* limit," which has

---

[6] Halff Report.

the added danger of having been unknown when the choices were being made. Confronted by necessity, only the technician is fitted to intervene, but does this fact itself not make the general debate quite futile? A discussion is still going on about whether the stabilization plan of 1963 was or was not a complete reversal of the Fourth Plan and a modification of its general direction. Is there not always a danger of a similar transformation? In the name of what authority should parliament reject such changes if it is not really qualified to appreciate in any technical detail the new economic facts and the changes in the plan prompted by revisions? To the extent that situations are broken down into details it becomes clear that analyses are not concrete. And this problem is surely a constant one; in the face of the rigorous and concrete studies made by the planners, whenever the problem is posed concerning the "politics-planning" relationship or the "planning-democracy" relationship, one either slips into verbalism and general solutions or else, by hypnotizing oneself with words, is satisfied with a notion of democratization which is completely artificial. There is not even a clear view about a decision as simple as the following: in political action, should one begin by a general discussion on the global decisions of the plan, or else by detailed discussions in different groups and sectors of society in order to give one an idea of demands and needs? It is easily seen that the two different approaches will lead to totally different results. That is why on this point it is difficult for me to agree with Meynaud when he says: "The plan is an instrument of government which becomes a factor of technical power when its elaboration and execution avoid the initiative and the surveillance of the political leadership." [7]

I think that is inherent in the nature of planning. Obviously, Meynaud is bound to add: "There is no doubt that the very nature of planning, and the coherence implied by it make such actions more difficult. One must not expect to find satisfactory

---

[7] Meynaud: *La Technocratie*, p. 206. Moreover, Meynaud still declares that all efforts up to this point have involved a consolidation of the technicians' power and that planning systems lead to the atomization of political power (p. 90).

solutions all at once; the reconciliation between what is 'politically desirable' and 'technically feasible' proves to be difficult; but it would be a serious failure to abandon once and for all the work of planning to the technicians. . . ." True, and I should very much like a solution to be sought, as I do not regard with pleasure this growth in the power of the technicians, though it seems to me even more serious to be satisfied with mere words. But Meynaud does not do this.

Having concluded this analysis, I believe that the formula of democratizing planning, or of bringing together politics and technique within a planning system is a characteristic example of a political illusion, of empty verbiage. It is a consolation that one gives oneself when confronted by the real growth of this planning power, and of the consequent questioning of democracy.

Index

A NOTE ABOUT THE AUTHOR

JACQUES ELLUL was born on January 6, 1912, in Bordeaux, France. He studied at the University of Bordeaux and the University of Paris, and he holds the degree of Doctor of Laws. Since 1946 he has been associated with the University of Bordeaux as professor of the history of law and of social history.

A NOTE ON THE TYPE

THE TEXT of this book is set in Caledonia, a typeface designed by W(illiam) A(ddison) Dwiggins for the Mergenthaler Linotype Company in 1939. Dwiggins chose to call his new typeface Caledonia, the Roman name for Scotland, because it was inspired by the Scotch types cast about 1833 by Alexander Wilson & Son, Glasgow type founders. However there is a calligraphic quality about this face that is totally lacking in the Wilson types. Dwiggins referred to an even earlier typeface for this "liveliness of action"—one cut around 1790 by William Martin for the printer William Bulmer. Caledonia has more weight than the Martin letters, and the bottom finishing strokes (serifs) of the letters are cut straight across, without brackets, to make sharp angles with the upright stems, thus giving a "modern face" appearance.

Composed, printed, and bound by
KINGSPORT PRESS, INC., KINGSPORT, TENN.

Typography and binding based on designs by
TERE LOPRETE